MIDDLE AGES

About the Authors

George Fox Mott has held three college deanships, and is a former member of the faculties of Stanford University (A.B., A.M.) and the University of Minnesota (Ph.D.), at which universities he also received his training, as well as of the San Diego Army and Navy Academy and Junior College, Emerson Junior College in Chicago, New Mexico A & M College, DePaul University, Florida State University, and the University of Maryland. At the present time he is managing partner of the research consultant firm of Mott of Washington & Associates. Among his publications are: *Survey of United States Ports*, and another volume in the College Outline Series, *New Survey of Journalism*.

Harold M. Dee served as professor of history and economics at San Diego Army and Navy Junior College and also taught history at Emerson Junior College in Chicago.

COLLEGE OUTLINE SERIES

MIDDLE AGES

An Outline-History from the Decline of the Roman Empire through the Reformation

GEORGE FOX MOTT, Ph.D.

HAROLD M. DEE, M.A.

Fourth Edition

BARNES & NOBLE, INC. NEW YORK

Publishers · Booksellers · Founded 1873

PREFACE

This is the fourth edition of a book which has had wide and continuing use by students everywhere since its publication in 1933. The numerous reprintings of previous editions attest to the correctness of the belief of the authors at the outset "that there was a definite need for a syllabus of the type here produced."

The present edition is in no sense a new book though it is an *enlarged* book in that two chapters have been added in order to summarize the whole period of the Reformation — including the Roman Catholic Reformation — rather than only the beginning of that period. This addition materially enhances its value and is in line with suggestions made by those using the book. In addition, of course, the bibliographies have been brought up-to-date and appropriately enlarged. Obviously though, they are selective rather than all-inclusive. A few errors of statement have been corrected. Aside from the foregoing, the book remains substantially the same as the improved third edition.

This fourth edition, like its successful predecessors, is a concise presentation of that most significant transitional era of history about which too many students know so little as to prevent them from understanding modern history in any but a most superficial "present" and "immediate past" sense. The edition here presented begins with the decline of the Roman Empire and deals with each important phase of medieval life through the Renaissance to and including the Roman Catholic Reformation.

The following extracts from the original Preface are appropriately explanatory and pertinent to the present edition:

The advantages of an outline have been combined with those of a text. The plan followed is based upon the conviction . . . that syllabi, as well as texts, are often more useful to those who know history than to those who are just learning to know it. The authors felt that this was unfortunate. Furthermore, it is of little permanent use for the student to read history indiscriminately. Therefore, this syllabus represents an effort to properly relate each phase of medieval history to every other phase; and it takes into consideration the students' actual needs.

• • • • •

The material is so arranged that one can pick and choose as

v

he likes, and still have a reasonably good comprehension of the relationship of one thought to another. In style of treatment and organization of material, the authors have put the historical data of the medieval period into thoroughly teachable form, on the college level of instruction.

• • • • •

A definite attempt has been made to give as much consideration as possible to the cultural development of the period, which helps to elucidate the changes taking place during the Middle Ages. Insofar as possible chronological order has been followed, and the different movements and countries have been so grouped. Furthermore . . . since most modern anthropologists and ethnologists have placed great emphasis upon invasions as one of the dynamics of social change, this phase has not been overlooked.

• • • • •

The Hundred Years' War has been considered as a part of the period to which it belongs chronologically . . .; for although it overshadowed any other development of its time, it was, nevertheless, only a part of the history of the period.

Acknowledgments for help received in connection with previous editions have long since been gratefully expressed by the authors. In preparation of the present edition, Dorothy Williams Mott has been most helpful.

TABLE OF CONTENTS

MAPS

PRACTICAL HINTS TO STUDENTS

This outline-history of the Middle Ages serves students in a variety of practical ways for the effective study of any part or all of that period of history generally thought of as medieval. *First*, it may be used *as a method of initial orientation to the study of the Middle Ages*. To accomplish this the college student reads the appropriate chapter in this outline first, then reads the corresponding chapters in one or more assigned textbooks. *Second*, it may be used *as a quick and accurate study aid prior to tests and examinations*. To meet this purpose the college student reads each topic in the outline dealing with subjects to be covered by the examination, then makes a summary in his own words and checks this with the assigned text, appropriate lecture notes, and the course prospectus. *Third*, it may be used *as an organizing syllabus*. To achieve this objective the college student makes use of the various units of the book as a convenient framework for the purposeful organization of information which may be acquired through lectures and assigned or selected readings. As no period of history is more involved, and as scholars have made available extensive readings in this important period of history, the practical value of the outline for this purpose is very real. *Fourth*, it may be used *as an authoritative synthesis of the history of the Middle Ages*. To fulfill this necessarily broad cultural objective, the college student reads as slowly or rapidly as his own previous knowledge permits. Through his use of the outline in this way, he will gain a general interpretation and understanding rarely possible of achievement otherwise except at much greater cost in both time and energy.

In connection with use of the book in any one of the first three ways, most of the more generally used college texts currently available are given in the "Tabulated Bibliography," which is correlated with a "Quick Reference Table," so that the student can locate readily the corresponding chapters of these standard texts. Of special significance to the more advanced student of the period, there is a supplementary list of references at the end of the book. These have been selected for their value to the inquiring mind with reference to some special period or area of knowledge of the Middle Ages. College students will find the bibliographies valuable aids to learning. They are designed to save "searching time" and thereby increase "learning time."

TABULATED BIBLIOGRAPHY
OF STANDARD TEXTBOOKS*

This *Outline* is keyed to standard textbooks in two ways.

1. If you are studying any of the following textbooks, consult the cross references here listed to find which pages of the *Outline* summarize the appropriate chapter of your text. (Roman numerals refer to the textbook chapters, Arabic figures to the corresponding *Outline* pages.)

2. If you are using the *Outline* as the basis for study and need a more complete treatment of a given phase or topic, consult the pages of any of the textbooks as indicated in the Quick Reference Table on pp. xiii-xv.

BOAK, A. E. R., HYMA, A. AND SLOSSON, P., *The Growth of Western Civilization*, 4th ed., 1951, Appleton-Century-Crofts.

Vol. One: VI, VII (1-5); VIII (7-16); IX (17-21); X (22-27); XI (81-85); XII (39-49, 57-73, 120-134); XIII (105-119); XIV (141-152, 160-165); XV (135-140, 166-172, 206-211); XVI (173-198); XVII (199-227); XVIII (220-227); XIX (153-159); XX (228-263); XXI (246-255); XXII (228-255); XXIII (256-263).

FERGUSON, W. K., AND BRUUN, G., *A Survey of European Civilization* (Part One) rev. ed., 1958, Houghton Mifflin.

V (1-5); VI (1-5); VII (17-19); VIII (11-16); IX (81-85); X (22-27, 86-91); XI (14, 28-31); XII (33-43); XIII (44-49); XIV (57-73); XV (92-104); XVI (120-134); XVII (105-119); XVIII (135-152); XIX (160-165); XX (166-171); XXI (190-198); XXII (173-185); XXIII (153-159); XXIV (199-205); XXV (206-219); XXVI (220-227); XXVIII (228-236, 246-255); XXIX (237-245); XXX (256-263).

HAYES, C. J. H., AND BALDWIN, M. W., *History of Europe (Vol. I)*, 1949, Macmillan.

V (1-5); VI (7-16); VIII (17-21); IX (22-27); X (28-43); XI (44-49); XII (147-152); XIII (62-80); XIV (81-91, 135-140); XV (105-119); XVI (160-165); XVII (120-134); XVIII (92-104); XIX (153-155); XX (166-171); XXI (206-219); XXII (173-189); XXIII (190-198); XXV (155-159, 228, 229, 252); XXVI, XXVII (199-227); XXVIII, XXIX, XXX (228-255); XXXI, XXXII (245, 256-263).

HOYT, R. S., *Europe in the Middle Ages*, 1957, Harcourt, Brace.

I (1-5); II (7-16); III (17-19); IV (20-21); V (22-31); VI (33-37); VII (135-137); VIII (39-43); IX (44-66); X (147-152); XI (67-80); XII (81-91, 105-111); XIII (160-165); XIV (64, 92-97, 120-125, 128-129); XV (135-139, 141-146); XVI (139-140, 166-171); XVII (153-155); XVIII (153-158); XIX (166-171, 217); XX (—); XXI (139-140); XXII (136-138); XXIII (160-165); XXIV (125-127, 173-175); XXV (129-134); XXVI (101-104, 153-155); XXVII (113-117, 193-195, 197-198); XXVIII (175-189); XXIX (155-159); XXX (190-198); XXXI (199-205); XXXII (206-227).

JOHNSON, E. N., *An Introduction to the History of the Western Tradition (Volume I)*, 1959, Ginn.

VII (1-16); VIII (17-19); IX (19-21, 28-43); X (44-49, 57-61, 120-126, 141-152, 160-165); XI (22-27, 52-55, 81-91, 105-119, 195-198); XII (57-80, 92-97, 120-134, 153-159, 173-195); XIII (98-104, 153-159); XIV (135-140, 166-171); XV (199-205); XVI (206-227).

---

*For a list of supplementary reference books, see p. 264.

LA MONTE, J. L., *The World of the Middle Ages*, 1949, Appleton-Century-Crofts.
I, II (1-5); III (7-16); IV (81-85); V (17-21); VI (22-27, 86-91); VII (81-85); IX (28-43); X (50-55, 67-73); XI (57-66); XII (44-49, 141-152); XIII (60, 61, 66, 135-140, 147-152); XIV (74-80, 92-97); XVI (120-134); XVII (123-126); XIX (105-110); XX (110-119); XXI (160-165); XXII (141-146); XXIII (99-101); XXIV, XXV, XXVI (98-104, 153-159); XXVII (128-134); XXVIII (125-127); XXIX (114-119); XXXII (135-140, 166-171); XXXVI (155-159); XXXVII (173-180); XXXVIII (181-189); XXXIX, XL (190-198); XLI (199-227).

LUCAS, H. S., *The Renaissance and the Reformation*, 1934, Harper.
Book I: Introduction (199-205); Part One: I-III (190-198); Part Two: IV-VII (153-159); Part Three: VIII (199-205); IX (141-146); X (166-172); XI (153-159); XIII (212-219); Part Four: XIV, XV (206-219); Parts Four, Five, and Six: XVI-XXVIII (212-219); XXIX-XXXI (220-227); Book II: Introduction and Part Seven: XXXII-XXXVI (228-245); Part Eight: XXXVII-XLI and Part Nine: XLII-XLVI (246-255); Part Ten: XLVII-LII (256-263).

MACKINNEY, L. C., *The Medieval World*, 1938, Rinehart.
Part One: I-III (1-5); IV (17-21); V (7-10); VI (11-16); VII (81-85); VIII (22-27, 86-91); IX (28-38); X (39-43); XI (44-49, 141-146); XII (44-49, 147-152); XIII-XVII (135-140); XVIII (160-165); XIX (50-56, 74-80); XX (92-104); XXI (50-56); XXII (50-56, 206-211, 228-236); XXIII (57-61, 120-127); XXIV (62-66, 128-134); XXV (105-112) XXVI (113-119); XXVII (220-227); XXVIII (128-134, 153-159); XXIX (173-189); XXX, XXXI (190-198); XXXII (166-171, 199-227); XXXIII (206-219); XXXIV, XXXV (212-219).

O'SULLIVAN, J., AND BURNS, J. F., *Medieval Europe*, 1943, Appleton-Century-Crofts.
I-IV (1-5); V-VII (7-16); VIII (17-21, 26-37); IX (28-31); X (4, 5); XI (17-21); XIII, XIV (17-21); XV-XVII (135-140, 166-171, 206-219); XVIII (33-43); XIX (62-66, 120-134); XX (67-80, 92-104); XXI (44-49); XXII (50-55, 74-80); XXIII (147-152); XXIV (160-165); XXV (141-152); XXVII (22-27, 86-91); XXVIII (105-119); XXIX (153-159); XXX (103, 104, 190-192); XXXI (173-189); XXXII (162, 163, 179, 180, 202, 203, 229).

PAINTER, SIDNEY. *A History of the Middle Ages*, 1954, Knopf.
I (1-16) ; II (81-85) ; III (28-43) ; IV (44-49, 141-152) ; V (50-55, 74-80) ; VI (62-73, 120-123) ; VII (86-91, 105-112) ; VIII (160-165) ; IX (92-104, 123-134) ; X (98-101) ; XI (173-189) ; XII (181-193) ; XIII (153-159, 228-230) ; XIV (166-171, 206-219).

STEPHENSON, C., *Mediaeval History*, rev. ed., 1951, Harper.
I, II (1-5); III (7-16); IV (17-21); V (81-85); VI (22-27); VII (17-21, 28-32); VIII (33-43); IX (81-91); X (44-49) ;XI (141-152); XII (74-80, 105-112); XIII (160-165); XIV (166-171); XV, XVI (135-140); XVII (92-97); XVIII (92-104, 113-119); XIX (199-205); XX (98-104, 113-134, 190-198); XXI (153-159, 173-180); XXII (173-189); XXIII (153-159); XXIV (190-219); XXV (199-219).

STRAYER, J. R., AND MUNRO, D. C., *The Middle Ages, 395-1500*, 1959, Appleton-Century-Crofts.
I (1-5); II.(7-21); III (22-27, 81-85); IV (28-37); V (39-55); VI (67-73, 86-91); VII (57-66); VIII (74-80, 92-99, 105-112, 135-152, 166-171); IX (120-126, 128-131); X (99-104, 113-119, 190-198); XI (126-127, 131-134); XII (153-165, 173-175); XIII (175-189, 199-205); XIV (206-227).

THOMPSON, J. W., JOHNSON, E. N., *An Introduction to Medieval Europe, 300-1500*, 1937, Norton.
I, II (1-5); III (17-21); IV (7-10); V (11-16, 57-61); VI (81-85); VII (86-91); VIII (28-32, 57-61); IX (28-38, 57-61); X (39-43); XI, XII (44-49, 141-152); XIII (50-56, 67-80); XIV (92-104); XV (120-127); XVI, XVII (128-134); XVIII (105-119); XIX, XX (160-165); XXI (228-263); XXII (74-80, 98-104, 237-245); XXIII (135-140, 166-172, 199-236); XXIV (135-140, 199-227); XXV (173-189); XXVI (173-198); XXVII(190-198); XXVIII (153-159, 228-255); XXIX (199-236).

THORNDIKE, L., *The History of Medieval Europe*, 3rd ed., 1949, Houghton Mifflin.
I (1-5); II (7-10); III (2-4, 11-16); V (81-85); VI (28-31); VII (17-21); IX (22-27); X (86-91); XI (81-85); XII (28-43); XIII (57-61); XIV, XV (44-49, 62-73, 120-134); XVI (50-55, 74-80, 111, 124, 125); XVII (160-165); XVIII (74-80, 105-119); XIX (98-104); XX (101-104, 190-193); XXI (123-127, 173, 174); XXII (128-134); XXIV (135-140, 166-171); XXV-XXIX (199-219); XXX (173-184); XXXI (153-159); XXXII-XXXIV (190-198); XXXV (185-189, 191-195); XXXVI (199-205); XXXVII, XXXVIII (206-227).

WALLBANK, T. W., AND TAYLOR, A. M., *Civilization Past and Present* (Vol. I), 3rd ed., 1954, Scott, Foresman.
VIII (1-21, 28-37); IX (81-85); X (22-27, 86-91); XII (28-43, 57-65); XIII (44-49, 141-152, 160-165); XIV (17-21, 50-55, 74-80, 92-119); XV (135-140, 166-171); XVI (120-134, 173-198); XVII (199-223); XVIII (228-263); XX (223-227).

QUICK REFERENCE TABLE

Italic type indicates pages.   **Bold Face** type indicates chapters.

See preceeding pages for list of complete titles and publishers.

QUICK REFERENCE TABLE

Italic type indicates pages

Outline Chapter	Topic	Hoyt	Johnson	La Monte	Lucas
I	Empire Before Invasions	1	5, 7	1	
II	Barbarian Peoples	*24–30*	7	*38–40*	
III	Barbarian Invasions	2	7	3	
IV	Rise of Papacy	3	8, 9	*24–35*	
V	Mohammedanism	5	*480–485*	6	
VI	Franks to Charlemagne	*40–43, 115–122*	9	*152–155*	
VII	Empire of Charlemagne	6, 7	9	*155–160*	
VIII	Disintegration of Empire	8	9	*161–166*	
IX	Feudal Life	9, 10, 15	10	12, 22	
X	Church from 800 to 1056	*4, 189–193,* 11	*526–540*	*170–178*	
XI	Anglo-Saxon England	*138–140*		*196–202*	
XII	Feudal France	*170–174*		*185–196*	
XIII	Feudal Germany and Italy	11, *234–238*		10	
XIV	Empire and Papacy to 1122	11	*524–544*	*251–262*	
XV	Christian Empire of East	3, *227–232*	11	4, 7, 8	
XVI	Saracenic Empire	*108–115, 232–241*	11	6	
XVII	Empire and Papacy, 1152	*276–284*	12	*262–267*	
XVIII	Conflict Ends, 1254	*340–347,* 26	13	25	
XIX	First and Second Crusades	*238–244*	*485–492*	19, *348–353*	
XX	Later Crusades		*474–480*	20, 29	
XXI	Norman Conquest to 1272	14, 24	*434–438, 556–564*	16, 17, 28	
XXII	France, 1108 to 1328	14, 25	*551–556*	27	
XXIII	Culture of Middle Ages	15, *19–23*	9 , 14	13, 32, 34	
XXIV	Age of Chivalry	15, *585–591*		22, 34	*115–126*
XXV	Peasant in Middle Ages	10, 13, *575–579*	10	12, 13	
XXVI	Church in Later Middle Ages	15, 17, 18	13	25, 26, 35	*49–106*
XXVII	Development of Towns	13, 23	10	21	
XXVIII	Education	16, 19, 20, 22	14	32	*127–139*
XXIX	France and England, 14th Century	21, 28	*564–570*	37	
XXX	France and England, 15th Century	21, 28	*564–570*	38	
XXXI	Europe, 13th-14th Centuries	26, 27, 30	13	26, 30, 39	*7–48*
XXXII	Beginning of Renaisance	37, 31	16	32, 33	*3–18,* 8
XXXIII	Education, Thought, Philosophy	22, 32	14, 16	32, 33	*193–217*
XXXIV	Literature, Art, Science	22, 32	15	41	*172–366*
XXXV	End of Renaissance	32	Vol. II		*367–416*
XXXVI	Martin Luther		Vol. II		*419–491*
XXXVII	Reformation in Germany		Vol. II		*423–476*
XXXVIII	Spread of Reformation		Vol. II		*493–620*
XXXIX	Roman Catholic Reformation		Vol. II		*621–703*

TO STANDARD TEXTBOOKS

Bold Face type indicates chapters.

Mac-Kinney	O'Sullivan	Painter	Stephenson	Strayer & Monro	Thompson son & Johnson	Thorndike	Wallbank & Taylor
1, 2, 3	1-4, 10	1	1, 2		1, 2	1, 3	8
104-108	5	1	3	2	4	2	8
108-139	6,7	1	3	2	5	4	8
4	8, 11-14	71-74 84-88	4, 7	2	3	7	14
8	27	36-37	6	3	7	9	10
178-186	8, 9	62-76	53, 132	4	5, 8, 9	6, 12	8, 12
187-198	18	76-81	136-152	4	238-262	12	333-335
10	18	88-93	152-158	5	10	12	336-340
11, 12	21	4	180-190	114-131	11, 12	15, 29	13
375-383	22	123-136	12	131-139, 155-172	10, 13	16	14
450-454		91-92, 172-176	10, 179	180-190	96, 268	221-225	344-345
472-476	19	151-164	177, 190	172-178	10, 16	15, 17, 22	346-348
370-375	20	164-172	8, 12	146-153	283, 13	268-270	340-344
375-390	22	132-136	12	153-161, 206-216	13, 32	16	14
7	135, 141 151	33-50	5, 9	137-142	6	5, 11	9
8	27	193-197	9	80-85, 142-146	7	10	10
391-397	20	276-282	17	8	391-407	18	14
397-407	20	282-288 290-291	17, 18, 20	8, 10	14, 22	19	14
25	28	200-214	227-234	226-240	515-538	19	398-400
26	28	214-219	18, 20	240-243, 336-343	538-559	19	400-402
454-469	19	176-186 261-276	17, 18	190-195, 278-296, 375-383	15	21	345-346 452-459
477-487	19	248-261	17, 21	296-305, 369-375, 423-427	474-514	22	460-463
254-339	15-17		15, 16	8, 10	23, 24	8	15
11	25	117-122	11	383-394	11, 12	15	360-365
12	23, 25	94-104	11	407-413	11, 12	15, 522	365-372
28	29	400-416	21, 23	10, 12	28	31	518-522
18	24, 32	226-247	13	394-407	19, 20	14	372-382
32	15	430-432 467-468	14	356-366	23	24	15
580-590	31, 32	323-349	21, 22	467-481	25, 26	30	16
590-605	31	349-360, 380-396	22, 26	481-496	25, 26	30, 35	16 537-538
30, 31	30	396-399	20, 24	13	902-953	32, 33, 34	464-483
32			19, 24, 25	14	23, 24, 29	35, 36	17
654-701		14	24, 25	14	23, 24, 29	37	17
671-747		14	24, 25	14	23, 24, 29	37	15, 17
27				14	23, 24, 29	38	17, 20
439-447		417-428			624, 978		18
					21, 22, 28		18
					21, 28		18
					21		18

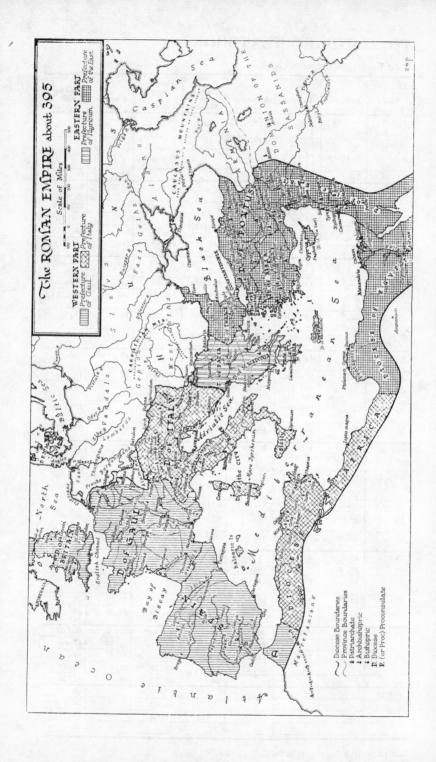

The ROMAN EMPIRE about 395

WESTERN PART
Prefecture of Gaul.
Prefecture of Italy.

EASTERN PART
Prefecture of Illyricum.
Prefecture of the East.

Scale of Miles

Diocese Boundaries
Province Boundaries
Patriarchate
Archbishopric
Bishopric
D. Diocese
P. (or Proc.) Proconsulate

CHAPTER I

THE EMPIRE BEFORE THE INVASIONS

"And there is no more majestic monument of human jurisprudence than the system of law which grew up in the Roman lawcourts." *

I. By the fourth century the vast Roman Empire[1] was held together by a strong government, as well as by certain cultural, social, and economic bonds.

A. With few exceptions[2] civilization was largely confined to the Roman Empire.
   1. There were no completely independent states, as such, in western Europe.
   2. The empire included most of western Europe and a great part of the Near East.
   3. All these peoples lived under one great empire-state, the Roman Empire.
      a. All paid taxes into the same treasury.
      b. They lived under the same law.
      c. Every part of the empire was protected by the same armies.

B. The empire was held together by many important bonds:
   1. Well organized, highly centralized government, which regulated almost every interest in life.
      a. The emperor made and executed the laws.
      b. He controlled finances and civil officials.
      c. He exercised control directly over citizens.
   2. Roman law was of paramount importance.
      a. There was but one law for the whole empire.
      b. Compared to earlier codes it was humane.
      c. Local differences were not considered.
      d. Law may be said to be the chief Roman contribution to civilization.
   3. Intercommunication was encouraged.
      a. Travel was comparatively easy, due to a system of good roads, and the *Pax Romana*[3] which made for the travellers' safety.

---

* *From* Morris, The Beginning of the Middle Ages, p. 5. copyright 1886, *used by permission of* Charles Scribner's Sons, *publishers.*
1 The Roman Empire About 395, Shepherd's Historical Atlas, sixth edition, pp. 42-43.
2 The Empire of the Sassanids in Persia; also the great civilizations of India and China.
3 The Roman Peace.

1

        b. Colonies were established at the borders.

        c. A uniform system of coinage and weights and measures was provided.

    4. Citizens of the empire viewed themselves as citizens of the world.

        a. Education was supported, and Greek teachers were allowed to spread civilization.

        b. Naturally, as a result, there was only one culture throughout the empire.

        c. The official language everywhere was Greek or Latin.

C. For administrative purposes the empire was divided into four great sections,[1] and each section subdivided.

    1. These four great sections were responsible to the emperor.

        a. Prefecture of the East.

        b. Prefecture of Illyricum.[2]

        c. Prefecture of Italy.

        d. Prefecture of the Gauls.

    2. Prefectures were further divided into Dioceses.

        a. These were ruled over by a vicar.

        b. They were under the control of the prefect.

    3. Each diocese was divided into provinces which were ruled over by the consular, or president, who was responsible to the vicar.

    4. Two local units were of importance.

        a. The Civitas was an urban center of government with territory subject to its authority. It enjoyed a great amount of self-government.

        b. The Villa was the country estate of a noble. Villas were nearly self-sufficient. Many officials were drawn from the nobles of villas.

II. Finally the Roman Empire lost the power to defend itself against the Barbarians, and gradually disintegrated as the result of forces within, rather than forces from without.

A. Probably the fundamental reason was that it had been founded upon the ruins of nation-states and empire-states that had already declined.

    1. Among these were Asia Minor, Carthage, the Hellenic cities of the Greek Peninsula, Sicily, and southern Italy.

    2. The empire had gradually developed from a patch-work of older nationalities, despotisms, and classic cultures.

---

[1] Excluding Rome and Constantinople, each of which was administered by a prefect of its own.

[2] Part of the Balkan Peninsula and the provinces of the lower Danube.

      a. They had not been able to save themselves from Roman attacks.

      b. They had little to give to reinvigorate the new empire-state.

B. It is significant that after the first century A.D. Italy furnished no emperors.

  1. The provinces were to furnish the leaders.

  2. The taste for luxuries and the distaste for military service among large numbers of the Roman citizenry contributed to this situation.

C. The decline of the old city-state and its civic religion contributed to the decline of the empire.

  1. The unsocial cults of the east invaded the empire and the old civic religion with its local patriotism and resulting high culture passed.

  2. The passing of civic religion was a factor in the decay of literature, of which there was a poverty in the later empire.

D. Some of the other causes which contributed to the empire's decline were:

  1. There was no satisfactory way of choosing the emperor, which led to civil war and internal weakness at the death of an emperor.[1]

  2. The system of collection of taxes was corrupt and oppressive.

      a. Luxurious courts called for heavy revenues.

      b. Weight of taxes ruined many landlords.

  3. There was a disappearance of the "middle class."

      a. The system of slavery imperiled laboring classes.

      b. Land came into the hands of the rich; agriculture declined.

      c. Improved conditions of slaves made life more difficult for laborers.

      d. Labor fell into disrepute.

  4. Depopulation and depletion of the soil were important factors.

      a. There was a definite falling off of population apparent in the "Augustan Age."

      b. This was furthered by war, plague, slavery, and taxation.

      c. Soil was not taken care of properly.

  5. The entrance of Germans into the empire to fill important positions in the army and civil service smoothed the way for the disintegration of the empire.

---

[1] Usually, emperors met their death through violence, and consequently many able emperors were killed before they had completed their work.

III.   However, the church found conditions favorable for its development.

A.   The necessity of a system of church government became evident and was established.
  1.   The early organization was simple, but was soon found insufficient.
      a.   Bishops, elders, and deacons were chosen.
      b.   An elaborate constitution was finally adopted.
      c.   Roman unity aided the task of the apostles.
  2.   The church government became highly centralized.
      a.   There were the pope, archbishops, bishops, and the priests.
      b.   Below these were the lay officials: the deacon and sub-deacon.
      c.   There were also several so-called minor orders.

B.   Finally the bishop at Rome became the acknowledged ruler of western Christendom.[1]
  1.   Christianity was recognized by Constantine, and by the end of the fourth century had become the state religion.
  2.   Later rulers forbade pagan practices altogether.
  3.   The clergy were given important privileges.
      a.   Exemption from taxation.
      b.   Permission to try certain civil cases.
  4.   Christianity showed advantages over other religions; it promised eternal happiness.

C.   The church, more than any other one force, was destined to preserve civilization.
  1.   It absorbed the conquerors.
  2.   It maintained education and kept the Latin language alive.

IV.   With the death of Theodosius, 395 A.D., there came a division of power in the empire.

A.   The two sons of Theodosius both became emperors, one in the east, the other in the west.
  1.   Arcadius, emperor in the east, 395-408.
  2.   Honorius, emperor in the west, 395-423.

B.   Constantinople was founded in 330 A.D., and became the capitol of the emperor of the east, but this did not mean that the two parts were to be entirely separated.
  1.   The idea of one government did not immediately pass away, but influenced men during the whole of the middle ages.

---

1 See Chapter IV for the Petrine Theory.

2. The eastern part of the empire withstood attack much
   longer than the western.
   a. Constantinople preserved civilization and became the
      most important city of Europe.
   b. Crusaders were impressed with eastern culture.
3. When the east "fell," in 1453, it was to the Turks, not to
   the Teutonic tribes.

   > *"The Roman state . . . was slowly undermined from
   > within . . . The recovery and health of this great but
   > deeply-diseased body seemed inconceivable; yet its
   > subversion and disappearance seemed equally so
   > amid the then forces of the world."* *

---

* *From* Morris, The Beginning of the Middle Ages, p. 5. Copyright 1886. *Used by
permission of* Charles Scribner's Sons, *publishers.*

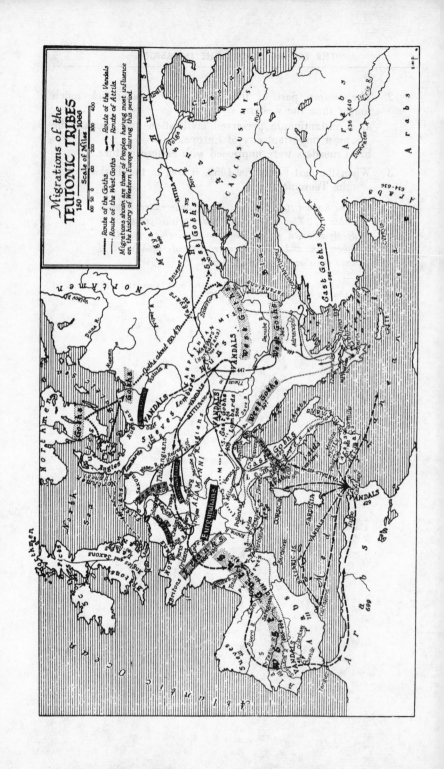

Migrations of the
TEUTONIC TRIBES

Scale of Miles
150   0   50   100   200   300   400   1050

Route of the Goths ....   Route of the Vandals
Route of the West Goths —   Route of Attila

Migrations shown are those of Peoples having most influence
on the history of Western Europe during this period.

CHAPTER II

BARBARIAN PEOPLES OF EUROPE

*"The early Germans were a hardy, vigorous race . . .
They were blonds with 'fierce blue eyes' and reddish
or golden hair, which they allowed to grow long, as
the visible mark of their freedom. They were fitful
and passionate in temper and often of a gloomy
nature . . . courage was the special virtue, and
cowardice the unpardonable sin."* *

I. **The barbaric peoples who fell upon the Roman Empire
came from Eastern and Northern Europe.**

A. These people were divided into many groups.
  1. Several were located along the North and the Baltic Seas.
    a. Northmen, Danes, and Jutes were residents of the
       Northern Peninsulas and adjacent islands.
    b. Vandals and Burgundians were to be found on either
       side of the Vistula.
    c. Lombards and Angles resided along the River Oder.
  2. East and West Goths were located on the border of the
     Black Sea.
  3. Finns lived near the headwaters of the Volga.
  4. Scythians and Tartars resided in a territory between the
     Dnieper and the Volga.
  5. Picts and Scots were settled in the western and northern
     parts of the British Isles.

B. The Teutons were Indo-Europeans or Aryans.
  1. They were a characteristically hardy, vigorous people who
     were very hospitable.
    a. Courage was their special virtue.
    b. However, they had certain vices, such as drunkenness
       and gambling.
  2. As they were nomads who lived mainly by hunting and fish-
     ing, their occupations were limited.
    a. Their herds were of poor quality.

---

* *From* Munro, The Middle Ages, p. 28. Copyright 1922. *Used by permission of* D.
Appleton-Century Company, *publishers.*

    b. Agriculture was practised, but not extensively.

    c. About their only trade was that of the smith.

        (1). They used iron for weapons.

        (2). Most of their ornaments were made of gold.

3. Generally they lived in villages; they disdained city life.

    a. Wooden houses were used in the summer—holes in the ground in winter.

    b. The Teutons' food was simple.

        (1). The favorite meat was horseflesh.

        (2). Game and fish were eaten only occasionally.

        (3). Grains and vegetables were an important part of their diet.

        (4). Honey was commonly used for sweetening.

    c. Their clothing, made by the women, consisted of fur, linen, and woolen garments.

4. Their religion was a combination of ancestor and nature worship, with a belief in many gods.

    a. Priests had great authority.

    b. Although noted for their vices, they were virtuous in many respects.

    c. They held intense regard for truth and faith.

    d. Women occupied an elevated position.

5. The government was very democratic, for the Teutons passionately loved liberty.

    a. The chiefs were chosen from the noblest families, and it is probably from these chiefs that the German kingship developed.

        (1). Leaders in battle were chosen for valor.

        (2). The chiefs' "companions" developed a relationship to the leader which later gave rise to the feudal organization.

    b. Public business was transacted in special assemblies attended by all freemen.

        (1). Here judicial matters were settled.

        (2). After being addressed by the leader they moved assent by the clash of weapons.

    c. Their judicial system was well established, but they had no police. The individual or the community had to bring offenders to court.

        (1). Guilt was determined by ordeals.

        (2). The death penalty was given to traitors and deserters.

        (3). The usual penalty was a fine; this was true even for murder.

        (4). Frequently a dispute was settled by fighting.

d. Every man wished to show valor in battle.
  (1). A quiet life was irksome to them; they sought battle.
  (2). Followers were obliged to match the courage of their chief.

C. The early German social organization was the "Sib," or enlarged family, corresponding to the Roman "Gen." It was their basic social as well as economic unit.
  1. Law was largely personal.
    a. It was unwritten, and held to a high degree the spirit of individualism.
    b. They did not hold, as did the Romans, that the will of the leader was law, or the later concept that all should be restrained by the written law codes.
  2. The Sib received the "Wergeld," divided a man's land on his death, and was responsible for the man's conduct.
  3. The chief formed a council of nobles, and this council prepared the laws and enterprises which the assembly as a whole assented to or dissented from.

II. The Goths were the first to penetrate the empire.

A. In prehistoric times the Goths supposedly lived in Scandinavia: the Visigoths, or West Goths, and the Ostrogoths, or East Goths.[1]

B. The Romans and Teutons were brought into early contact.
  1. The Romans mingled with the Germans in many ways.
    a. There was some contact through missionary work.
    b. The travel of traders was an important and very profitable contact.
    c. Their knowledge of Rome hastened the invasions.
  2. Whole tribes were sometimes allowed to enter the empire.
    a. They were enrolled in Roman armies.
    b. Frequently they held important civil posts.
    c. Sometimes they gained distinction and even intermarried.
  3. By the end of the third century the frontier was intact, but the enemy was threatening and there was a necessity for fortifying the frontier.
    a. Barbarian attacks began as early as 113 B.C.
    b. Others were driven back by Caesar.
    c. The Emperors Trajan and Hadrian strengthened fortifications.

---

[1] Germanic Migrations and Conquests, 150-1066, Shepherd's Historical Atlas. p, 45, sixth edition, 1927.

4. The prestige of Rome had been threatened.
   a. Rome relied upon the prestige of her name, to a certain extent, for her defense.
   b. The invasions were checked partly by fighting and partly by tribute.
   c. Rome used the principle of "divide and rule."[1]

   "The traditional policy of the Romans had been very effective. For several hundred years they had used with great effect their policy of 'divide and rule,' divide et impera." *

---

[1] Agents were sent among the Germans to precipitate trouble and thus prevent union among the various tribes.
* *From* Munro, The Middle Ages, p. 35. Copyright 1922. *Used by permission of* D. Appleton-Century Company, *publishers*

CHAPTER III

BARBARIAN INVASIONS AND THE DISINTEGRATION OF THE EMPIRE.

*"The marvellous prolificness of the Germans, added
to their lack of intensive methods of cultivating the
soil, precipitated the movement known as the wandering of the nations."* *

I. Various motives caused the Teutonic peoples to enter the Empire.

A. Sometimes economic necessity was the direct cause.
   1. They needed new lands.
      a. Pasture land for herds made migration necessary.
      b. Increased population made a large extent of territory imperative.
         (1). Agriculture was in a primitive stage.
         (2). Soil had been practically exhausted.
   2. Often they sought better homes and easier conditions of life.
      a. The great wealth of the empire was known to them.
      b. The temperate climate of Italy appealed to them.
      c. They desired to participate in Roman civilization.

B. Often their sole object was to plunder—or, perhaps, their love of adventure drove them on.

C. Frequently a tribe was driven into the empire by other barbaric peoples.
   1. The Huns were constantly pressing other tribes before them.
   2. Many were freely admitted by the Romans as a sort of buffer against the more barbarous tribes.

II. Vast numbers of the West Goths were forced across the Danube into the Roman Empire about 376 A.D.

A. The Visigoths[1] asked to cross the Danube and were given permission by the Emperor Valens.
   1. The Huns had forced them to the banks of the river.

---

* *From* Henderson, A Short History of Germany, p. 11. Copyright 1928. *Used by permission of* The Macmillan Company, *publishers.*
[1] For the migrations of the Visigoths and other tribes discussed in this chapter, see Shepherd's Historical Atlas, p. 45.

2. They were seeking safe homes.
   a. Ambassadors were sent to the emperor.
   b. They asked to be received by him as his subjects.

3. Then the Visigoths poured into the empire with Valens' permission.'
   a. The warriors were carelessly allowed to retain their weapons.
   b. They were mistreated by Roman officials, which caused them to revolt.

B. The Emperor Valens met his death in the battle of Adrianople, 378 A.D., the direct result of the Roman officials' mistreatment of these tribes.

   1. The Romans were defeated and the emperor slain.
   2. This battle of Adrianople demonstrated the value of cavalry as a weapon of war.
   3. "So now, with rage flashing in their eyes, the barbarians pursued our men, who were in a state of torpor, the warmth of their veins having deserted them." [1]

C. Theodosius was then elected emperor.

   1. He checked the invasions and made peace with the barbarians.
      a. He favored them during his reign.
      b. They fought loyally for him on many occasions.
   2. Theodosius died in 395, and was succeeded by his two sons who were both under age, and weaklings.
      a. His death was mourned by the Goths.
      b. The empire was divided between his two sons.
         (1). Arcadius became Emperor of the east with his capitol at Constantinople.
         (2). Honorius became Emperor of the west with his capitol at Ravenna.

D. Alaric, a barbarian, captured Rome in 410 A.D.

   1. Alaric was the leader of the Visigoths.
      a. They began their migrations in 395, which lasted for more than a generation.
      b. Their invasions extended over a large portion of the empire.
      c. They were stopped by Stilicho (a Vandal), an able general; but Honorius became distrustful of him, and had him put to death in 408.

---

[1] *From* the description by Americanus Marcellinus of the Huns and of the movement of the Goths. Robinson, Readings in European History, p. 35. Copyright 1906. *Used by permission of* Ginn and Company, *publishers.*

       d. Alaric then seized his opportunity and marched upon Rome.

  2. Finally, Rome was taken in August, 410.

       a. The capture was made possible by cutting off the food supply of the Romans.

       b. Honorius offered terms, but they were not accepted.

       c. The conquerors pillaged for several days.

       d. Many Romans were killed, many houses burned; but to their credit the Visigoths respected the principal churches, and frequently showed mercy to captives.

  3. Later movements of the Visigoths were extensive.

       a. They moved southward after the sack of Rome—perhaps Alaric intended to conquer Africa, but his fleet was destroyed in a storm.

       b. He died shortly afterward.

       c. Then they left Italy and passed into Gaul (412).

       d. From there they went to Spain under Athaulf.

       e. From this time Spain and Southern Gaul were held by the barbarians, independent of the Emperor.

III. The Vandals entered the empire in 406.

A. The frontiers had been left comparatively undefended.

  1. Consequently, the Vandals crossed the Danube, 406.

  2. After being defeated by the Visigoths they entered Roman Africa, which was too weak to defend itself, 429.

B. Finding the city defenseless, they captured Rome, 455.

  1. They ransacked the city for fourteen days.

  2. Taking all the treasure they could find, the Vandals set sail for Carthage.

  3. Many captives were carried away, destined to be sold into slavery.

C. After the death of Gaiseric, 477, they degenerated rapidly, and became amalgamated with the Roman population. Their name passed away as that of an historic race.

IV. After the invasions of the Vandals and the Burgundians, Rome was to be the victim of the Huns, the most barbaric of all the Barbarians.

A. The Huns were one of a series of Turanian or Mongoloid peoples who menaced Europe at intervals: Magyars, Tartars under Genghis Khan and Tamerlane; and more recently, the Seljik and Ottoman Turks.

  1. Of Asiatic stock—pagans and nomads—they fought wholly for plunder.

    2. Under Attila, "the scourge of God," they were united into a strong force.

B. Attila made several successful advances against Theodosius II.[1]
    1. He crossed the Danube, exacted a heavy tribute, and forced the emperor to give up the right bank of the Danube.
    2. Marcian was more successful against the Huns; he declared he had "gold for his friends, and a sword for his enemies."

C. The Battle of Chalons, 451, was one of the most momentous in history: it saved Europe for civilization.
    1. Aetius, called "last of the Romans," forced Attila to retreat.
    2. Aetius was a very able general. He had previously used Huns in his armies.

D. The end of the Huns as a menace came as a welcome relief to all Europe.
    1. In the following year Attila invaded Italy.
    2. Rome was saved by Pope Leo.
        a. Contemporary authors tell us that the Huns were stricken with disease and famine, and sued for peace.
        b. Pope Leo, known as the protector of Rome, became the mediator with the Huns.
    3. Attila died in 453, and with his death the Hunnic Empire crumbled to pieces.

V. Clovis, a Frank, developed a Frankish empire out of part of what had been Gaul.

A. The conquests of Clovis were extensive.
    1. Around the lower Rhine there were several tribes who came to be known as Franks.
    2. Clovis, the founder of the Frankish nation, succeeded in numerous conquests.
        a. The conquest of Gaul was comparatively easy because of its divided condition.
        b. With the defeat of Syagrius, 486, the Franks were masters of the country.
        c. Little was left of the empire of the west.
    3. Three peoples now held dominion in Gaul: the Visigoths, the Burgundians, and the Franks.

B. Clovis was converted to orthodox Christianity, and the results were more far-reaching than even Clovis could have foreseen.
    1. This was the most important event in his reign.
    2. He was converted through the influence of his wife.

---

[1] Not to be confused with Emperor Theodosius (The Great)—379-395. Theodosius II was famed especially for his publication in 438 of a collection of Roman Imperial laws. These included edicts on religion indicating the triumph of Christianity within the Roman system.

     a. The king had registered a vow that he would accept the God of his Burgundian wife if successful in the battle of Tolbiacume.

     b. He called upon God when the battle was going against him, promising to accept Christianity if victorious. He won the victory and kept his promise.

  3. With him, his sister and 3000 warriors were baptized.

  4. Clovis became a champion of the Catholic faith, but mainly for political purposes, as his brutality is proverbial.

  5. The way was opened for a close alliance between the Roman papacy and the kingdom of the Franks.

VI. The "Fall of the Roman Empire" is a misnomer, as it did not "fall" in the strict sense—it disintegrated.

A. The year 476 has frequently been given as the date of the so-called "fall of the Roman Empire."

  1. In this year the empire of the west all but ended, except in name.

     a. Power had long been in the hands of the barbarian generals.

     b. There was only one empire, but it was in a desperate position.

     c. The greater part of the empire was controlled by barbaric kings.

  2. The eastern emperor sent Theodoric to recover Italy from the German kings.

     a. The new champion was king of the Ostrogoths, residing in the eastern empire.

     b. The whole nation of the Ostrogoths set out on their long journey to Italy.

     c. By 493 Theodoric was ruler of all Italy.

  3. Theodoric set up a good government in Italy.

     a. He unified Romans and Goths.

     b. Under him Italy was prosperous.

     c. He granted religious freedom.

     d. Theodoric was a good man in spite of the many deeds of violence attributed to him.

     e. He was really in advance of his age.

B. The causes of the disintegration of the empire were many.

  1. Too numerous political divisions encouraged decentralization of authority.

  2. Slavery had displaced middle classes—yeomanry.

  3. Depopulation had resulted from riotous living.

  4. Unjust taxation was entirely too common.

5. Incoming barbarians displaced true Romans.
6. The coming of Christianity is sometimes given as an in-
    direct cause.
    a. It displaced the old civic religion, which made for
        patriotism and civic virtue.
    b. Monasticism and virginity led to race suicide.
    c. Barrenness in learning resulted from the great impor-
        tance placed upon theology.
    d. Probably, Christianity had the least effect, and per-
        haps was even helpful in some respects.

> *"It must not be supposed of these wandering German
> conquerors that, wherever they came, they utterly
> stamped out the Roman civilization."**

---

* *From* Henderson, A Short History of Germany, p. 12. Copyright 1928. *Used by permission of* The Macmillan Company, *publishers.*

CHAPTER IV

THE RISE OF THE PAPACY; CONVERSION OF ENGLAND AND GERMANY

"Gregory was the first of the great popes of the Middle Ages. His work may be summed up under two heads: (1) To make the bishop of Rome a temporal sovereign in Rome and Italy; (2) To prepare the West to receive the spiritual primacy of Rome." *

I. The church was gradually laying the foundation for its future supremacy.

A. It was known as the Catholic, or all-embracing church.

    1. Rulers had made the church legal.

    2. Safeguards were set up for the church and the clergy.

B. The church had several sources of strength.

    1. It met the wants of those who lived under it.

    2. Christianity had brought a fear of death and judgment.

       a. The religion of the pagan was merely an affair of this life; he visualized no future life.

       b. Greeks and Romans thought the next life uninteresting.

       c. They thought they should enjoy the present without regard to the future.

       d. Christianity laid emphasis upon man's existence after death: this resulted in monasticism.

    3. Membership in the church was held to be the one agent of salvation.

    4. Performance of miracles helped to convert people to Christianity.

II. The church soon sought independence.

A. The church and the Roman government were at first friendly.

    1. They respected and supported each other.

       a. The emperor adopted the policy of paternalism.

       b. The church undertook to root out paganism.

---

* From Bemont and Monod, Medieval Europe, p. 121. Copyright 1930. *Used by permission of* Henry Holt and Company, *publishers.*

    2. Then the church sought independence.
       a. The church resented the barbarian rulers.
       b. It freed itself from civil government, performing many
          secular duties.

B. The church began to perform functions of government.
    1. It offered itself as a substitute when efficient civil govern-
       ment no longer existed.
    2. Keeping order fell to the well-organized church.
       a. It performed functions which had formerly belonged
          to the state.
       b. Conditions were such that the church could greatly ex-
          tend its power.

III. The bishop of Rome became the head of the church.

A. The bishop of Rome claimed to be the divinely ordained head
of the Christian church. The claim was based upon three main
assumptions:
    1. That Peter was designated by Christ as chief of the
       Apostles.
    2. That Peter was the first bishop of Rome.
    3. That Peter handed down the power and influence he en-
       joyed to succeeding bishops.

B. There was a distinction between the bishop of Rome's position
as religious and as governmental head of the church.
    1. Probably, at first, he enjoyed no greater jurisdiction than
       other metropolitans, such as the archbishop of Alexandria,
       or the archbishop of Antioch.
       a. However, he was destined to be recognized both as
          spiritual and governmental head of the church.
       b. He was the only patriarch[1] in the west; therefore, he
          had no competition.
    2. Since Rome was the seat of the government of the empire,
       it seemed natural to think of her bishop as the first bishop
       in the world.

C. Leo the Great was the first to give a clear-cut expression to the
Petrine theory.
    1. He contended that bishops of Rome were apostolic succes-
       sors of St. Peter, giving them preeminence over the other
       bishops.[2]

---

[1] As several political provinces were grouped together to form a larger division
(eparchy), so several ecclesiastical provinces, with archbishops at their respective
heads, were grouped together to form a larger province, with an over-archbishop at
its head. For this officer and his diocese the words, *Patriarch* and *Patriarchate*, were
used in the fourth century.
[2] Antioch, Jerusalem, Alexandria, and Constantinople.

2. This theory was in time accepted as the basis for the supremacy of the bishop of Rome.

IV. The authority of the pope was temporal as well as spiritual.

A. The pope was the man of highest rank in Rome.

1. He represented the only institution which retained virility.
2. Other institutions represented universal corruption and decay.
3. The pope became the virtual ruler of Rome by the end of the sixth century.
   a. He had great power.
   b. This power was due largely to the personality of Pope Gregory the Great.

B. Gregory the Great contributed greatly in bringing temporal and religious prestige to the papacy.

1. Patricians and freemen alike were much surprised when he withdrew from the world.
   a. He was the son of a rich Roman senator.
   b. Previously he had held high positions.
   c. He feared he was becoming vain and worldly.
2. Gregory's fortune was spent in establishing monasteries.
   a. Seven monasteries were founded by him.
   b. He succeeded in bringing Lombard Italy, Visigothic Spain, and Anglo-Saxon England again under the sway of the Roman church.
3. He saw, and helped bring about Rome's transition from ancient to medieval Rome.
   a. A transformation took place with the election of Gregory, 590 A.D.
   b. Ancient Rome as capitol of the empire gradually changed into medieval Rome as the capitol of Christendom.
4. Gregory was noted as a writer, a statesman, and a missionary.
   a. He enjoyed an unrivaled reputation as a writer.
   b. He assumed the title "Servant of the servants of God," which is used by popes to this day.
   c. As an enthusiastic monk, he relied upon the monks in his great work of converting the heathen.
   d. He was, in fact, a really great statesman.

V. The church, with the aid of the monks, brought about the conversion of the Barbarians.

A. Monasticism made rapid progress in the fifth and sixth centuries.
   1. It was favored by the church fathers.
       a. Many withdrew from the world.
       b. The monastery was the natural refuge of the spiritually minded, those of a scholarly disposition, and those who disliked the dangers of the time.
   2. It is difficult to overestimate the influence of the monks.
       a. They were leaders in many branches of activity.
       b. Many eminent philosophers, scientists, historians, statesmen, and poets were among them.
       c. Important advances in agriculture were made.

B. Western monks were governed by the St. Benedictine rule.
   1. At first monasticism lacked organization.
       a. Monasticism originated in the east. Consequently, eastern rules were generally used.
       b. Conditions in the west, however, were different from those in the east.
   2. The Benedictine rule was established to govern the western monks.
       a. It was based upon three fundamental vows: poverty, chastity, and obedience.
       b. Government of the monastery was administered by the abbot; his will was supreme.
       c. In important matters the abbot called together the whole congregation for counsel before making his decision.

C. Gregory and the monks succeeded in converting England to Christianity.
   1. Upon becoming pope, Gregory sent forty monks to England.
       a. Gregory grieved over the Angles being sold into slavery.
       b. The monks were kindly received.[1] They were assigned an ancient church at Canterbury, 597.
   2. The conversion of Ethelbert of Kent was important.
       a. He was the most powerful petty king on the island.
       b. Augustine[2] became archbishop of the English.
       c. Canterbury became the English capitol of Christendom.

---

[1] Due to the influence of the Christian wife of the heathen king of Kent, Ethelbert.
[2] Not St. Augustine.

3. Augustine's influence became great in all lands which recognized Ethelbert's supremacy.

4. The Roman church won a victory over the Celtic customs in 664.
   a. Irish monks had departed from Roman usages.
      (1). Conflict was inevitable between the Irish and the Roman monks.
      (2). Neither side would make concessions.
   b. The assembly at Whitby, 664, resulted in the acceptance of the Roman idea.
      (1). The King of Northumbria brought about the concession.
      (2). Gradually Celtic customs were abandoned in England, and eventually in Scotland, Wales, and Ireland.
   c. England remained faithful to the Bishop of Rome until Henry VIII broke away in the sixteenth century—largely for personal reasons.

D. Boniface brought about the conversion of Germany.
   1. He was commissioned by Pope Gregory II to preach the gospel to the heathen tribes.
      a. He was appointed by the pope as the presiding bishop of Germany, 722.
      b. Charles Martel assured him of full protection and assistance. They worked for mutual advancement.
      c. Boniface cut down Odin's Oak and used it to build a chapel.
   2. Irish monks had preceded Benedictine monks in Germany.
      a. The Irish monks were now driven out or converted.
      b. Benedictine monks were installed in place of the Irish.
      c. New homes were founded for the Benedictine monks. Fulda, founded in 744, became the most important.
   3. Boniface, after completing his work, met a martyr's death at the hands of the Frisians in 755.

   "The Popes were the Emperor's subjects; they awaited his confirmation, like other bishops; they had more than once been the victim of his anger. But as the city became more accustomed to a practical independence, and the Pope rose to a predominance, real if not yet legal, his tone grew bolder than that of the Eastern patriarchs." *

* *From* Bryce, The Holy Roman Empire, p. 37. Copyright 1904. *Used by permission* of The Macmillan Company, *publishers.*

CHAPTER V
ORIGIN AND INFLUENCE OF MOHAMMEDANISM

> *"According to the tradition of his companions, Mahomet was distinguished . . . . His memory was capacious and retentive, his wit easy and social, his imagination sublime, his judgment clear, rapid, and decisive. He possessed the courage both of thought and action; and, although his designs might gradually expand with his success, the first idea which he entertained of his divine mission, bears the stamp of an original and superior genius."* *

I. The Mohammedans early became an important factor in the development of Western Europe.

A. This new religion developed in the east.
   1. It became a serious menace to the Roman Empire.
   2. The causes of its rapid growth were numerous.
      a. Geographical, political, and physical conditions were conducive to its growth, as were the customs and character of the Arabians.
      b. Their leader, Mohammed, was a man of remarkable personality.

B. In desert Arabia the hardy Arab had dwelt from time immemorial.
   1. These people lived in a constant struggle with nature.
      a. Arabia was an elevated plateau—mostly a desert waste.
      b. There were no forests and little vegetation.
      c. The Arabs were reputed to be descendants of Ishmael —the "wild man of the desert."
   2. The Arabs lived in a state of independence and freedom from the rest of the world.
      a. They had never bowed to a foreign conqueror.
      b. This was due to their local position, and, as some believe, to the fulfillment of prophecy.
      c. There was no central government; each tribe governed itself.
         (1). The family was the unit in times of peace.

---

* *From* Gibbon, The Decline and Fall of the Roman Empire, p. 394.

(2). Polygamy was practiced.
d. Two classes existed in the seventh century.
(1). The Bedouins, who lived in tents, were nomads.
(2). The House-dwellers were found only near the coast.

3. Before the rise of Mohammed, they were liberal and tolerant in their religious belief.
a. Their ancient religion was Sabaism—star worship.
b. It assumed many forms, being a mixture of nature-worship and fetishism.
c. All, however, believed in one supreme God, Allah.
d. There were also devotees of other religions in Arabia (Jewish, Christian, Persian), as absolute toleration prevailed.

II. The prophet Mohammed, as he came to be known, developed a new religion.

A. He called upon the people to abandon their idols and recognize the one true God.
1. He thought he was called upon to preach.
a. He retired one month each year to meditate and pray.
b. On one occasion he had a vision in which he believed an angel commanded him to preach.
2. His wife encouraged him in his desire to spread the new religion.
a. He began preaching God's power through nature.
b. In three years he made only fourteen converts.
c. No supernatural powers were claimed by him.
(1). He was known as the prophet of God.
(2). There was little new in his religion.
3. Opposition caused the prophet's flight from Mecca[1] to Medina. This is known as the Hegira.
a. He began to preach against idols.
b. As opposition grew, his life was endangered.
c. He fled to Medina in 622 with Abu-Bekr, who was destined to become his successor.
d. From this flight the Mohammedans still date their lunar year of 364 days.
e. The teachings of the prophet might have perished had not Medina "embraced with faith and reverence the holy outcasts of Mecca."

B. The Mohammedan holy book is known as the Koran.
1. After Mohammed's death his revelations were collected and published by his successor.

---

[1] Mecca had long been held as somewhat sacred by Arabian tribesmen.

a. These revelations came to the prophet over a period of twenty-three years.
b. It became the religious guide of all Mohammedans.
c. The Koran contains frequent repetitions and contradictions, and most of it is commonplace. Nevertheless, some parts are very beautiful.

2. The material is borrowed chiefly from Jewish and Christian scriptures.
a. Much of the Koran was "inspired" by legendary sources.
b. The two main points of faith are: "There is but one God, and Mahomet is his prophet."

3. In it there was incorporated a definite moral code.
a. Temperance was emphasized.
b. The fatalism of the Mohammedan religion, however, has proved a blight upon its followers.

III. The great spread of Mohammedanism occurred after Mohammed's death in 632.

A. After the Hegira, Mohammed was well received in Medina.[1]

1. Soon the whole city recognized him as its leader and prophet.

2. His religion was to be established by the sword.
a. After seven years there was little opposition.
b. Mecca[2] swore allegiance to him.
c. Conquest and voluntary submission of the remainder of Arabia soon followed.
d. In 632, the year of his death, 114,000 Musselmans[3] marched under his banner.

B. Abu-Bekr succeeded Mohammed and the Mohammedan conquest began.

1. There was a general reorganization of government.
a. Many revolted after Mohammed's death, because they resented the restrictions and taxation placed upon them.
b. Abu-Bekr reduced all Arabia to obedience again.
c. The Arabs became united into a nation for the first time.

2. They soon made notable conquests in the east.[4]
a. They destroyed the empire of the Sassanids.
b. The Roman Empire was robbed of many provinces.

---

[1] "Known under the name of Yathreb before it was sanctified by the throne of the prophet."
[2] The city from which he was forced to flee in 622.
[3] Musselman signifies in Turkish language "a true believer."
[4] See Shepherd's Historical Atlas, pp. 53, 54, and 55.

      (1). Within fifteen years Syria, Palestine, Crete, Cyprus, Rhodes, Armenia, and Egypt were taken.

      (2). Success was due to the fatalism of the Moslems and to the weakness of the Roman Empire.

    c. The Ommiads established their capital at Damascus, 661-750.

      (1). Rule became more centralized; the office of caliph became hereditary.

      (2). All Arabia recognized the authority of Damascus.

      (3). Luxury became common; democracy was lost.

      (4). However, further advance was possible.

    d. The Abbassides succeeded the Ommiads with their capital at Bagdad, 750-1258. Ultimately there were three caliphates, with capitals at Bagdad, Cairo, and Cordova.

    e. They laid siege to Constantinople which withstood their attacks.

3. Eventually they succeeded in their attempted conquest of northern Africa.

    a. The conquest began in the latter part of the seventh century, lasting about fifty years.

    b. Carthage was destroyed in 697.

    c. The Berbers of northern Africa were converted to Mohammedanism.

    d. The Arabian fleet was supreme in the Mediterranean by 708.

    e. Latin civilization then disappeared in northern Africa.

4. The conquest of Spain followed their other victories.

    a. They passed from Africa over into Spain; the conquest was easy.

    b. The Visigothic kingdom in Spain was weak.

    c. Tarik landed near Gibraltar in 711, opening the whole country to the Arabs.

    d. The oppressed Jews aided the invaders.

    e. Soon, practically the whole peninsula was occupied by the Moslems.

5. Their attempted invasion of Gaul failed when they were defeated in the Battle of Tours.

    a. Moslem ambition began to look beyond the Pyrenees.

    b. Narbonne was occupied in 720.

    c. The Mohammedans were defeated by Charles Martel in the Battle of Tours (or Poitiers) in 732.

      (1). The importance of this battle can hardly be overestimated from the point of view of the future of Christianity.

> (2). Further advance was checked by the revolt of the Berbers.[1]

6. The Mohammedan forces next invaded Sicily and Italy, but were finally expelled.
   a. They came later than other invaders.
   b. They renewed their raids upon the Mediterranean Islands in the eighth and ninth centuries. Crete was occupied in 826.
   c. Sicily was under conquest by the Aghlabids, 827-902.
   d. They conquered Bari about 841, and then attacked Rome in 846.
   e. The Saracens were expelled from Italy about 915—permanently.

IV. The Mohammedan religion differed greatly from the Christian, particularly in its organization.

A. In its fundamental tenets it was similar in many respects.
   1. But, there was no priesthood, no images, and no elaborate ritual.
   2. Its simplicity recommended it to the simple desert folk.

B. The reward of the Moslem heaven was much more real than that of the Christian.
   1. In fact, there was a real inducement to die, because of the pleasures their heaven held out to the faithful.
   2. Fatalism was a great factor in their military success.

V. The Mohammedans left a lasting impression upon the culture of Western Civilization.

A. Many centers of Mohammedan culture were located in Spain.
   1. Cordova was the Bagdad of the west.
      a. The ninth and tenth centuries saw the greatest development.
      b. The library of Al Hakam is illustrative.
   2. Seville became the center of luxury.
   3. Toledo was a famous seat of learning.
   4. The University of Cordova was world famous.

B. The Mohammedans were patrons of science and medicine.
   1. They used the experimental method.
   2. Achievements were gained in astronomy, chemistry, and physics.
   3. They contributed to invention and discovery.

---

[1] They had been enlisted in the Arab armies, and now regretted their lost independence.

C. They were renowned architects.

    1. Decorative art was to be found in many places.

    2. Their architecture was notable.

        a. The great mosque—Cordova.

        b. The Giralda and Alcazar—Seville.

        c. The Alhambra—Granada.

D. In the eleventh century Latin Christians took the offensive against the Mohammedans, and in time the latter were expelled from Europe, but not for several centuries.

> "'The sword,' says Mahomet, 'is the key of heaven and of hell: a drop of blood shed in the cause of God, a night spent in arms, is of more avail than two months of fasting and prayer: whosoever falls in battle, his sins are forgiven; at the day of judgement his wounds shall be resplendent as vermillion, and odoriferous as musk; and the loss of his limbs shall be supplied by the wings of angels and cherubim.' The intrepid souls of the Arabs were fired with enthusiasm: the picture of the invisible world was strongly painted on their imagination; and the death which they had always despised became an object of hope and desire." *

---

* *From* Gibbon, The Decline and Fall of the Roman Empire, p. 425.

CHAPTER VI

THE FRANKS TO THE TIME OF CHARLEMAGNE

*"Clovis was a nominal convert to Christianity . . .
But his religion . . . seems to have exerted no influence in restraining the natural ferocity and blood-
thirstiness of his disposition, as all the rival monarchs or chieftains whom he could conquer or en-
trap were sacrificed to his jealousy and ambition."* *

I. The Franks were destined to found a strong state in Western Europe.

A. The early history of the Franks is very obscure.

    1. In 500 A.D. there were various "tribe-nations"[1] living in the territory now occupied by the French.

        a. Gallo-Romans

        b. Visigoths

        c. Burgundians

        d. Alemanni

        e. Salien and Ripuarian Franks

        f. Thuringians, etc.

    2. The Franks[2] originally occupied only a small part of Gaul.

        a. In 500 they probably occupied four cities in north-eastern Gaul.

        b. They were governed by four separate kings.

        c. Clovis was the most powerful of the four kings.

            (1). He made war upon the remains of the Roman power in Gaul.

            (2). Soissons was his capitol.

    3. By 511 nearly half of modern France was part of Clovis' new empire.

B. Clovis, who rose from an obscure petty kingship to control of a large territory, ruled as king of the Salien Franks from 481 to 511.

    1. He was eminently successful, making many conquests.

        a. Clovis became king at fifteen years of age. His people were still pagans, and backward in civilization.

---

* *From* Wilson, Outlines of History. p. 255.
[1] See map p. 53—Shepherd's Historical Atlas.
[2] In contrast to other tribes, the Franks expanded through annexation rather than migration, and subsequently abandonment of their home territory.

      b. He gained by conquest the Roman lands to the south. (This part of Gaul had never been conquered by the Germans).

      c. Theodoric, the Ostrogoth, interfered, but Clovis conquered the greater part of Gaul. However, Theodoric succeeded in shutting the Franks off from the Mediterranean.

  2. The most important event in Clovis' reign was his conversion to Christianity. He became the champion of the Catholic faith.

      a. He made the new faith a pretext for war.

      b. The Roman subjects were ready to obey Clovis, as they looked upon him as the agent of God.

C. The sons and grandsons of Clovis were not truly great.

  1. Clovis died in 511; his four sons divided his possessions among themselves.

  2. The period was noted for civil strife, although the Franks increased their territory.

  3. By 558 Lothair secured the whole kingdom.

  4. At Lothair's death in 561 the kingdom was again parceled out among his four sons.

II. A new era was ushered in when Pippin, the first of the Carolingian line, replaced the "Do Nothing" Merovingians.

A. The power of the Merovingians[1] steadily declined.

  1. Power grew weaker with the division of the kingdom at the death of Louis.

  2. Dagobert, who was king over all the Franks, 628-38, was the last to enjoy independent authority.

      a. After him came the "Do nothing kings," (Rois faineants) 639-751.

      b. They were mere figure-heads—puppets in the hands of the mayors of the palace in the three kingdoms, Austrasia, Neustria, and Burgundy.

  3. The mayor of the palace exercised royal authority.

      a. However, he did not have the royal name.

      b. After the death of Dagobert the office of mayor of the palace in Austrasia became hereditary in the family of Pippin the Elder.

  4. Pippin the Younger seized the office and practically ruled Austrasia.

---

[1] Merovingian was the name given to the first dynasty of France. This was in 486 A.D.; the first king was the Salien Frank, Clovis—his rule described above.

       a. He became master of Neustria also, after a long war, 687-714.

       b. Finally, he ruled over the whole of "Frankland."

       c. Pippin the Younger strove for centralization and consolidation.

          (1). Tried to make his government absolute.

          (2). Worked for a homogeneous people.

B. Charles Martel continued the policy of his father, Pippin.

    1. He put down many rebellions—Frisians, Neustrians, Thuringians, Bavarians, Alamanni, and Aquitains.

    2. The winning of the Battle of Tours, 732, was one of the greatest victories of western civilization.

       a. The Mohammedans were turned back.

       b. Thus, their power north of the Pyrenees was broken by Charles Martel.

    3. At the death of Charles Martel his authority over "Frankland" finally fell to his son Pippin the Short.

       a. He had divided the power between his two sons, Carloman and Pippin.

       b. Carloman resigned and went into a monastery, which left Pippin in sole power.

C. Pippin attained the Kingship of the Franks in 751.

    1. Pippin had desired to become king.

       a. He sent an embassy to Rome to ask Pope Zacharias who should be king—the old line or the real rulers, the Mayors-of-the-Palace.

       b. The pope favored Pippin—the one with power, instead of the Merovingian who had no power.[1]

    2. Pippin called an assembly of nobles at Soissons to carry out the pope's will.

       a. The last phantom Merovingian was deposed.

       b. Pippin was formally elected and annointed king of the Franks.

III. Pippin dealt with the Lombards, Saracens, and others in a masterful manner.

A. The Franks allied themselves with the papacy.

    1. The Lombards had threatened the pope.

       a. They had conquered Ravenna and looked toward Rome.

       b. The eastern emperor failed to protect Italy.

       c. The pope was unable to defend either the people or the territory.

---

[1] This set a precedent of great historic moment. It seems to recognize the papal authority to set up and depose temporal rulers; hence, the theory of the ascendancy of the church over the state.

2. The pope asked for the aid of Pippin, who made two successful expeditions against the Lombards.

    a. The Lombards were forced to give up several cities, including Ravenna.

    b. They promised to refrain from attacking Rome.

B. As a result, the conquered territory was turned over to the pope.

    1. The keys to the conquered cities were solemnly carried to the pope and placed upon St. Peter's tomb, together with a deed of gift.

    2. This was to be known as the famous "donation of Pippin."

C. Pippin carried on many other successful wars.

    1. He expelled the Saracens from Narbonne in 759.

    2. He reduced all Aquitaine to submission.

        a. It required five years of fighting.

        b. This completed the work of Charles Martel.

    3. He put down revolt in Bavaria.

    4. He was successful against the Saxons.

D. Pippin showed himself to be an able ruler.

    1. He won recognition from the Caliph at Bagdad and the Emperor at Constantinople.

    2. His work prepared the way for Charlemagne, whose renown has to a great extent obscured the services of the father.

E. Upon the death of Pippin in 768, the realm was divided between his two sons, Charles and Carloman.

> *"In 768 Pepin the Short, the great King of the Franks, passed away to make room for his greater son, whom the common usage of history knows in Latin as Carolus Magnus, or . . . Charlemagne."* *

---

* *From* Davis, A History of France, p. 29. Copyright 1919. *Used by permission of* Houghton Mifflin Company, *publishers.*

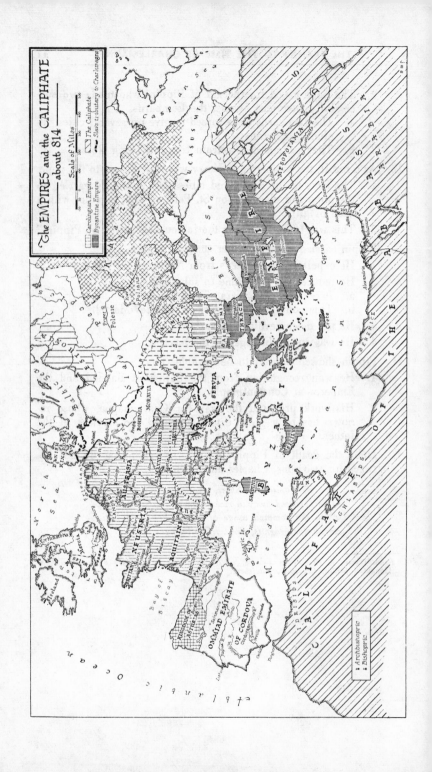

The EMPIRES and the CALIPHATE
about 814

Scale of Miles

Carolingian Empire
Byzantine Empire
The Caliphate
Slavs tributary to Charlemagne

† Archbishopric
‡ Bishopric

CHAPTER VII

THE EMPIRE OF CHARLEMAGNE

*"His reign marked an epoch between the ancient
world and the modern, and his commanding personality stamped its impress deeply upon his own age
and cast its shadow over several subsequent
centuries."* *

**I. Charlemagne continued the policy of his father and his
ancestors.**

A. He was the heir of old policies rather than the originator of
new.

    1. The consolidation of the Frankish kingdom was necessary.

    2. He adopted the policies started by the mayors of the palace.

    3. The legend of the Roman Empire was still present; so he
set out to build up a universal empire.

B. Charlemagne became the sole ruler of the Franks in 771.

    1. Carloman died in 771.

    2. Charles stripped his brother's widow and children of their
inheritance, and added this territory to his own domains.

II. He completed the military work of his predecessors.

A. His major conquests were against the Lombards and Saxons.

    1. The war against the Lombards was a continuation of Pip-
pin's work in aiding the pope.

        a. Desiderius, Lombard king and a friend of Carloman,
had reconquered the Lombard cities.

            (1). These Pippin had formerly forced him to sur-
render to the pope.

            (2). This conquest by Desiderius was an attempt to
aid Carloman's widow in regaining her children's
inheritance.

        b. This condition Charles considered just cause for war.
Desiderius was captured and Charles forced the
Lombards to recognize him as their king, in 774.

---

* *From* Davis, A History of France, p. 29. Copyright 1919. *Used by permission of*
Houghton Mifflin Company, *publishers.*

33

2, His Saxon wars, lasting over thirty years, were successful.
   a. The conquests of the Saxons were Charles' greatest military achievements. Their lands extended from beyond the Elbe almost to the Rhine.
   b. The Saxons were still heathen.
      (1). They had been a constant source of annoyance.
      (2). Frequent inroads of destruction had been made by them into Frankish territory.
   c. The war was carried on with great fury.
      (1). At Verdun, in 782, about 4500 Saxons were executed in one day.
      (2). The Saxons, once conquered, would not keep the terms of peace; thus, the long period of the war.
      (3). Finally, when the youth of Saxony revolted, Charles scattered throughout the empire 10,000 of those living on the Elbe.
   d. At length peace was granted the Saxons who submitted to the Frankish institutions, as well as to Christianity.

B. Charles continued the "donation" to the pope.
   1. He renewed Pippin's donation at the pope's request.
   2. Theoretically, he gave most of Italy to the pope, but actually, he never relinquished his control over the territory.

III. Charles carried on many frontier wars.

A. His first war was occasioned by a revolt in Aquitaine.
   1. This territory had been recently conquered by his father.
      a. These people revolted.
      b. He was forced to compel submission.
   2. Charles was successful in putting down this revolt; the province was firmly annexed.

B. Charles carried on wars in Spain, 778-811.
   1. This war has lived in song. (Chanson de Roland, great epic poem of the French).
   2. Roncesvalles—778.
      a. Here Charles was compelled to retreat.
      b. Count Roland was slain.
      c. This defeat was never avenged by Charles.
      d. Establishment later of the "Spanish March."

C. For about forty years Charles was almost constantly engaged in military conflict of some kind.
   1. In Bavaria.
   2. Against the Danish king, Godfried.

3. With the Slavs and the Avars.
4. Added territory beyond the Danube.
5. Aided Egbert, Saxon king, to regain his throne in England.

D. He succeeded in building up a vast empire.

1. Even before his coronation his territory might be spoken of as an empire.
2. He had conquered all the barbarous tribes in Germany between the Rhine and the Vistula, and the ocean and the Danube.
3. At the end of the eighth century conditions were ripe for the installation of a new emperor in the west.

IV. Charlemagne became emperor in the West.

A. The pope, Leo III, was in need of his protection.

1. Conspiracy in Rome had endangered the pope.
2. Charlemagne, in 800, visited Rome to punish the evil doers.

B. Charlemagne was crowned emperor on Christmas day, 800.

1. The coronation took place in St. Peter's Church.
   a. Charles was attending the Christmas festival.
   b. The pontiff placed upon his head a crown of gold, and saluted him by the titles of Emperor and Augustus.[1]
2. This act was considered as the revival of the empire of the west, after an interruption of about three centuries.[2]

V. Charles set up an imperial system of government.

A. He developed the methods of his predecessors.

1. He summoned the general assemblies regularly. They were composed of nobles and some clergy—not all freemen.
2. Counts were employed as his chief officials.
3. He made many important changes.
   a. The institution of the privy council had its origin here.
   b. Territory was divided into counties. Marks were put on the borders.
   c. He employed the *missi dominici*.
      (1). Into each district were sent each year two missi, one to check on the other.

---

[1] This was in accordance with the formula observed for the Roman emperors, but Charles did not seem to be entirely pleased with the title from the hands of the pope. It may have interfered with his plans. Certainly, it established a precedent which tended to make his successors subservient to the pope. However, Charles kept the church in control. He used the church to cement his heterogeneous subjects together.

[2] See pp. 54-55 Shepherd's Historical Atlas.

        (2). They represented the emperor.
            (a). They held court and corrected abuses.
            (b). Acted as a check upon the counts.
      d. The missi greatly aided centralized government.[1]

B. Charles' financial system was thorough.
   1. There were few expenses to be paid by the imperial treasury.
      a. Public works were taken care of locally.
      b. Soldiers cared for their own maintenance.
      c. There was no navy.
   2. Charles' income consisted of:
      a. Fines and gifts.
      b. Produce from his estates—the most important.
   3. His capitularies were very famous.
      a. The famous "Capitulary de Villis" was an order for the taking of inventories of his estates.
      b. They were a great source of information to Charles, and throw much light upon the economic and social condition of the time.
   4. He displaced the old tribal laws by territorial regulations.

VI. Charles was greatly interested in education and the social activities of his day.

A. He was "large and robust, and of commanding stature," and when crowned emperor was about 58 years of age.
   1. His appearance was always stately and dignified.
   2. His habits were simple.
      a. Was temperate in eating and drinking.
      b. Fond of exercise—especially swimming.
   3. His ideals were high, and he laid stress upon morality and piety for his subjects.
      a. He was of a very serious nature—conscientious.
      b. He compelled his subjects to take an oath of fidelity to him as emperor.
      c. The one defect in his character was sexual lawlessness which was characteristic of the chieftains of his race.

B. He was intensely interested in education and wanted to increase the knowledge and influence of his people.
   1. He opened schools for nobles as well as for the lower classes.

---

1 Brunner sees the origin of the circuit judges in England, and consequently of those of the U.S., in these missi and the courts which they held during their circuit. But Stubbs and others deny that the missi had any influence, even indirect, upon the English institution. It is certain that Charles introduced into the courts many of the elements which are found in the courts today. He applied much of the procedure found in Roman law.

        a. He took lessons in grammar and attempted to learn to write.

        b. He brought about a reform in writing which resulted in many beautiful manuscripts.

    2. Throughout his reign he frequently indicated his high regard for the old Roman civilization.

    3. An academy was formed at his command.

        a. There assembled at his court many learned men.

        b. This greatly stimulated education.

    4. He also established many churches.

C. We can describe Charlemagne's reign as "A patch of light in a vast gloom."

    1. His greatness lies in his nobility of aim, his great energy, and his wisdom; however, there has arisen in literature a "Legend of Charlemagne" attributing much to him which he does not deserve.

    2. In the greatness of his character and in his manysided activities we may compare him to a Caesar or an Alexander.

    3. His name has had a magic influence upon subsequent generations.

    4. His main purpose was to unite into a new people the best characteristics of the German stock and the older civilizations.

D. Charlemagne died of fever at the age of seventy-one in 814.

    1. He had reigned forty-seven years.

    2. The imperial position went to his only surviving son, Louis the Pious.

> *"Charlemagne's reign fills but a short time in the long period of the Middle Ages, but it binds the whole together. In him is completed the process which runs through the first half, the Germanization of the Roman Empire."* *

---

* *From* Adams, Medieval and Modern History, p. 70. Copyright 1903. *Used by permission of* The Macmillan Company, *publishers.*

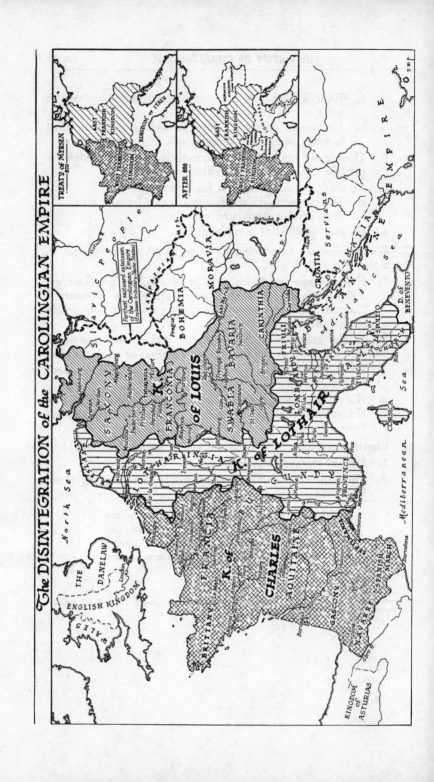

The DISINTEGRATION of the CAROLINGIAN EMPIRE

CHAPTER VIII

THE DISINTEGRATION OF CHARLEMAGNE'S EMPIRE

"The posterity of Charlemagne were unequal to the task of preserving the empire which he had formed, and it speedily fell asunder by its own weight . . . . about thirty years after the death of Charlemagne (A.D. 814) . . . the empire was divided among his descendants, and out of it were constituted the separate kingdoms,—France, Germany, and Italy, by the treaty of Verdun, August 11th, 843." *

I. With the passing of Charlemagne, his empire was destined to disintegrate.

A. Charlemagne was succeeded by Louis the Pious.

    1. He was the only legitimate son at Charlemagne's death.
      a. The empire passed to him.
      b. There are great differences of opinion regarding his character.
        (1). He would probably have been a good ruler under less responsibility.
        (2). He had been successful as king of Aquitaine.

    2. There are various reasons for his partial failure.
      a. First, he dismissed his father's councilors.
        (1). He believed they were corrupt.
        (2). He alienated the strongest supporters of the throne.
        (3). He had little in common with the East-Frankish nobles.
      b. Second, his great piety proved a handicap.
        (1). It led him into subserviency to the pope, which caused him to lose prestige, consequently power.
        (2). He was better fitted for the monastery than the throne.
      c. Third, his own sons—Lothair, Louis, and Charles, "The Bald"—were greedy for power even during their father's life time, and so precipitated much civil discontent.

---

* *From* Wilson, Outlines of History, p. 260.

B. The building up of the empire had been a difficult task.
  1. Charlemagne brought to a successful conclusion the task begun by Charles Martel and Pippin.
  2. Its administration was a difficult task—even for Charlemagne.
    a. It was necessary to put down rebellion and watch officials.
    b. Counts and other officials were often corrupt.
    c. The title of emperor had added no real power.
      (1). He was simply king over various nations.
      (2). The title gave him little but prestige at best.
C. There were numerous forces working against unity.
  1. Political conditions were a handicap.
    a. The different people were not welded together into a single nation.
    b. People were more imbued with the spirit of local patriotism than empire patriotism.
  2. Feudalism was developing.
    a. Many counts, dukes, bishops, and abbots were semi-independent of the empire.
    b. Many people had lost their freedom; hence, they depended upon the wealthy and the strong.
  3. Economic conditions were not the best.
    a. Transportation was difficult.
    b. People were thrown on their own resources for economic needs.
    c. The counts and barons were practically independent locally.
  4. The principle of territorial division was unfortunate in this sense.
    a. Charlemagne made a solemn act of partition, 806.
    b. Only Louis, however, survived him, but this principle was continued.
    c. Finally, there were many petty kingdoms instead of one empire.

II. Under Louis the Pious and His Sons, The Empire was divided.

A. Louis the Pious divided the empire among his three sons soon after he became emperor.
  1. The first division came in 817.
    a. The largest portion went to Lothair.
      (1). With his share went the title of emperor.
      (2). This was a new principle.
      (3). Lothair held supremacy over his brothers.

    b. Louis and Pippin received Aquitaine and Bavaria.

    c. Bernard, nephew of Louis the Pious, was neglected.

    d. This division caused jealousy among the brothers and Bernard.

  2. The second marriage of Louis the Pious, 818, was a further cause for family quarrels.

    a. In 823 a son was born, destined to become Charles the Bald.

    b. Redivision was necessary to secure a suitable kingdom for the new son.

    c. The next ten years saw repeated divisions and more family quarrels.

  3. New divisions did not satisfy the brothers.

    a. The attempts were in vain.

    b. Louis died in 840 and the wars continued.

    c. The strength of the nation was exhausted in civil strife.

        (1). Fontenay, 841—here the three brothers met, but the battle was not decisive.

        (2). It is said that on that battlefield "the supremacy of the Franks perished."

        (3). Henceforth the Franks would not be able to protect themselves against invaders.

  4. The brothers finally settled their quarrel by the treaty of Verdun, 843.[1]

B. The treaty of Verdun shows the early beginnings of the modern map of Europe.

  1. The division was destined to be more or less permanent.

    a. Louis[2] the German received the eastern part—now Germany.

    b. Charles the Bald, the western portion—now France.

    c. A portion of land dividing these countries went to Lothair.

        (1). He also received the title of emperor and the territory of Italy.

        (2). There were these several divisions, but still the people thought of only one empire.

  2. Charles and Louis reaped an advantage in the division.

    a. Their territory was compact.

    b. Their subjects were more homogeneous.

    c. Lothair's subjects were of many nationalities.

  3. This treaty led the way for modern nations.

    a. France was clearly separated from Germany.

    b. Both were separated from Italy.

---

1 See p. 56—Shepherd's Historical Atlas.
2 For reasons of consistency, the authors have used the French *Louis* rather than the German spelling *Lewis* which is used by certain authorities. Either spelling is accepted.

    c. The strip between was destined to have no unity—it was to be the battleground between France and Germany.

III. The difficulties of the empire were increased by the invasions of the Northmen.

A. Invading barbarians came from almost every direction, but principally from the north.

    1. Saracens troubled southern frontiers.

    2. Hungarians were invading from the east.

    3. The Northmen were the greatest offenders of all.

        a. They were the last of the German invaders.

        b. They made their attacks by sea—due to their situation.

        c. Most important of these peoples were the Danes, Swedes, and Norwegians.

B. The Northmen had visited many lands and had founded important colonies.

    1. All the coasts within their reach were visited.

        a. All the British Isles.

        b. The Atlantic coast of Europe and Africa.

        c. The whole Mediterranean.

        d. Iceland, Greenland, and even North America.

    2. They already had many colonies.

        a. In Iceland, Scotland, and Ireland.

        b. The two most important were in England and Normandy.

    3. Everywhere people were concerned about defending themselves from the Northmen.

        a. Walls and castles were built.

        b. Skillful leaders were developed.

C. The Northmen entered Gaul—even laying siege to Paris.

    1. There had been early invasions.

        a. They invaded France during Charlemagne's time.

        b. Made occasional attacks during the reign of Louis the Pious—obtained considerable booty.

    2. After 840 they made regular attacks.

        a. Pillaged the city of Rouen, 841.

        b. Sacked Nantes, 843.

        c. Paris captured, 845.

    3. Their depredations were numerous.

        a. They were still pagans and did not recognize the sanctity of churches and convents.

            (1). Enslaved monks, plundered monasteries.

            (2). Murdered the bishop at Nantes.

  b. "They destroyed houses, and razed monasteries and
      churches to the ground, and brought to their death the
      servants of our holy religion by famine and sword or
      sold them beyond the sea. They killed the dwellers in
      the land and none could resist them."[1]
  c. After sacking cities, they withdrew from the district,
      but only when there was nothing of value left.

IV. In 875 the empire was practically at an end.

A. Charles III ruled as emperor from 881 to 887.
  1. The siege of Paris was the main event of his reign.
      a. After a long siege, Charles succeeded in making peace
          with the barbarians of the north.
      b. A powerful party rose in opposition.
      c. He was compelled to abdicate in 887.
      d. He died in 888.
  2. Later generations made a hero of Charles.

B. The imperial title was finally left vacant.
  1. A few ambitious men were crowned emperor after 888.
  2. Most of them owed their title to the pope.
  3. The title carried little prestige and no power.
  4. The office was left vacant for more than a generation until
      Otto the Great was crowned emperor, 962.

C. With the election of Hugh Capet, 987, the Carolingians dis-
    appeared from history.

> *"By the middle of the ninth century the Frankish*
> *Empire had become a colossal anachronism. Side by*
> *side with, and working simultaneously with, forces*
> *of decay and dissolution, were other forces working*
> *for the reintegration of government and society upon*
> *a new basis more in harmony with the conditions of*
> *the time and the spirit of the age. Out of the soil*
> *made by the corruption of old things a new and far*
> *richer feudal Europe was destined to spring up."* *

---

[1] *From* the Annals of St. Vaast—Readings in European History, Vol. I, Robinson, p.
163. Copyright 1906. *Used by permission of* Ginn and Company, *publishers.*
* From Thompson, Economic and Social History of the Middle Ages, p. 250. Copyright 1928. *Used by permission of* D. Appleton-Century Company, *publishers.*

CHAPTER IX

FEUDAL LIFE AND INSTITUTIONS

*"Sir, I become your man and promise to you fealty
for the future as my lord towards all men who may
live or die, rendering to you such service as the fief
required, paying to you your relief, as you are the
lord."* *

I. **Feudalism, The outgrowth of existing conditions and
customs, contained three fundamental elements: the
personal element, the economic element, and
the governmental-military element.**

A. The relationships of people to the king indicated decentralization of the government.

   1. The people were often responsible only to their immediate
   lord or suzerain.

   2. The lords governed their own landholdings with little or
   no restraint.

   3. Naturally, this system hindered the development of strong
   monarchies.

B. Economic relations may well be expressed by the phrase
"Feudal tenure of land"—the theory being: a tenant, or holder
of any piece of land, had only its use, although he paid certain
dues as rent to the lord, or suzerain, from whom he had received it.

   1. However, economic life was almost at a standstill. Cities
   lost their importance; there was less demand for trade than
   formerly.[1]

   2. Finally, many cities passed out of existence. The only
   occupation open to the inhabitants was agriculture.

C. The other important element responsible for feudalism was the
governmental-military element.

   1. Political disorganization was evident.

      a. Political organization among the Germans consisted of
      personal loyalty to a chief—usually a war leader.

---

* *From* Robinson, Readings in European History, p. 90. Copyright 1906. *Used by permission of* Ginn and Company, *publishers.*

[1] Each community had become almost economically self-sufficient, and trade was less
necessary.

          (1). He owed his prestige to his personal qualities.

          (2). To this leader the people lent their assistance, and he in turn gave them the protection of his military ability.

     b. With the decay of the Roman political system, the Germans reverted to their old customary political organization.

  2. The empire failed to guard life and property.

     a. Other agents arose to perform these functions.

     b. The church took over many civil duties.

     c. Strong lords protected the weak.

  3. The armed and mounted man was a part of the times.

     a. Fortified houses and walled towns were everywhere.

     b. People resorted to petty feudal warfare.

  4. Conditions were, perhaps, partially due to the chaotic state of the two centuries following Charlemagne.

II. Feudalism was not uniform in all countries, but there were certain characteristic features.

A. The relationships existing between the lord and vassal were probably the result of the fusion of Roman and German customs.

  1. Beneficium and Comitatus were important.

     a. The Comitatus was used in the later Roman Empire.

          (1). Freemen who owned no land became the dependent of some rich neighbor.

          (2). In return the freeman was guaranteed food, clothing, and protection.

          (3). This system was adopted by the Germans.

     b. The Beneficium.

          (1). Much land was turned over to the church.

          (2). Use of the land was granted to the former owner by the monastery—the beneficium.

          (3). Kings and other land owners disposed of their land in a similar way.

     c. This was the first state in the development of medieval landowning.

  2. There were many other terms employed to indicate certain relationships between lord and vassal.

     a. Fealty—the sworn obligation to an overlord for the grant of land.

     b. Fief—the portion of land lent out.[1]

     c. Commendation—the protection which the poor man was obliged to seek from the wealthy man. This indicated the dignity of the Comitatus relationship.

The right to rent the fief was inheritable—unlike the benefice.

    d. Benefice—the custom of granting land for a lifetime.

    e. Aids—the vassal's payment to the lord to help the lord meet extraordinary expenses.

    f. Vassal—a person subordinate to an overlord, bound by oath to furnish the overlord certain restricted services befitting his station as a noble, such as those of a military or financial nature.

    g. Subinfeudations and subvassal.

        (1). One who held a fief might become a lord by granting a portion of it to a vassal—sub-infeudation.

        (2). The vassal of a vassal was called a sub-vassal.

    h. Homage and the feudal bond.

        (1). Homage—the vassal placed his hands in those of the lord and took the oath of fidelity.

        (2). The act of homage constituted the feudal bond.

    i. Serf—a person bound to the land, representing an intermediate position between freeman and slave.

B. Military duty was one of the most important characteristics of feudalism.

    1. Each feudal estate had its own army.

        a. Each vassal was required to serve in the lord's army for a fixed period each year.

        b. Each vassal was obliged to equip himself and pay his own expenses.

        c. This system of recruiting an army had serious drawbacks.

            (1). The vassals were bound to serve the king for only a limited period.

            (2). Many refused to follow the king in a foreign war, claiming they were bound only to defend the king.

            (3). There was no real unification of command.

            (4). There was no unitary organization of supply—a very vital factor in any warfare.

            (5). Economic activity was seriously interfered with during a war, as the soldiers were also the executives in the economic scheme.

            (6). The feudal system of warfare delayed the development of a standing army—a necessary component of a strong government.

    2. Wars became so numerous that the church intervened and set apart certain days when there was to be no fighting.

        a. The church was the only restraining influence.

        b. A period of this kind was called the "truce of God."

        c. Law was enforced by threat of excommunication—partially successful.

3. The "Peace of God"—parts of the land were set off where no fighting was allowed.

C. Feudal justice was often executed by ordeal.
  1. "Trial by ordeal."
    a. This was one of the most frequently used methods of determining guilt.
    b. It was believed that if a person came through an ordeal uninjured, or if his wounds healed in a certain time, he was innocent.
  2. There were many different kinds of ordeals.
    a. Putting an arm in boiling water.
    b. By combat.
    c. Walking across red hot iron and many others.
    d. Doubtless here is the origin of the terms, "Raking him over the coals" or "being in hot water."
  3. Compurgation, or wager of battle, was also used.
  4. Penalties were usually fines, even in cases of murder. The "wergeld" was the payment for murder, varying according to the position of the murdered.
  5. Judicial procedure differed from the Roman custom.
    a. The accuser did not need to prove a charge.
    b. The accused individual must prove his innocence.

D. There was to be found in all feudal countries a sharp division between the various classes of people.
  1. Drastic distinctions were always evident.
    a. Nobles enjoyed a great many special privileges and rights.
    b. Many privileges continued until the time of the French Revolution in France, and, in the case of Italy and Germany, until well into the nineteenth century.
    c. The most conspicuous of the privileges was partial exemption from taxation.
  2. Life of the nobles was relatively luxurious; that of all others, except the clergy, generally wretched.
    a. Nobles, in times of peace, amused themselves by games, tournaments, feasting, and hunting.
    b. The other classes, except the clergy, spent their entire time in making a living.
    c. The nobles lived in castles and manor houses; the less fortunate classes usually lived in one-room huts.

III. Feudalism developed gradually, but once developed spread rapidly over Europe.

A. It was not developed according to any conscious plan.
  1. The institution was not established by royal decree or general agreement between all landowners.

2. It grew up gradually and irregularly.

3. The owner of vast estates found the system to his advantage and so employed it.

B. The central government's power and influence gradually declined.

    1. The king ceased to deal directly with his people.

        a. He governed indirectly through the lords.

        b. It became the duty of men to obey lords rather than kings.

    2. Apparently the kings did not realize the danger.

        a. They thought of their kingdom as private property, and made grants freely.

        b. A very strong monarch was needed to hold such a society together.

C. Feudal relations became all-important.

    1. Lords bound themselves together by a network of relations.

        a. This relation was based on landholding.

        b. They owed protection and services to one another because of the various fiefs they held.

        c. Theoretically, they were subjects of the king; practically, only those served him who held land directly from him.

    2. There were thousands of fiefs in Europe at the close of the tenth century.

        a. They were very unequal in size.

        b. The great lords pieced together a great number of districts.

        c. Registers were necessary:

            (1). To show what lords owed to others.

            (2). And more important, to show what his numerous vassals owed to him.

IV. Feudalism, as an institution, presented certain advantages as well as many definite disadvantages.

A. The main advantage was that the "institution" brought people together, and so offered mutual protection.

    1. People collected into groups.

        a. They became habituated in living together.

        b. This condition paved the way for cities and towns in the future.

    2. Agriculture was advanced.

        a. Much new land was brought into use.

        b. Drainage and clearing was accomplished.

        c. A greater demand for labor resulted, which meant an improvement of the serf.

3. Progress lacked the spur of private ownership and personal gain.
4. . Chivalry was developed.
    a. The clergy insisted that the knight be a manly Christian, that he should respect and defend the church, fight against the heathen, and protect those in distress.
    b. The social virtue of courtesy and good manners was developed.
    c. Position of women was raised.

B. The greatest disadvantage of feudalism was the ever-present conflict and war.
    1. War was the natural state of the feudal world.
        a. It formed the chief occupation of the restless aristocracy.
        b. Feudal lords were meant to be a guarantee of peace, but often they were the cause of violent conflict.
        c. Dissension was evident even among members of the same family.
    2. War was not unlawful.
        a. French and German law did not prohibit war.
        b. Provisions were made for its gentlemanly conduct.
        c. Tournaments gave vent to war-like nature during times of peace.
    3. It was the constant state of war that weakened the central government to a great extent.
        a. Kings were always trying to suppress powerful lords.
        b. There was no organized police.
        c. Money was lacking for government functions, weakening the king and hence the government.

C. The status of the farmer was unsatisfactory and even degrading.
    1. There was little in his condition to develop that keen sense of worth and personal pride that characterized the Roman peasant in the days of the Republic.
    2. Little could be looked for in the way of national spirit or patriotism from such an abject mass of people.
    3. Feudal rights such as the "Droit du Seignor" and other impositions on the peasant were degrading and humiliating, and debased personal character to a low level.

> "The feudal system as a whole was a class-system in which the lord of the manor was supreme. The condition of the peasant was one of undiluted and almost hopeless misery." *

---

* *From* Shaw, Trends of Civilization and Culture, p. 229. Copyright 1932. *Used by permission of* The American Book Company, *publishers.*

CHAPTER X

THE CHURCH FROM THE NINTH TO THE ELEVENTH CENTURY

"The condition of the Papacy during the middle years of the tenth century was such as to cry aloud to heaven for betterment." *

I. The church greatly extended its territory and power from 800 to 1056

A. Many new peoples adopted Christianity during this period.

    1. Christianity was introduced into Denmark and Sweden early.

        a. Ausgar, "Apostle of the North," became Archbishop of Hamburg, 846.

        b. However, Sweden was not completely Christianized until the middle of the twelfth century.

    2. Christianity influenced Norway but little until the tenth century.

        a. Olaf established it firmly.

        b. Olaf the Saint completed the work between the years 1014 and 1030.

    3. Greenland was Christianized about 1000.

    4. Magdeburg was selected by Pope John XIII as the See of the primate of Germany in 967. From this time on the archbishopric became the missionary center of the Slav region of the Elbe.

    5. In 973 Prague became the Bohemian religious center with the establishment of an archbishopric.

    6. Posen, Poland, became an important religious center.

    7. Christianity became the legal religion in Hungary about 1000.

B. The ninth century was described by Voltaire as the "Age of Bishops."

    1. The church greatly increased in wealth.

        a. It possessed much land and exercised great feudal authority.

---

* *From* Henderson, A Short History of Germany, p. 52. Copyright 1928. *Used by permission of* The Macmillan Company, *publishers.*

b. Finally, the church became enormously wealthy.
  (1). Charles the Great demanded that tithes be paid into the church.
  (2). The church treasury received incomes from feudal lands, gifts, and payments for rites and services.
  (3). The sale of "Indulgences" was also a source of revenue.

2. The church gained great power by regulating conduct.
  a. It insisted on penance for wrong-doing.
  b. The unruly were punished in numerous ways.
    (1). By terrors—horrible conditions after death were described to sinners.
    (2). By excommunication—those who would not recognize the authority of the church were refused membership.
    (3). By interdict—extending excommunication to the whole community or country.

3. The church showed its influence by regulating feudal warfare.
  a. The "Truce of God."[1]
  b. The "Peace of God."[1]

4. In addition the church performed many definite services.
  a. The welfare of society was enhanced.
    (1). Members of the clergy were leaders in the community.
    (2). The church was the social center.
    (3) Education was carried on by the clerics.
  b. The monks were more influential than the secular clergy.
    (1). People flocked to the monasteries for protection.
    (2). The monks acted as nurses and doctors, and extended hospitality to weary travelers.
    (3). The monasteries were the educational centers.

5. In short, the church was the one outstanding civilizing force in an age of disorganization.

II. The contest between the emperors and the popes began in the ninth century.

A. Under the early Carolingians the church and state had cooperated.

1. Charlemagne maintained some authority over Rome.
  a. He received his crown from the pope.
  b. Officials were sent to Rome to represent the emperor.

[1] See Chapter IX.

      c. The coins show the condition—on one side appeared the name of the emperor; on the other the name of the pope.

  2. Later emperors took matters more definitely into their own hands.

      a. Still, emperors continued to be crowned by the popes.

      b. Lothair, however, exercised more authority.

         (1). He ruled the city of Rome.

         (2). He maintained the final supremacy of the emperor.

  3. After Lothair, control drifted into the hands of the popes.

      a. Internal strife occupied the attention of the emperors.

      b. "The patrimony of St. Peter" gradually developed.

         (1). The lands of Italy outside of Rome had been governed by the emperor.

         (2). Due to Carolingian weakness, the popes gradually extended their control.

         (3). Successive donations and recognitions finally gave the popes power over the whole patrimony.

B. The Saracens attacked Rome during the pontificate of Leo IV, 845-855.

  1. The Saracens succeeded in the conquest of Sicily.

      a. They invaded Sicily in 827.

      b. The island was still subject to the Byzantine Empire.

      c. The Greeks thus lost their last important stronghold.

  2. The Saracens finally invaded Italy, but were soon expelled.

      a. Conquest was made easier by ruling factions in southern Italy.

      b. By 851 the city of Rome was in danger.

      c. The Carolingian, Lewis, allied himself with the Pope, Leo IV. Lewis made war against the Saracens and the Lombards, but died in 875 before the completion of the task.

      d. Pope Leo IV and Lewis had won the most important victories.

      e. Finally, Basil, the Greek Emperor, drove the Saracens out of Italy.

C. The church wanted a series of precedents which would free it from lay control.

  1. The "False Decretals"[1] furnished the needed precedents.

      a. The collection was composed of genuine and forged documents concerning important questions of the day.

      b. Most laymen considered the documents authentic at that time.

---

[1] Also known as the "pseudo-Isidorian Decretals."

2. Nicholas I, 858-867, won a complete victory for the church.
   a. The Photian schism in Constantinople was an important phase.
      (1). Photius, head of the Byzantine church, was deposed by Nicholas.
      (2). The Roman Church was charged with heresy. This helped to bring about the later schism between east and west.
   b. Nicholas indicated the authority of the papacy by showing that a Christian king (Lothair) was subject to the judgment of the church, 863.
   c. Hincmar, Archbishop of Reims, was also condemned.
   d. Thus, Nicholas set up the precedent of the right of the pope to intervene in all church affairs.
3. The papacy had won great power, and the outlook seemed promising, but the church was hampered by the Saracen invasions.

III. There were three great sources of weakness in the medieval papal organization.

A. Much of the church property was feudalized.
   1. This made ecclesiastical appointments the football of local politics and the ambitions of feudal lords.
   2. The nobles came to demand the right of investiture, because of the temporal powers possessed by the church lords. This infringed on the authority of the church, for bishops were practically counts.
B. The church struggled to prevent the marriage of the clergy, as this would tend, in the case of heirs, to make the offices hereditary and divide the lands.
C. Church offices were often purchased from the feudal lords who controlled the appointments, and sometimes from the churchmen themselves.
   1. This was called the sin of "Simony."
   2. The correction of these abuses was undertaken by Nicholas II who placed the election of the popes in the hands of the "College of Cardinals."
   3. Married clergy were forbidden to perform the services of the church.
   4. Many attempts were made to remove the appointment of bishops from the influence of the king and feudal lords.

IV. The ever-increasing differences between the Latin and Greek churches culminated in a complete separation in 1054.

A. The Iconoclastic controversy began about 720.
   1. Images adorned the churches.

       a. Both statues and pictures were used.

       b. Some thought it their duty to discard all such representations of saints or divinity.

    2. Leo the Armenian (or Isaurian) attempted to rid the church of all images.

       a. Great opposition was aroused.

       b. Riots resulted.

    3. The outcome was a partial compromise.

       a. The struggle lasted for over a century.

       b. Pictures were allowed, but statues were discarded from the churches.

    4. The east and the west disagreed over this question.

B. The controversy between Nicholas I and Photius added to the trouble.

C. In 1054 the schism became final.

    1. Relations had been strained for centuries.

       a. At the Synod of Constantinople, 867, the Roman Church was accused of heresy.

          (1). Enforced celibacy of the priests was denounced.

          (2). The doctrine that the Holy Ghost proceeded both from the Father and the Son was especially denounced.

       b. Attempts were made to patch up the differences but they were futile.

    2. In 1054 each church excommunicated the other, which made the schism final.

       a. Latin churches and convents in Constantinople were closed.

       b. Relations were hostile from this date.

V. The last quarter of the ninth century and the first quarter of the tenth was a period of degradation of the papacy.

A. During this period there was practically a disappearance of the empire in the west.

    1. The emperors received their crown from the pope.

       a. Emperors had little authority.

       b. The papacy was the exalted power.

    2. The power of the emperors was not restored until the coronation of Otto the Great, 962.

B. Local factions in Rome controlled the papacy.

    1. After John VIII, 872-882, the popes were weak.

       a. They usually ruled for a short time only.

       b. The papacy passed under the control of Roman nobles.

      c. Partisan popes were desired by rival factions, so they might enjoy the income flowing into Rome.

  2. For a time the papacy was controlled by women.

      a. Marozia became all-powerful in Rome.

      b. This power was checked by Marozia's son, Alberic "Princeps."

  3. Alberic held great influence from 932 to 954.

      a. The activity of the popes was restricted to spiritual affairs.

      b. His son, Octavian, became pope as John XII. Thus temporal power again passed into the hands of the pope.

VI. The church was destined to undergo reform.

A. The whole church was influenced by feudal usages.

  1. Bishops and abbots were often corrupt.

  2. Monks were not always of good character.

B. Reform movements had great influence on the whole church.

  1. Cluny, a Burgundian monastery founded in 910, had leaders who worked for righteousness.

      a. It was an "exempt" monastery, and therefore owed obedience only to the pope.

      b. It became a champion of papal authority.

  2. The "Congregation of Cluny" was an important development.

      a. Previously, each monastery had been independent, but now all monasteries founded from Cluny were subject to its control.

      b. It provided for the supervision of monasteries.

         (1). Existing monasteries passed under its control.

         (2). The "congregation" became very powerful, and worked for various reforms.

> *"It seemed as if the popedom would share the fate of the empire of Charles the Great; that the great office . . . would sink under the weight of its degradation and shame, and that the system of which it was the keystone would break up and perish. Two things saved it . . . One was the revival . . . . of the imperial authority . . . . The other . . . was the growth and spread of a strong spirit of austere reform of manners in the Church itself . . . specially embodied in the great monastic order or 'congregation of Cluny.'"* *

---

* *From* Morris, The Beginning of the Middle Ages, p. 198. Copyright 1886. *Used by permission of* Charles Scribner's Sons, *publishers.*

The BRITISH ISLES about the TENTH CENTURY

CHAPTER XI

ANGLO-SAXON ENGLAND TO 1066

*"The colonizing energy of the English immigrants,
combined with their savage destructiveness, altered
the civilization and the racial stock far more than
any other Nordic invasion of the period. Goth and
Lombard in Italy, and Frank in Gaul had not destroyed the city life, the Christian religion or the
Latinized speech of the conquered . . . It is . . . difficult to exaggerate the injury done to Romano-British
civilization."* **

I. **After the Roman legions were withdrawn, several Saxon
kingdoms developed independently of one another.**

A. The barbarian invasions of the Roman Empire served to cut off
England from the empire.

   1. In the fourth century England had been protected by Roman
soldiers.

     a. Roman legions were led into England by Maximus.

     b. Although England was not completely Romanized, the
country did receive protection from Rome.

   2. The barbarian invasions caused the withdrawal of the
Roman legions.

     a. Thus, England was left to protect herself, and so ceased
to be a part of the Roman Empire—about 410.

     b. However, Emperor Honorius was asked to send help,
but his soldiers were needed to protect territory nearer
Rome.

B. From the time of the withdrawal of the Roman legions, the barbarian invasions became more frequent.

   1. The invaders were mainly Angles, Saxons, Jutes, and
Frisians.

     a. They came from the Netherlands, Germany, and Den-
mark.

     b. At first they were content to ravage the country, but
soon began to migrate there in large numbers, especially the Saxons.

---

* *From* Trevelyan, History of England, p. 42. Copyright 1926. *Used by permission of*
Longmans, Green and Company, *publishers.*

  c. By 600 about one half the Island was occupied by these barbaric tribes from the continent.

C. Seven kingdoms were formed out of this territory wrested from the original Britons—hence, the so-called Saxon Heptarchy.[1]

  1. These kingdoms were usually and originally independent, but occasionally a powerful monarch was a virtual overlord, and exercised great influence throughout Briton.

    a. This influence was often marked by the payment of tribute.

    b. Occasionally there were other indications of one ruler's influence over his neighbor.

  2. The seven important kingdoms were: Northumbria, Mercia, East Anglia, Kent, Essex, Sussex, and Wessex.

    a. Three kingdoms eventually became predominant: Wessex, Mercia, and Northumbria.

      (1). Wessex rendered tributary the small states of the southwest.

      (2). Mercia held influence over, or directly controlled East Anglia.

      (3). Finally, Egbert, King of Wessex, obtained an acknowledgment of superiority over both Mercia and Northumbria.

      (4). Still, those three important kingdoms remained under their ancient line of sovereigns.

II. Saxon-England was too weak to resist the Danish invasions.

A. These invasions began toward the end of the eighth century, and eventually, the "Danelaw" was established.

  1. The number of invaders steadily increased.

    a. Their attacks became more terrifying.

    b. By about 850 the Danes were remaining over winter, and forcing the Saxons to provide for them.

    c. Liking the country, permanent settlements began.

    d. They allied themselves with the Celtic peoples.

  2. A Danish section of England resulted.

    a. They established themselves in both the East and North.

    b. Much of the territory became more Danish than English in population, custom, and law.

    c. The territory was then acknowledged independent by the West Saxon kings, and an agreement on boundaries was concluded in 866.

[1] See Shepherd's Historical Atlas, p. 60.

      d.   All matters in this Danish territory were settled by Danish law, and so became known as the Danelaw.[1]

B. King Alfred of Wessex, later called the Great, pursued the work of regaining England for the English.

    1. Previous kings had been unsuccessful, but under Alfred, 871-900, the tide of conquest turned.

        a. When he came to the throne the Danes had been almost universally successful.

        b. Nearly all Englishmen except Alfred lost heart.

        c. Finally, in 878, the Danes were defeated in battle, and so withdrew for a time to plunder on the continent.

    2. Alfred's reforms were of great importance.

        a. Perhaps he is best known for his achievements in peace.

        b. He brought about reforms in law. Existing laws were codified, and important additions were made in many instances.

        c. He revived learning, founded monasteries, and translated several books into the English tongue.

        d. It was under his influence and patronage that a new literature developed.

    3. Alfred's work was carried on by his successors, Ethelred and Edmund.

        a. The next seventy-five years witnessed many changes: Danish territories were won back; the Christian church was established; government became more settled; and a literature gradually took form.

        b. The customs brought into being at this time developed into some of the most fundamental and permanent institutions of the future English race.

    4. Edgar the Peaceful continued the work from 959 to 975.

        a. There had been frequent revolts preceding his reign.

        b. He was recognized as king of all England; and, in addition, as overlord of the kings of Scotland and Wales.

C. The later Danish invasions were relatively unimportant except that they infused new blood into the English nation.

    1. They brought little that was Danish or new into England.

    2. The reign of Canute the Great, although he was Danish, was highly beneficial.

        a. It gave a welcome respite from much suffering that had developed under the less capable English kings.

        b. He gave good government, made few changes, and often appointed Englishmen to office.

---

[1] Ibid.

    c. He ruled as a native king, and honestly endeavored to restore conditions as they were in the days of Edgar the Peaceful.

    d. Because Canute's sons proved unworthy, the nation gladly saw the kingdom bestowed upon Edward.

  3. Edward, later called the Confessor, reigned from 1042 to 1066, but was weak and incompetent in every way.

    a. Having been raised in Norman court life he preferred Norman ways and adopted many of them.

    b. During his reign many Normans were given offices in England, which prepared the way for the conquest.

    c. Harold, who was destined to be the last Saxon king, succeeded to the throne.

III. The development of English institutions was greatly influenced by the Christian church.

A. The early institutions were primitive in character.

  1. The invaders were in a state of barbarism.

    a. There was great slaughter of the English people.

    b. They held to their own customs, disliked cities, and many of the old centres of population were destroyed.

    c. For the most part they were farmers, not traders; consequently, roads were not maintained.

  2. Political institutions were somewhat different.

    a. The freemen were warriors.

    b. The king had considerable power, being surrounded by an aristocratic class.

    c. Bondsmen and slaves were numerous.

  3. Their literature was largely legendary and unwritten.

B. England was converted to Christianity in the seventh century.

  1. Irish monks had preceded Augustine.

    a. For a time there was a contest between the Irish and the Roman monks.

    b. Theodore of Tarsus brought about the unification of the English Church.

  2. The work of the "Venerable Bede," the most learned man of his age, was important to the age.

    a. The school at Jarrow was made famous by his residence there.

    b. He wrote many books—"The Ecclesiastical History of the English Nation" is the best known.

    c. It has been said that he was "first among English scholars, first among English theologians, and first among English historians."

3. The English became active in missionary work.
   a. They were very successful among the Germans.
   b. The English Church seemed destined for a bright future.

C. Later Anglo-Saxon institutions were of a higher order.
  1. Anglo-Saxon institutions prevailed throughout England.
    a. The Hundred was the most important political division.
      (1). The court was held frequently: composed largely of landowners and was presided over by the sheriff (or Shire-reeve).
      (2). Compurgation was often used in case of lack of evidence; ordeals were gradually introduced.
    b. Further divisions were the shires and boroughs which also had their own courts.
    c. Danish territory was also divided into shires.
  2. The position of the king was important, but he was regarded mainly as a peace officer.
    a. He was regularly advised by his wise men (witan)— who framed laws and levied taxes.
    b. The first tax to be levied was the **Danegeld**.
      (1). This money was used to buy off the invaders.
      (2). Unfortunately, however, this tribute meant only temporary relief, as civil strife continued until the time of Canute, when peace and tranquility were restored for a time.

> *"Canute* (1017-1035) *. . . became more of an English-man than a Dane, and proved to be a most adroit ruler, one of the wisest and ablest England had known . . . During his reign England was the center of a great though transitory northern Empire. All the Scandinavian lands, the northern isles, Scotland, and Ireland, acknowledged him as overlord."* *

---

* *From* Hulme, History of the British People, p. 45. Copyright 1924. *Used by permission of* D. Appleton-Century Company, *publishers.*

CHAPTER XII

FEUDAL FRANCE — TENTH AND ELEVENTH CENTURIES

"There is no more interesting or important phase of mediaeval history than the gradual emergence of the modern national state from the feudal anarchy into which the great empire of Charlemagne fell during the century after his death." *

I. France as a nation may be said to date from the Treaty of Verdun, 843.

A. Charles the Bald received the west Frankish territory.

    1. He developed this heritage into a separate state which was to be known as France.[1]

    2. The following century saw the decline of the Carolingians and the growth of feudalism.

B. The development of the French monarchy was gradual and of evolutionary character.

    1. In 987 the direct Carolingian line came to an end.

    2. The change in kings was not a revolutionary event, but the later Carolingians were poor and unfortunate, and finally succumbed to their rich and capable vassals—the Capetians.

    3. Hugh Capet may be considered the founder of the new national line of French monarchs under whom the French nation developed.

C. Geographically France was pretty definitely defined.

    1. Natural boundaries served to separate it on three sides: the ocean, the Pyrenees, and the Mediterranean.

    2. The eastern frontier had no distinct natural boundary.

        a. There was natural rivalry between France and Germany.

        b. The absence of a natural boundary led to disputes which have never been satisfactorily settled.

    3. More important than boundaries, however, is the fact that the French are a distinctly Latin people, and in most respects definitely different from their neighbors.

---

* *From* Robinson, History of Western Europe, p. 120. Copyright 1918. *Used by permission of* Ginn and Company. *publishers.*

[1] "Hugh Capet inherited from his ancestors the title of Duke of France, which they had enjoyed as the military representatives of the later Carolingian kings in 'France,' which was originally a district north of the Seine. Gradually the name France came to be applied to all the dominions which the dukes of France ruled as kings." Ibid p. 121.

II. The election of Hugh Capet (987) brought with it many difficulties for the Capetian line of Kings.

A. Great misery was to be found everywhere among the people.
   1. Conditions were the worst, perhaps, that Europe has ever seen.
      a. People suffered many calamities, even under Charlemagne.
      b. They not only had to resist foreign invasions, but also carried on many offensive expeditions.
      c. Many people became ecclesiastics to avoid military conscription.
   2. Conditions grew steadily worse after Charlemagne.
      a. The central government was weak, for dukes and counts were no longer checked by a vigorous administration.
      b. The poor landowners were forced to bow to the powerful lords.
   3. Each frontier lived under the dread of a possible attack by the enemy.
      a. The Saracens threatened on the south.
      b. The Hungarians were a menace on the east.
      c. The Normans were feared from the north.

B. At the close of the tenth century France was far from constituting a united nation, politically.
   1. There was no effective central government.
      a. Local government was not in the hands of public officials, but private landlords.
      b. The powerful nobles, entrenched in their castles, were a law unto themselves.
      c. The power of the princes was the chief obstacle to the growth of a royal power.
      d. The king did not exercise direct authority over the people in any way.
   2. The feudal principalities were numerous. [1]
      a. The duchies—Normandy, Burgundy, Brittany, Aquitaine, and Gascony.
      b. The counties — Flanders, Blois, Champagne, Anjou, Tolouse, and Barcelona.
      c. The third great class of counts were the bishops, who held and sometimes controlled great amounts of land.

C. Thus the Capetians were confronted with two great problems in creating modern France.
   1. They must recover and unite the territory of France by getting control of the land from the great barons.

---

[1] See p. 61—Shepherd's Historical Atlas.

      a. This was often a work of real conquest.

      b. Conditions were further complicated by the position of the duke of Normandy who was also king of England.

  2. They had to create and develop a real central government for France.

      a. New institutions of government were badly needed.

      b. The work of constitution-making fell to the king.

      c. The barons, instead of helping form the constitutions, were forced to complete submission.

III. The first four Capetian kings accomplished comparatively little.

A. These kings were:

  1. Hugh, 987—996.

  2. Robert, 996—1031.

  3. Henry, 1031—1060.

  4. Philip, 1060—1108.

B. These kings were not altogether unconscious of their problems, but their situation prevented them from doing much to remedy the condition.

  1. They did strengthen the hold of the Capetians upon the throne of France.

      a. This, in itself, was no small contribution.

      b. The work was necessarily slow.

      c. However, the tendency was toward a strong monarchy.

  2. They continued the alliance with the church.

C. The relations of the Capetians with Normandy were of great importance.

  1. The duke of Normandy was the most important vassal.

      a. The Norman dukes long remained faithful vassals.

      b. The relations with the Norman dukes, usually kings of England, determined many Capetian policies for the next century.

  2. While the kings remained at home the great nobles added to their power by conquest.

      a. The Normans and Aquitains won glory and booty in Spain.

      b. The Normans acquired much territory in Italy and Sicily—later the kingdom of the two Sicilies.

  3. The policy of the early Capetians is important.

      a. Hugh received the title of king without material power to support his position, but he and his successors used their position to build up this power.

b. They usually secured the support of the clergy.

c. Each king had his son crowned during his lifetime.

d. They avoided placing power in the hands of powerful nobles, and limited the nobles' authority wherever possible.

IV. More important than political changes were the church reforms and the development of new towns.

A. Many church reforms were attempted.

1. Hugh was favorable to the movement and was generous to the church.

   a. He maintained privileges of the clergy.

   b. His methods were sometimes high-handed, but his spirit was usually cooperative.

2. Monastic reform was instituted.

   a. The congregation of Cluny helped reform the monks and the monasteries.

   b. Both Hugh and Robert aided the attempt.

3. The church attempted to alleviate the suffering from feudal warfare.

   a. The "Peace of God."

   b. The "Truce of God."

4. Celibacy, Simony, and Lay Investiture were questions of great import.

   a. Celibacy, insisted upon by the kings, was met with a determined resistance from the clergy.

   b. An attempt was made to check Simony, but this interfered with the incomes of the king and great nobles.

   c. Although Lay Investiture caused a great struggle, there was no open conflict.

B. The period was one of great development, especially of the towns.

1. Flemish towns came into being, for pressure of the Northmen in the low countries compelled people to seek shelter in the old Roman fortifications.

   a. They soon became used to living in close communities, and thus the fortifications became towns.

   b. These towns became centers of commerce and industry.

2. The population of these centers became active influences.

   a. Certain classes were constantly traveling—nobles, merchants, and clergy.

   b. Peasants left their homes, finding employment in the towns and cities.

   c. Many pilgrimages were undertaken—to the Shrine of Saints, to Rome, and even to the Holy Land.

3. The career of Gerbert illustrates the advancement of the peasant class.
   a. Gerbert was peasant born, but through study and travel he won great renown as both student and churchman.
   b. His high offices enabled him to enter into the politics of France, Germany, and the papacy.
   c. He became Pope in 999 and took the name of Sylvester II.
   d. He became known as a wizard: education was greatly indebted to him, but he was too much disposed to profane learning for his position as pope.

> *"The material progress of France in the two hundred years between the vanishment of the Frankish monarchy in the ninth century and the end of the eleventh . . . . was not inconsiderable. In material condition and in the formulation of customary social and economic practice into forms of law . . . . the evidences of improvement are many and various."* *

* *From* Thompson, Economic and Social History of the Middle Ages, p. 312. Copyright 1928. *Used by permission of* D. Appleton-Century Company, *publishers.*

CHAPTER XIII

FEUDAL GERMANY AND ITALY FROM 919 TO 1056

*"In an age when there was practically no increase
of territory, no war, excepting internal revolts, no
foreign policy, it is difficult to find a thread through
the mazes of German history."* *

**I. Germany had not become a nation at the end of the
ninth century.**

A. It was composed of four peoples,[1] clearly defined by name, history, and institutions.
1. The Allemannians or Swabians dwelt between the Vosges
Mountains and the Lech.
2. The Bavarians lived to the east of the Lech.
3. The Franconians were the eastern Franks.
4. The Saxons occupied the northern part of Germany.
5. The annexation of Lorraine added a fifth.

B. Two of the four peoples, the Franconians and Saxons, were particularly important.
1. Franconia was of first rank.
a. Here were situated famous cities and dioceses.
b. Kings of Germany were elected here for two centuries.
2. Saxony was the only duchy of hereditary nobility. Later
German kings came from Saxony.

C. The feudal system had a strong hold on Germany.
1. Peasant proprietors had practically, if not completely, disappeared.
2. The clergy had become part of the feudal hierarchy.
3. Agriculture was the only source of wealth; commerce and
industry were unknown.

**II. The German state was founded by Henry I, the Fowler,
919.**

A. The crown changed from Frankish to Saxon rulers.
1. Conrad, the Frank, turned over the crown to Henry the
Saxon, his cousin.

---

* *From* Henderson, A Short History of Germany, p. 49. Copyright 1928. *Used by permission of* The Macmillan Company, *publishers.*
1 See pp. 62-63—Shepherd's Historical Atlas.

Prominent broken line enclosing shaded areas of map shown above indicates
boundary of the Empire (exclusive of most of Italy).

K. of Burgundy (K. of Arles)
Became united, 933
To the Empire, 1033 to 1034

Duchy of Bohemia
Western section under Poland, 1003 to 1004.
Moravia under Poland, 1003 to 1029

Bavarian East March (Ostmark):
(MARGRAVATE OF AUSTRIA)
Hungarian, 907 to 955
Duchy, 1156

March of Carinthia
Established about 970
Separated from Carinthia, 1035

Duchy of Carinthia
Separated from Bavaria, 976

March of Carniola and March of Istria
Separated from Carinthia, 1040

March of Styria (From 1055)
Duchy, 1180

March of Verona
To Bavaria, 952
To Carinthia, 976

   2. Henry was elected "king of the Saxons and Franks."

      a. He was first recognized by only part of the Germans.

      b. At the end of six years of war he gained recognition from all of them, and so accomplished the founding of the German state.

B. However, Germany was not a nation in the modern or political sense until long after 1800.

   1. Germany was little more than a great number of practically independent states.

   2. Germany was not a true nation until the confederation under the leadership of Prussia became known as the German Empire, which included the previously independent kingdoms, principalities, and free towns.

C. Henry organized and fortified Germany.

   1. He adopted offensive and defensive measures against foreign foes.

   2. He founded and fortified many cities.

      a. He has been called the "Founder of Cities."

      b. Cities were in reality little more than garrisons.

   3. He replaced the infantry with cavalry.

III. With the election of Otto I in 936 the prestige of the crown increased.

A. Otto was the eldest legitimate son of Henry I.

   1. He was proposed by his father and elected by the assembly of nobles.

   2. The ceremonies of the election indicate the position of royalty during the period.

B. Otto weakened the power of the dukes and suppressed the uprisings in 941.

   1. He took possession of the duchies and gained territory from the Slavic tribes.

   2. He did not attempt to abolish the duchies, but they were placed in the hands of his family.

      a. Some were returned to the original dukes, but they were usually divided, thus limiting their power.

      b. None of the duchies offered a long succession of able rulers; consequently, the duchies fell into the hands of the king.

C. The Hungarian invasions were ended during his reign.

   1. The Hungarians had been called in to aid the revolt of the princes, but Otto defeated them in 955 at Lechfeld.

2. The Hungarians then settled down in their own territory.
    a. They laid the foundations of national development.
    b. Today they are a most important factor in eastern Europe.

D. Otto proved himself more than a good soldier by organizing a central government.
    1. He established Counts of the Palace who watched over the royal domains and revenues.
    2. The church was administered for the benefit of the state.
        a. To prevent the new agents from making personal use of their power, he gave the most important church offices to members of his own family.
        b. The greater number of administrative offices were given to bishops.

IV. The condition of affairs in Italy soon took Otto to Rome.

A. Italy was in feudal anarchy from 887 until 962.
    1. The experience of Italy and the papacy, after the deposition of Charles the Fat, 887, forms the most gloomy chapter in European history.
        a. Princes from across the Alps assumed the Italian crown at different times.
        b. Mohammedan invasions added to the confusion.
        c. Three Italian kings were crowned emperor during the period, and then the title of emperor disappeared in the west until assumed by Otto in 962.
        d. The Greek Empire controlled portions of Italy, and the Saracens held Sicily.

B. Conditions in Rome were also unsettled.
    1. The feudal system dominated Rome.
        a. Domains were granted by the popes to bishops, abbots, and laymen.
        b. Power in Rome lay in the hands of the nobility, or "Senators," as they called themselves.
        c. There was no middle class.
    2. Popes were nominally elected by the clergy and the people, but more often mobs forced their candidates upon the electors.

V. The Empire of the West was revived by the coronation of Otto I, 962, an event of great significance in medieval history.

A. Otto came to the assistance of the pope.
    1. After crossing the Alps in 951 he was generally acknowledged as king of Italy, but was forced to return to Germany to put down a revolt.

    2. Ten years later the pope called Otto to his assistance.

        a. Otto relied upon the German church for support, and worked to bring it under the control of the pope. This was one reason for his desire for the imperial title.

        b. Consequently, Otto immediately freed the pope from his enemies.

        c. He was crowned emperor at Rome, Feb. 2, 962.

    3. However, Otto practically ruled Rome.

        a. He insisted that his over-lordship should be recognized by the pope. Thus he demanded the right to keep an ambassador at Rome to watch Roman affairs.

        b. After 964, for a period of about forty years, the popes were nominated by the German kings.

B. The coronation of Otto carried with it most important results for Germany.

    1. A great burden was imposed upon Otto's successors, for it was practically impossible to control Germany, Italy, and the papacy.

        a. The central government was very weak.

        b. There was no fixed revenue nor body of law of national scope.

    2. Eventually all was lost.

        a. Germany became a group of small states.

        b. Italy gained its independence.

        c. The papacy became independent of both.

C. Otto added southern Italy to his domains.

    1. This brought all Italy under his control.

    2. The addition came about largely through negotiations and the marriage of his eldest son to a Grecian princess.

    3. His personal characteristics are noteworthy.

        a. Firm and dignified bearing.

        b. Powerfully built figure.

        c. Long wavy beard.

        d. Eyes that moved incessantly, opening and closing "as if they were watching their prey."

VI. Under the Ottos the German kingship became hereditary, but in 1002 it reverted back to the Franconian line.

A. Otto II, 973-983, continued his father's work.

    1. He attempted to add to his territory in Italy.

        a. Seized Naples and Tarentum.

        b. Was finally defeated by the Saracens, 982.

        c. Set about preparing a fleet to recoup his losses.

        d. Died, 983, before his work was accomplished.

    2. His son, Otto III, who was only three years of age, suc-
       ceeded him.
       a. A revolt of the nobles was put down.
       b. Otto was established on the throne.

B. Peace was established under Otto III, 983-1002.
    1. Otto was well educated.
       a. Greek, Latin, and German were familiar to him.
       b. He was imbued with the spirit of imperial dignity.
       c. Much personal attention was given to Rome without
          neglecting Germany.
    2. In 996 he was crowned emperor.
       a. He elevated his cousin Bruno, Gregory V, to the papacy.
       b. Most popes had been born in Rome or the papal states.
          (1). Bruno was of Syrian ancestry.
          (2). This gave a more universal idea to the papacy
             and Catholicism.
       c. The new pope immediately crowned Otto emperor.
    3. Otto established his capitol at Rome and built a palace
       there.
       a. The old imperial court was reestablished as was the
          old administrative system.
       b. His power began to decrease outside of Italy.
          (1). New invasions began on the frontiers.
          (2). France won independence.
          (3). He even lost power in Italy.

C. As Otto died leaving no heir, an election was necessary.
    1. There were three claimants.
    2. Henry, duke of Bavaria, was elected and ruled till 1024.
    3. He turned to the church for aid.
       a. However, he kept it dependent on the state.
       b. He simply reformed the church for the benefit of the
          state.
          (1). Certain rights of election were removed from the
             church.
          (2). The bishops he chose served the state first.
    4. Henry was crowned emperor in 1014.
       a. Germany was strengthened by Henry, but he was little
          interested in Italian affairs.
          (1). The power of nobles was restricted.
          (2). Participants in private wars were punished.
       b. Henry sought the title of emperor.
          (1). In 1013 he led a small army into Italy.
          (2). He was crowned in Rome by Benedict VIII, 1014.
          (3). Later he went to the aid of the pope against the
             Greeks.

5. Henry II was the last of the Saxon line.
   a. This house had given great glory to Germany.
   b. Charlemagne's empire had almost been restored.

VII.   The German kingship passed to Conrad of Franconia.

A. Conrad II was king of Germany from 1024 to 1039.
   1. The course of affairs was not changed by the accession of the Franconian kings.
      a. Henry II left no heirs; therefore, an election was necessary.
      b. For over a hundred years the kingship was again elective.
   2. Conrad annexed the kingdom of Burgundy.
      a. Under Conrad and his son, Henry III, the empire probably reached its greatest height.
      b. Even the kings of Poland recognized his suzerainty.
   3. Conrad was succeeded by Henry III.
B. In the reign of Henry III, 1039-1056, the imperial power reached its height.
   1. Henry was confronted with the great problem of church reform.
      a. The power of the emperor might have been greatly affected by the proposed changes.
         (1). The church had become very wealthy.
         (2). The church wished fiefs to be made hereditary, which would have taken power from the kings.
      b. Hence, Henry interfered when the control of the emperors was endangered.
   2. Henry won a decisive victory by appointing the popes.
   3. Germany had become a nation although the church was to contest this power soon.
      a. Henry's successor was only a child, which resulted in civil discord.
      b. The church seized the opportunity to increase its power.

   "Under Henry the Third the Empire attained the meridian of its power . . . . Abbeys and sees lay virtually in his gift. Intestine feuds were repressed by the proclamation of a public peace . . . In Rome no German sovereign had ever been so absolute . . . A Roman synod granted to Henry the right of nominating the supreme pontiff; and the Roman priesthood . . . . were forced to receive German after German as their bishop, at the bidding of a ruler so powerful, so severe, and so pious." *

---

* *From* Bryce, The Holy Roman Empire, pp. 150, 151. Copyright 1904. *Used by permission of* The Macmillan Company, *publishers.*

CHAPTER XIV

CONFLICT OF EMPIRE AND PAPACY, 1056—1122

*"The struggle is rather on the part of the emperor
to recover and to retain an imperial position from
which he is being slowly but irresistibly pushed,
than to prevent any rival power from establishing a
similar imperial position beside him."* *

**I. This conflict grew out of a sincere and almost universal
movement to reform the papacy and the church.**

A. The church had been drawn into the feudal system; thus, the
lords not only appointed bishops, but conferred spiritual powers
—or became bishops themselves.

　1. The church lost strength during the time of Henry III.
　　a. This was due largely to the vast land-holdings of the
　　　clergy.
　　b. Bishops became the vassals of the king.
　　　(1). They were forced to pay homage the same as other
　　　　vassals.
　　　(2). Monasteries were sometimes placed under the pro-
　　　　tection of a lord.

　2. Fiefs held by the church were not hereditary.
　　a. Churchmen could not marry; on their death someone
　　　was chosen in their place.
　　b. In spite of church rules, bishops and abbots had come
　　　to be selected by kings and lords.
　　　(1). Outwardly regular canonical elections were per-
　　　　mitted.
　　　(2). But the feudal lord dictated the candidate.

　3. Investiture was affected by the temporal control.
　　a. Little distinction was made between the transference of
　　　property and the spiritual functions which went with it.
　　b. Church offices usually were not attractive unless
　　　property went with them.

---

* *From* Adams. Civilization During the Middle Ages, p. 244. Copyright 1922. *Used by
permission of* Charles Scribner's Sons, *publishers.*

    c. The lord often conferred upon a bishop the ring and the crosier, the emblems of spiritual authority.

B. Simony was one of the greatest weaknesses of the church.

    1. Simony may be defined as the buying and selling of church offices.

        a. Considerable revenue went with the landed estates and church offices.

        b. Men of noble birth frequently sought church positions.

        c. Bribery of the king or lord possessing the right of investiture was common.

    2. The revenue was often more coveted than the office.

        a. The king did not sell offices outright.

        b. He expected permanent fees, which were usually paid from the abundant revenues of the estate.

    3. The results of simony were unfortunate.

        a. It led to the corruption of the clergy.

        b. Even the lower clergy did not escape the system.

            (1). Priests were expected to pay for their appointments.

            (2). This led to improper exactions for the performance of their duties.

    4. However, in this period, lay investiture was practically a political necessity.

        a. Many bishops and abbots were officers of the king's government, so the king had to have the right to appoint them.

        b. The governing of church lands was a difficult political problem, and the appointment to office from members of the regular clergy would not have given the necessary executive ability.

C. Another danger threatening the power and resources of the church was the marriage of the clergy.

    1. It had been repeatedly condemned.

        a. But there was no Catholic state in which this rule was rigidly observed.

        b. The practice was most widespread in Lombardy.

    2. Reformers of the time pointed out that this weakened the church, as the lands would become hereditary unless the clergy remained unmarried.

        a. The property of the church was being dispersed.

        b. The clergy wished to provide estates for their children.

    3. Reformers advocated that reform come from Rome.

        a. However, it came from Cluny.

       b.   Gregory VII was greatly influenced by the doctrines emanating from Cluny.

    4. The question of marriage of the clergy had been settled in many instances by public opinion.

       a.   The parishioners had insisted that the clergy put away their wives or give up their benefices.

       b.   This probably accounts for the fact that no mention was made of this question in the Concordat of Worms, 1122. This was also true of the question of simony.

II. The interference of Henry III in papal affairs brought important consequences.

A. Henry settled the question of the three rival popes.

    1. The three popes were:

       a.   Benedict IX, 1033-1045.

          (1). A boy of only 10 or 12 years who was thoroughly evil-minded.

          (2). His family maintained his position until he proposed to marry; the Romans then drove him out of the city.

       b.   Sylvester III, 1044-1045 (Antipope).

          (1). A rich neighboring bishop.

          (2). He secured his own election.

       c.   Gregory VI, 1045-1046.

          (1). This third claimant was a learned and pious priest.

          (2). Bought out the claims of Benedict IX.

    2. This state of affairs called for Henry's interference.

       a.   He went to Italy in 1046.

       b.   A council was summoned at Sutri.

          (1). Benedict and Sylvester were deposed.

          (2). Gregory resigned his office.

    3. Henry secured the election of Clement II, 1046-1047.

       a.   He was a German bishop.

       b.   He immediately crowned Henry emperor.

B. The settlement of the question of the popes was a very important event.

    1. A rival to the imperial power was created.

       a.   The papacy was lifted out of Italian politics.

       b.   It was destined to become the greatest power in western Europe.

       c.   The papacy met with many difficulties in establishing its power.

    2. Pope Leo IX, 1049-1054, was the most important of Henry's appointees.

a. He believed that the popes should rule not only over bishops and abbots, but also over kings and emperors.

b. He was very popular.

(1). He refused to take his office by appointment.

(2). Humbly, he entered Rome and was elected by the people, carrying out the rule of the church.

C. Hildebrand (Gregory VII) helped establish the prestige of the papacy.

1. He was the faithful chaplain of Gregory VI and followed him into exile after Gregory resigned his office.

a. He evolved the idea of a universal and theocratical monarchy.

b. At Gregory's death Hildebrand went to Italy as a companion of Pope Leo IX, 1049.

2. Hildebrand was made subdeacon and cardinal, and soon held first place next to the pope.

a. He was sent to France as legate.

b. Shortly after he went to Germany to secure the election of Stephen IX, 1057.

(1). Here he found complete disorder.

(2). He became convinced that the empire could not carry on successfully without church reform.

3. Nicholas II had performed two services for the church.

a. He freed the church from the state by a decree of the Lateran council, 1059, which gave the power of electing popes exclusively to the cardinals.

(1). It was necessary for only the people and clergy to give their consent.

(2). The emperor retained only nominal rights of confirmation.

(3). The decree was to cause much conflict between the emperor and the church.

b. The papacy secured the support of the Normans.

(1). Nicholas II forgave them for their wars against the church.

(2). As allies they furnished troops and money to the church.

4. Nicholas finally succeeded in doing away with lay investiture and marriage of clergy.

a. These reforms caused greater opposition than had the manner of electing the pope.

b. The difficulty of these reforms became apparent when Hildebrand ascended to the papacy. He became pope as Gregory VII, in 1073.

III. Gregory VII's (Hildebrand) theories of papal power led to open conflict with Henry IV.

A. Henry IV began his personal rule in 1065.

  1. Henry III died in 1056, leaving his wife, Agnes, and their six-year-old son to rule.

  2. Henry IV was declared of age in 1065 and began his reign of lifelong difficulties.

    a. His first trouble was with the Saxons who accused him of oppression.

    b. The pope interfered, and Henry promised obedience, but victory over the Saxons and the attitude of the pope brought about renewed independence.

      (1). Of course, it is true Henry was guilty of gross insincerity in his representation to the pope.

      (2). Henry was an opportunist.

  3. Henry had trouble with the popes who had preceded Gregory VII over the question of lay investiture.

    a. Bishops and abbots were often officers of the government.

    b. They were the chief allies of the king.

    c. The struggle continued under Gregory VII.

B. Gregory VII's exalted ideas of the papacy caused constant conflict with Henry IV.

  1. Gregory issued orders to correct these abuses in the Lenten Synod of 1075.

    a. His purpose was to complete the reform of the church.

    b. He looked upon his office as supreme, and believed in the infallibility of the church.

    c. He did not hesitate to use force when he deemed it necessary.

  2. Gregory's policy of church government was aggressive.

    a. He was a man of action.

    b. He often used legates effectively to carry out his policies.

      (1). They were obeyed as high officers of the church.

      (2). The pope was represented at foreign courts by these legates.

    c. He wielded the greatest power of any pope.

      (1). In fact, Gregory actively watched over the interests of all Christendom.

      (2). He disregarded the separation of Greek and Latin churches.

    d. He wished to reign, but at the same time he wished to reform the clergy and the church.

3. The convictions of Gregory VII are noteworthy. They serve as a key to his later acts.
   a. He believed himself to be the representative of St. Peter, the chief of the Apostles.
   b. He thought St. Peter spoke through him and that his position gave him unique powers.
      (1). Supreme powers of excommunication and absolutism.
      (2). Believed he could control the destiny of any subject.
4. The quarrel of investitures was a bitter one.
   a. Gregory in 1075 reproached Henry IV for his conduct.
   b. Gregory VII was then deposed by a German council at Worms, 1076.
      (1). The violence of the legate's language gained friends for the king among the bishops, and had the German bishops not lost heart Henry might have maintained his pretention to power over the papacy.
      (2). Gregory was deposed because of his irregular election[1] and upon charges of immorality and ambition.
      (3). The bishops renounced allegiance to him.
   c. Henry was then deposed and excommunicated by the church. This brought the question of authority to a head.
      (1). At first the bishops and German princes turned against Henry.
      (2). Finally, however, he was given another chance.
         (a). He was not allowed to rule until he had made peace with the pope.
         (b). If he failed to do this within a year he was to forfeit his throne.
   d. Henry went to Canossa, 1077, and submitted to the pope. His motive was to keep the German nobles from combining with the papacy against him.
      (1). Meanwhile the German princes had elected another king, Rudolph of Swabia.[2]
      (2). The next few years saw bloody struggles between the followers of the rival kings. In 1080 Gregory again excommunicated Henry.

---

[1] Gregory's election was not in accord with the decree of 1059.
[2] Gregory was careful to recognize both kings. Later he was called upon to choose between the two kings. This set up a precedent for papal power. It gave the pope the virtual choice of the emperor.

  e. Henry created an antipope and marched upon Rome.
    (1). He entered Rome after a long struggle and set up
    his pope, who crowned him emperor, 1084.
    (2). Soon after, Gregory died, disappointed in his
    hopes—shown by his last words: "I have loved
    justice and hated iniquity, therefore I die in exile."

C. The question of investiture was finally settled in the Concordat
of Worms, 1122.

 1. Henry died in 1106.
  a. His difficulties had continued even after Gregory's death.
  b. He spent the rest of his life trying to maintain order in
   Germany and Italy.
  c. To add to his difficulties his son revolted against him.
   (1). Civil war resulted.
   (2). Finally he abdicated.

 2. The investiture question was settled under Henry V.
  a. Henry V wished supreme power. In 1110 he invaded
   Italy, marching upon Rome.
  b. Pope Pascal II wished to end the quarrel.
  c. After prolonged conflict the trouble was settled by compromise.

 3. The Concordat of Worms, 1122, was most important.
  a. The emperor consented to permit the church to elect
   bishops and abbots and to invest them with the spiritual
   emblems.
  b. The elections, however, were to be held in the presence
   of the king, but he could not use simony or violence.
  c. The king was also permitted to invest the new church
   officers with his fiefs and secular powers by a touch of
   the scepter.

   *"Though the new age was to prove itself bitterly
   hostile to certain of the papal pretensions, its immediate triumph was not so full of danger, even to
   these pretensions, as the triumph of the emperor
   would have been, and, in the end, could not be so
   destructive to the other side of the papal power, its
   ecclesiastical supremacy."* *

* *From* Adams, Civilization During the Middle Ages, p. 245. Copyright 1922. *Used by
permission of* Charles Scribner's Sons, *publishers.*

CHAPTER XV

THE CHRISTIAN EMPIRE OF THE EAST TO 1095

"The story of the Eastern Empire is at least as interesting as that of any medieval State, or perhaps more interesting because its people were more civilized and intellectual than other Europeans and had a longer political experience behind them. On the ecclesiastical side it offers the longest and most considerable experiment of a State-Church that Christendom has ever seen." *

—PROFESSOR J. B. BURY

I. Byzantine history is a record of great accomplishments.

A. The history of this empire is unfortunately described by Gibbon as a "tedious and uniform tale of weakness and misery," but recent evidences prove this definitely untrue.

   1. Of course there were certain religious persecutions and some military disasters, but they were relatively few.[1]
     a. The wars with the barbarians lasted much longer than in the West—until the fifteenth century.
     b. In addition the East met the first attack of the pagan and Mussulman invaders.
     c. However, the East civilized the barbarians and spread Christianity.

   2. Modern scholars take a different view of the eastern empire than did earlier chroniclers.
     a. Constantinople preserved the civilization of Greece and Rome until the nations of the west could assimilate the culture of the past.
     b. The eastern empire showed remarkable strength and power in overcoming its obstacles.

---

* *From* The Cambridge Medieval History, Vol. IV, p. xiv. Copyright 1923. *Used by permission of* The Macmillan Company, *publishers.*

[1] "The appreciation of method and system which the Byzantines inherited both from the Greeks and from the Romans is conspicuously shown in their military establishment and their conduct of war. Here their intellectuality stands out in vivid contrast with the rude dullness displayed in the modes of warfare practised in the West ... In the period in which the Empire was strong ... its army was beyond comparison the best fighting machine in Europe. When a Byzantine army was defeated, it was always the incompetence of the general or some indiscretion on his part, never inefficiency or cowardice of the troops, that was to blame." Ibid, p. xi.

B.   Constantinople was the first city of Europe for centuries.
   1.   Its geographical position made it practically impregnable.
      a.   It was surrounded on three sides by water; and defensive walls were built on the only land side.
      b.   It was located at the crossroads of the civilizations of the East and West.
   2.   It was the center of active commerce.
      a.   Great revenue came to the government; the city prospered; wealthy merchants were produced.
      b.   The city was the greatest trading point in the world for several centuries.
   3.   Its sound financial condition meant adequate protection.
      a.   The army was perhaps the best in the world.
         (1). It was strengthened by other peoples.
         (2). Training of the army was scientific.
      b.   The navy was also well organized, protecting the city's commercial position.

C.   In reviewing the East's great achievements two points are particularly noteworthy:
   1.   The excellent system of government and its "systematic administration of justice enforced by fixed legal procedure."
   2.   The constant repulse of its foreign foes whenever they appeared.

II.   The government of the East was characterized by a centralized system.

A.   The East sought unity in the strength of its government.
   1.   Justinian's laws were continued and perfected.
      a.   His institutes were translated into Greek.
      b.   A new code was drawn up by Basil II, known as the Basilica.
      c.   The emperor's court was brilliant.
   2.   The government was weakened by two main causes.
      a.   There were no rules for the succession of the crown.
         (1). This is known as the "Malady of the purple."
         (2). With the death of the emperor, it was necessary for his successor to establish himself.
      b.   The church was a source of strength to the Eastern Empire in some respects, but it was also a source of weakness.
         (1). The church would not allow its usages to be changed. Consequently it separated from the Roman church in 1054.
         (2). Sometimes the result was civil strife—the war of the Iconoclasts is an example.

        (3). In other cases the church was a unifying influence, but it did not act as a check on political government, as in the West.

        (4). The Greek church lacked powers of growth; it was not a leader in education.

   3. Nevertheless, the centralized system was usually efficient.

     a. The Greeks had adopted the Roman plan of organization.

     b. The government was divided into many bureaus, which usually continued to function even when there was trouble in the succession of the crown.

B. Law and order prevailed.

   1. This was essential to promote commerce.

   2. Foreigners were assimilated.

     a. Foreigners were subject to Roman law.

     b. Many foreigners entered the empire, but accepted the tradition of "one empire."

     c. The empire became definitely cosmopolitan.

     d. The real bond which held the empire together was religious unity.

   3. The nobility did not succeed in playing an important political role.

     a. The nobility gradually assumed a feudal character.

     b. But the Byzantine Empire remained an absolute and centralized government.

III. The Eastern Empire was constantly threatened by foreign invaders.

A. Swarms of savages poured down upon the empire from the north.

   1. The Slavic tribes came in the sixth century.

     a. Being fearful of other tribes, they dwelt in swamps and other inaccessible places.

     b. They never took the offensive, except when commanded by foreigners.

     c. For the most part they were colonizers, and finally established a strong Slavic kingdom within the empire.

   2. The Avars were troublesome.

     a. They began a long series of desolating raids.

     b. They were nomads from the north, driven out of Asia by the Turks.

   3. The Bulgarians came early in the seventh century.

     a. They were a Finnish people.

     b. They settled in the midst of the Slavs.

     c. Constantinople was threatened at times.

4. The Petchenegs and the Russians were sometimes a menace.
   a. Frequently they attacked the frontiers.
   b. They were repelled with difficulty from the very walls of the capitol.

5. The empire withstood these attacks, but often after the sixth century, seemed on the point of succumbing to the barbarians from the north.

B. In the meantime, more terrible foes were advancing from the south.

1. The Arabs suddenly fell upon the empire.
   a. They took most of its lands for a time.
   b. By the beginning of the eleventh century most of the lands were recovered.

2. The rise of the Turks in the middle of the eleventh century drove back the Romans. This was a disaster from which the empire never fully recovered.
   a. The Greeks were forced out of the eastern and central parts of Asia Minor.
   b. Armenia was lost forever.

3. Long Persian wars had exhausted the empire.
   a. Consequently, the Moslems had little difficulty in their early conquests.
   b. Even so, Constantinople did not fall; it continued to be the "bulwark of Europe."

IV. The Byzantine Empire rendered great service to European civilization.

A. The whole eastern part of Europe owes its civilization to Constantinople.

1. Russia and the Balkan countries came under the influence of Constantinople.

2. It had many connections with western Europe.
   a. The east preserved art and culture during the medieval period.
   b. Trade and commerce spread the civilization of the east.
   c. The Crusades were partly responsible for improving the civilization of the west.

3. The east was conservative.
   a. It preserved literature and learning; law and government.
   b. It showed an evolving process.
   c. There was no great break in religion as in the west.

B. Constantinople endured for centuries after the so-called "fall of Rome."

1. It served as protection to western Europe.
2. It set an example of a superior civilization to a barbarian world.
3. To a certain degree Rome may be said to have lived on in Constantinople.
4. Constantinople's life and culture were altered to a certain extent by Christianity.

> "The Byzantine hierarchy long justified its existence by providing its millions a more general enforcement of law and order, a surer administration of justice, a more genuine effort to make government exist for the benefit of the governed than in any other Christian or Moslem land during the early Middle Ages, save possibly in the best days of the personal rule of Charlemagne, and in the reigns of one or two of the ablest Abbasside Kalifs." *

* *From* Davis, A Short History of the Near East, p. 67. Copyright 1924. *Used by permission of* The Macmillan Company, *publishers.*

CHAPTER XVI

THE SARACENIC EMPIRE AND ITS CULTURE

"If civilization is to be defined as 'the conquest of nature by art for the advantage of mankind,' the sum total of Saracenic contributions to the world's progress is varied and significant." *

I. The establishment of the caliphate in Spain marks the first real break in the unity of Islam.

A. The Ommiads were overthrown by the Abbasids.

　　1. The rulers at Damascus became weakened.
　　　　a. Their civilization had improved but they were weakened by civil strife.
　　　　b. Repeated attempts were made to overthrow the Ommiads.
　　　　c. Finally the Ommiads were overthrown by the Abbasids, who were descendants of Mohammed.

　　2. Abu'l Abbas became caliph.
　　　　a. He was called Saffah (the bloody).
　　　　b. Only a few Ommiads escaped Saffah.
　　　　c. One of these became ruler in Spain.

B. The caliphate of Cordova was established in 752.

　　1. Spain became independent of the Abbasids.
　　　　a. This was the first break in the unity of Islam.
　　　　b. Gradually the old Mohammedan Empire broke up.

　　2. The Mohammedans were isolated in Spain.
　　　　a. This event was very important in the history of western Europe.
　　　　b. Their isolation made them less dangerous to Christian Europe.
　　　　c. However, the reconquest of the Mohammedans was not complete until 1492.

C. Mohammedan civilization reached its apex under Persian influence at Bagdad.

　　1. The capital was moved from Damascus to Bagdad.

---

* *From* Davis, A Short History of the Near East, p. 161. Copyright 1924. *Used by permission of* The Macmillan Company, *publishers.*

2. The splendor of Bagdad made it second only to Constanti-
    nople.
    a. Here, in 766, was completed a city surrounded by a
        wall.
    b. The situation was excellent—fertile country and ade-
        quate protection.

3. The Arabs played a comparatively small part in Moham-
    medan culture.
    a. The Syrian Nestorian Christian, the Hindu, and the Per-
        sian influence dominated.
    b. Aristotle greatly influenced their culture.
    c. They developed interest in theology, philosophy, his-
        tory, law, mathematics, medicine, and the natural
        sciences.
    d. Literature developed to a considerable extent.
        (1). Ancient books were translated into Arabic.
        (2). The "Thousand and One Nights" (Haroun-al-
              Rashid was the hero) portrays the civilization of
              Bagdad rather accurately for the most part.

4. The culture of the East was really an international culture.
    a. Eastern Europe was influenced by Chinese culture. This
        was particularly true of Persia.
    b. The eastern Renaissance developed in the ninth century,
        spreading from India westward.

II. Cordova became the Bagdad of the West.

A. The binding force of Mohammedan culture and religion kept
    Islam somewhat united even after the political disruption of the
    Caliphate.
    1. This was evident in Sicily and Spain where the Jews acted
        as intermediaries between Mohammedans and Christians.
        a. They were translators and commentators.
        b. Their philosophy was parallel with the Mohammedan.

B. The ninth and tenth centuries were the periods of Cordova's
    greatest bloom. It was the most civilized city in Europe.
    1. Famous libraries were developed. That of Al Hakam was
        the greatest in the world in the tenth century.
    2. Seville later became the center of luxurious life.
    3. Toledo became a center of learning.
    4. Higher schools of education were developed everywhere.

III. The Saracens were influenced by older civilizations.

A. Their early history was concerned largely with war and con-
    quests.

1. At Bagdad their manner of living was changed.
    a. Little zest for fighting caused them to become engaged in peaceful pursuits: industry, commerce, and travel.
    b. Pleasure supplanted religious restraint.
2. They accepted the civilization of the conquered lands.
    a. This was particularly true of Persia.
    b. They adopted and adapted from all with whom they came in contact.
    c. They became religiously tolerant.
        (1). Jews and Christians were both welcome.
        (2). They often held important positions and many found employment in trades and professions.

B. Extravagance became the fashion.
1. They no longer lived a frugal life.
    a. The income of the caliph was enormous.
    b. Money was spent lavishly.
2. This extravagance was shown in all phases of daily life.
    a. Magnificent palaces were built; fine houses and grounds were common.
    b. Furniture and dishes were frequently the most costly.
    c. Expensive, richly-dyed cloth took the place of simple garments.
    d. Extravagance was also shown in food and drink.

IV. **The changed mode of living contributed to the development of commerce and industry.**

A. They built up a well-developed commerce.
1. Bagdad was well situated for commerce.
    a. It was the center of many trade routes.
    b. To its harbor came vessels from many parts.
    c. Many overland caravans also visited Bagdad.
2. Restrictions on commerce were comparatively few.
    a. There were no tolls, and only one monetary system.
    b. Commerce was an estimable business.
3. An idea of the extent of commerce can be gained by the many European countries in which Arabic coins have recently been unearthed.

B. The demand for goods stimulated manufacturing.
1. The Jews were the first manufacturers but later the Arabs entered the industry.
    a. The Arabs were great traders.
    b. They manufactured to meet the demands of trade.
2. Many of their manufactured articles have become famous.
    a. Damascus steel—goldsmith's products.

      b. Expensive, richly-dyed clothes.

      c. Rugs and wall decorations.

  3. Many other articles were manufactured, such as paper, sugar, and perfumes.

C. Agriculture was developed to a scientific state.

  1. Fruits and vegetables were introduced and acclimated from the various countries they had visited.

  2. Agriculture was fostered by the government.

      a. The industry was held in high esteem.

      b. Scientific works appeared.

      c. Modern methods were developed: irrigation, grafting, and fertilizing.

V. Mohammedan culture was famous for its science, literature, and art.

A. The Arabs' achievement in the sciences is noteworthy.

  1. Manufacturing necessitated scientific knowledge.

      a. The Arabs were at first imitators, learning much from the Greeks and other peoples.

      b. They later became contributors to the advance of learning.

      c. Much of their manufacturing required scientific development.

  2. Medicine was first practised by non-Moslems, but later by Arabs.

      a. Specialists developed—the oculists were very successful.

      b. Practitioners often became very wealthy.

  3. Natural sciences were studied and developed.

      a. The foundations of the science of chemistry were laid.

      b. Astronomy was given great impetus by the founding of observatories. Attempts were made to measure the size of the earth.

  4. Mathematics is much indebted to their contributions.

      a. "Arabic numerals" was one of the most important.

      b. The "Treatise on Algebra" was used as a text book for centuries, even in the Christian world.

      c. Spherical trigonometry was developed.

B. The Mohammedans were interested in both literature and art.

  1. The caliphs patronized learning.

      a. They founded many schools which were of the nature of research institutes and colleges. This movement preceded the European universities by about two centuries.

      b. Their curriculum was varied.

      c. The Koran was the most important text for grammar and law.

2. There was great activity on the part of the Moslems to recover Greek manuscripts.
   a. These, when procured, were translated and preserved.
   b. This work of the Moslems aided the revival of Greek in western Europe.

3. The pilgrimage to Mecca was a big factor in the spread of culture, as well as a great social consolidating force.
   a. Many people went primarily in search of knowledge.
   b. These pilgrimages drew people from all corners of the Moslem world.

4. Literature and art developed in Spain.
   a. Here there was a great amount of decorative art and literature.
   b. The Great Mosque at Cordova, the Giralda and Alcazar of Seville, and the Alhambra of Granada are excellent examples of its effect.

5. Libraries were extensive in Arabic Spain.
   a. Private libraries were common.
   b. In the tenth century there were seventy public libraries containing many volumes.

VI. A sudden decline of Mohammedan culture came in the eleventh and twelfth centuries.

A. The causes of the decline were similar to those of the decline of Rome.
   1. Strong rulers were rare.
      a. The extensive empire needed strong rulers.
      b. Weak rulers were unable to exercise absolute authority in all the provinces.
      c. Life in the harem sapped the strength of the rulers.
   2. There was no rule of succession.
      a. Many were tempted to seize the throne.
      b. Rulers could not always depend upon the governors of the provinces; some were almost independent.
   3. In the tenth century there were three caliphs: Bagdad, Cairo, and Cordova, instead of one, as formerly.
   4. The outburst of intellectual activity throughout Latin Christendom also weakened the Mohammedans.

B. Although the caliphs had gradually lost power, the Mohammedan religion had gained strength.
   1. Religious dogma became firmly fixed.
      a. The Koran was followed strictly, and the orthodox view prevailed.
      b. This favored religious stability but inhibited progress.

2. Warfare between theology and science appeared.
   a. Freedom of thought was stifled by orthodox theologians.
   b. Progress, freedom, and tolerance continued longer in Spain than elsewhere, for the Moslems of Cordova "refused to be bound by the letter of the Koran."

C. Saracen culture is of importance because of its influence on western civilization.
   1. Early Christian scholars were in close touch with the culture of the Moslems.
      a. Particularly true of Gerbert (Pope Sylvester II), Constantinus Africanus, Adelard of Bath, and Daniel Morley.
      b. Sometimes too much importance is given to Mohammedan influence; Byzantine influence was equally great.
   2. The Christians learned much from Islam, particularly along scientific and industrial lines.
      a. This was especially true in Spain.
      b. The greatest contact came during the Crusades, when Christian and Moslem lived side by side in peaceful relations.
      c. Many English words derived from the Arabic and Persian languages are significant.

> *"The most marked trait in their culture, however, is its composite character. They borrowed or adapted from all the peoples with whom they had come into contact. It has been well said that they overran the domains of science as rapidly as they had conquered the kingdoms of the earth."* *

From Munro, The Middle Ages, pp. 215, 216. Copyright 1922. *Used by permission of* D. Appleton-Century Company. *publishers.*

CHAPTER XVII

CONFLICT BETWEEN EMPIRE AND PAPACY IS RENEWED IN 1152

"At a time when the feudal system was at its height . . . the minds of many men were strongly held by two theories . . . the Holy Catholic Church and of the Holy Roman Empire . . . As to the relation of these two governments to one another, the dividing line between these two empires, there was no definite idea. Each laid claim to the very highest and widest rights . . . . In such a situation a conflict was inevitable." *

I. **The period between 1125 and 1152 was one of contest for the throne of Germany.**

A. With the death of Henry V, 1125, three families were presented to the electors.

    1. The Guelfs, Hohenstaufens, and the Saxons.

        a. The Guelfs were powerful in Germany, and the Hohenstaufens had been faithful to the empire.

        b. The Saxon family, however, bore a spirit of independence.

    2. Lothair II (House of Saxony) was elected in 1125.

        a. He supported the papacy and ecclesiastical reform.

        b. Lothair, although sixty years old when elected, maintained his warlike spirit.

        c. Frederic (Hohenstaufen) seemed certain of election, but the clergy opposed him from the beginning because of his support of Henry V.

B. Hostilities between the Guelfs and Ghibellines began soon after the election in 1125.

    1. The Hohenstaufens became known as the Ghibellines.[1]

        a. The Guelfs were partisans of the papacy.

        b. The Ghibellines were its foes.

        c. The election of Lothair II led to a long struggle between the two.

---

* *From* Adams Civilization During the Middle Ages, rev. ed., pp. 224, 225. Copyright 1922. *Used by permission of* Charles Scribner's Sons, *publishers.*
[1] *From* "Waiblingen," a castle of the Hohenstaufen family.

2. Conrad III (Ghibelline) was elected in 1138.
   a. This election dashed the hopes of the Guelfs.
   b. Conrad's opponent was Henry the Proud, Lothair's son-in-law.
3. Intense rivalry resulted between Guelf and Ghibelline.
   a. This weakened Lothair and Conrad.
   b. It gave the nobles and the church greater power.
4. Finally Frederick Barbarossa was elected in 1152, and peace seemed near.
   a. He was the nephew of Conrad II, the offspring of a Ghibelline father and Guelf mother.
   b. His succession was hailed with joy, as he was energetic and tactful.

II. Frederick attempted to bring the Empire back to its former glory and influence.

A. "Frederick Barbarossa was 'the noblest embodiment of the mediaeval kingship, the most imposing, the most heroic, the most brilliant of the long line of German emperors.' "
   1. His character was outstanding.
      a. His intelligence and education made him worthy of the crown.
         (1). He was resolute; had a remarkable memory; was religious and charitable.
         (2). He was tall and slender, with pleasing features and personality.
      b. He regarded himself as the successor of the Caesars, of Justinian, of Charlemagne, and of Otto the Great, believing his office to be divinely established.
   2. He was prepared for his position inasmuch as he had participated in important affairs for many years, and was well known and highly respected.

B. However, in carrying out his policies he encountered all the old difficulties and many new ones.
   1. Troubles in Germany caused him concern.
      a. He had to put down rebellions among his vassals.
      b. They took a great amount of his time, energy, and resources.
   2. He had to meet the opposition of the popes, which was vigorous and determined.
   3. Trouble in Italy increased his difficulties.
      a. Recent emperors had often had great difficulty in establishing their power in Italy.
      b. The increasing importance of the towns in northern Italy caused endless trouble.

C. In 1154 Frederick entered Italy to establish his authority, and
so renewed the strife between empire and papacy.

    1. Frederick had secured some measure of peace and order in
Germany.

        a. This was accomplished mainly by favoring the bishops
and his powerful vassals, the Guelfs.

        b. However, he wanted to win renown by a successful ex-
pedition; and, consequently, he set out for Italy and
opened a conflict which lasted for nearly twenty years.

        c. At first he was successful.

            (1). He became king of Pavia.

            (2). At Rome he was crowned emperor by the pope,
but the opposition of the Roman people caused
him to withdraw from the city.

    2. Rome and the Lombard towns of the north caused him much
trouble.

        a. The government of the cities had become partially
democratic, and they resisted his interference.

        b. Arnold of Brescia caused both Frederick and the pope
to cooperate for a time.

            (1). Arnold of Brescia held exalted opinions.

                (a). That civil power should be vested in princes
and republics.

                (b). That the church should depend upon tithes
for its support, and that it should not own
land.

            (2). He was banished from Italy and went to France.

            (3). A revolution in Rome gave Arnold his oppor-
tunity. The pope was fatally wounded, and Arnold
returned to Rome as the leader of the people.

            (4). Finally, the pope placed Rome under the interdict
which broke the power of the commune.

            (5). The pope and Frederick cooperated in this one
incident.

        c. After helping to settle conditions in Rome, Frederick
hastened back to Germany.

            (1). He left Pope Hadrian to deal with his unruly
people.

            (2). This desertion by Frederick increased the ill feel-
ing between them.

    3. Frederick summoned teachers of Roman law and representa-
tives of the towns to decide his rights as emperor at the
Diet of Roncaglia—1158.

        a. The Lombard cities were very strong; in fact, they
were almost independent.

(1). These cities were allies of the papacy and foes of the emperor.

(2). They had developed a remarkable commercial system which had brought about a wealthy class of merchants.

b. At the Diet of Roncaglia it was decided that the powers that had been exercised by the towns belonged to the emperor.

(1). Measures were then taken to restore the feudal regime in Italy.

(2). Podestas (officers immediately responsible to the emperor) were established in the cities. These officers met with much objection, as they usually came from outside the city.

c. When Milan resisted in 1162, it was totally destroyed by Frederick as a lesson to the other cities.

(1). Milan refused to receive the podestas.

(2). The city held out for two years, but finally was compelled to surrender unconditionally.

(3). Frederick refused to listen to the prayers of the citizens.

(4). The population was scattered throughout four villages.

4. The Lombard towns revived the Lombard League in 1167.

a. Pope Alexander III became closely allied with the League.

(1). The people of Rome received him as their liberator.

(2). The league became the center of the opposition which the emperor had aroused by his vigorous methods.

b. The only hope for the Lombard towns was in union, and Milan was speedily rebuilt.

(1). The League and the pope encouraged the Milanese in this work.

(2). There were also other leagues formed. The Lombard League allied itself with the Veronese League and with Venice.

(3). To help keep the emperor in check a fortified city was built, named Alexandria, 1168.

c. However, Frederick was busy at home for some time, and therefore did not begin the struggle again until 1174.

5. Finally, Frederick again determined to assert himself, but was defeated by the League at Legnano in 1176.

   a. He found the new "straw town" too strong, and Frederick
       was hopelessly defeated at Legnano.
   b. The question of the mastery in Lombardy was settled.
   c. The Peace of Constance, 1183, resulted in a complete
       triumph for the League and the pope.
       (1). The towns received back practically all their
            power, although they acknowledged the emperor's
            overlordship.
       (2). Frederick was also compelled to recognize the
            pope, Alexander III.
       (3). Thus the union between the towns and the pope
            brought victory to both.

D. Frederick was now free to turn his attention to Germany.
   1. He turned to combat the lay aristocracy in Germany, and
       to make new alliances against the pope.
       a. The German princes had been poor supporters.
       b. Henry the Lion, Frederick's most powerful vassal, had
           taken part in none of the expeditions outside of Italy.
       c. Henry, proud and confident of his power, refused to
           appear before the diet when summoned to answer. He
           was, consequently, placed under the ban of the empire
           and deprived of his property after having been cited
           three times according to feudal custom.
       d. His Saxon duchy was divided and Henry was stripped
           of most of his power.
           (1). He was compelled to submit to the emperor as his
                partisans deserted him.
           (2). He sought the emperor's pardon at the Diet of
                Erfurt, where he was condemned to three years of
                exile.
           (3). Although eventually allowed to return, he was
                given back only part of his lands, and never re-
                gained his former position.
   2. The six years of truce with the Lombard cities was about
       to end, so Frederick was faced with new tasks.
       a. Frederick wished to secure peace for Italy as he had for
           Germany.
       b. Negotiations were opened and the Treaty of Constance
           was entered into in 1183.
           (1). Autonomy of the cities of the League was acknowl-
                edged.
           (2). Frederick conferred upon them legal powers in
                the towns, as well as outside the walls.
           (3). The towns in turn were to support the empire.

    c. This peace was advantageous for the emperor.

        (1). Once more he held a strong position in Italy.

        (2). However, it had been a concession even to the decrees as set forth at Roncaglia.

3. News of the capture of Jerusalem in 1187 prevented further conflict with the pope, and Frederick was to enjoy a partial realization of his earlier dreams.

    a. Jerusalem was captured by the Turks under Saladin.

    b. The third crusade began, and Frederick Barbarossa left Europe for Jerusalem.[1]

    c. Unfortunately, at the height of his good fortune, he was drowned in the river Chalycadnus in Seleuvia, in Asia Minor, through the force of the chill of the water, in 1190, and so ended one of the most remarkable careers recorded in history.

> *"If not a great statesman, . . . Frederick Barbarossa was a great personality, and as such he has inspired successive generations of German nationalists. 'Long after his death Germans believed that Frederick was sleeping in a cave in the Untersberg . . . . and that he would awake to save his country in time of need.'"* *

---

[1] Frederick's part in the third crusade will be discussed in Chapter XX.

* *From* Ault, Europe in the Middle Ages, pp. 360-361. Copyright 1932. *Used by permission of* D. C. Heath and Company, *publishers.*

CHAPTER XVIII

CONFLICT BETWEEN EMPIRE AND PAPACY ENDS 1254

"The opening years of the thirteenth century are commonly known as the age of Innocent III, for circumstances, as well as the remarkable ability of the man himself, combined to place him at the center of nearly all the important developments of the period." *

I. **The extension of the Hohenstaufen power into southern Italy proved disastrous.**

A. Henry VI succeeded Frederick I as king of Germany and Italy.

   1. To carry on his struggle with the papacy, Frederick had formed alliances in southern Italy.

     a. His eldest son, Henry, was married to Constance, heiress to the kingdom of Sicily.

     b. Constance was crowned Queen of Germany in 1186.

     c. This threatened coalition against the papacy between north and south was interrupted by the third crusade.

     d. The hopeless attempt to keep Germany and Italy under the same head was continued under Henry VI.

     e. New conflicts eventually caused the downfall of the House of Hohenstaufen.

   2. Henry VI, like his father, had his troubles in both Germany and Italy.

     a. Henry the Lion broke his oath to Frederick; he returned to Germany and organized a rebellion against the emperor.

       (1). However, the Guelf party was soon under the control of Henry.

       (2). Then Henry went into Sicily.

     b. In Sicily, Tancred, a Norman, led a revolt against Henry.

       (1). The pope and Richard the Lion Hearted of England allied themselves with Tancred.

       (2). Henry failed to establish himself in Sicily. In fact, his army was almost annihilated by disease.

---

* *From* Sellery and Krey, Medieval Foundations of Western Civilization, p. 175. Copyright 1929. *Used by permission of* Harper and Brothers, *publishers.*

(3). Richard's capture on his return from the Holy Land, plus the death of Tancred, 1194, enabled Henry to regain control of Sicily.

c. Sicily was a prize for which the Hohenstaufens had long labored.

(1). There was a very high culture there, and it was a natural naval base for Mediterranean operations.

(2). Frederick II drew much revenue from Sicily and instituted many valuable political practices.

(3). After Tancred's death Henry achieved his object. He established in Sicily a new aristocracy composed of faithful German adherents, 1197.

d. In the meantime Henry was forced to return to Germany in 1192 to put down rebellious vassals.

(1). The German princes refused to recognize the permanent union of southern Italy with Germany.

(2). Neither would they make the crown hereditary for the Hohenstaufens.

B. Death overtook Henry before he completed his extensive plans.

1. He had established himself as undisputed master of Italy and Germany.

2. He planned to conquer the Orient and extend his influence over Europe.

a. He thought the time had come to avenge the Latin crusaders and his father, Frederick Barbarossa, for the Byzantine treachery.

b. He hoped to seize Constantinople and at the same time conquer Jerusalem.

c. He brought about war between Richard of England and the king of France.

3. In 1197 when he was about to set out on the crusades he died, at the early age of thirty-two.

II. Pope Innocent III, 1198-1216, exerted great political influence.

A. After the death of Henry, the German crown was again contested.

1. Imperial succession was in dispute between Henry's brother, Philip, and Otto, son of Henry the Lion.

a. Germany was "like a sea lashed by every wind," and it seemed doubtful if peace and order could be restored.

b. Finally, Philip was elected king of the Romans; but the Archbishop of Cologne brought about another election, resulting in the choosing of the rival claimant, Otto of Brunswick, son of Henry the Lion.

      c.   The old struggle between Guelfs and Ghibellines was renewed just as Innocent III, a great pope, ascended the throne.

   2. Asked to decide, the pope, favoring Otto, gave him the decision.

      a.   Both kings bid for the support of the new pope.

      b.   The pope, fearing Hohenstaufen power, decided in favor of Otto, the Guelf.

      c.   Otto expressed his gratitude to the pope. Philip was murdered in 1208, and so left Otto the undisputed king.

   3. Later the pope abandoned Otto for the young son of Henry VI.

      a.   Otto was crowned emperor in 1208, but immediately made an enemy of the pope by playing the emperor in Italy.

      b.   Innocent then repudiated Otto and made young Frederick, son of Henry VI, king in 1212.

      c.   However, the pope exacted many promises from Frederick to prevent him from becoming as powerful as his father had been.

      d.   These promises were to be a handicap to Frederick later on in carrying out his policies.

B. For many years Pope Innocent III was the virtual arbiter of western Europe, a claim asserted before only by Gregory VII.

   1. His views were noteworthy.

      a.   He was well educated.

         (1). He had studied grammar and theology, and was a student of civil and canonical law.

         (2). He had written books on theology, law, and discipline. The most famous of his works was "On the Wretchedness of the Human Lot."

      b.   His views resembled those of Gregory VII.

         (1). He believed the priesthood superior to lay power.

         (2). He thought he had the right to interfere in affairs of princes and all secular problems.

         (3). These ideas triumphed: the independence of the papacy was established, and his authority was extended over Europe and all Christendom.

   2. Even John of England was forced to submit to Pope Innocent.

      a.   The monks of Canterbury chose an archbishop without consulting King John.

      b.   Their appointee went to Rome to be confirmed by the pope. Meanwhile John forced another election, making his treasurer archbishop.

      c. Innocent rejected both and set up Stephen Langdon as archbishop. Then John drove the monks of Canterbury out of England.

      d. England was placed under the interdict; John was excommunicated, and the pope threatened, unless John recanted, to displace him with Philip Augustus of France.

      e. John humbly submitted to the pope. He handed England over to the pope and received it back as a fief.

  3. Innocent extended his political power over most of Europe.

      a. His ambitions were near attainment.

      b. He maintained his asserted rights to interfere in important political affairs in various European countries.

      c. The fourth Lateran Council, 1215, might be called an international congress.

        (1). It was held in Innocent's palace.

        (2). It was attended not only by hundreds of bishops and abbots, but representatives of kings, ruling princes, as well as the towns.

        (3). Both religious and political problems were discussed.

          (a). Church abuses and heresy were fought.

          (b). The decrees confirmed Frederick II as king and excommunicated Otto IV.

  4. Innocent III died in 1216, the year following the Fourth Lateran Council.

      a. Otto IV also died soon after, 1218.

      b. This left Frederick II free to act as he saw fit.

      c. Frederick was little inclined to obey the pope, so Innocent left a great amount of trouble to his successors.

III. The conflict between Frederick II and the papacy was in the nature of a death struggle.

A. Being educated in the Norman kingdom of Sicily, Frederick had developed a peculiar character.

  1. He was only three when his father, Henry VI, died and left him under the guardianship of Innocent.

      a. He grew up in the midst of a life of intrigue, and this environment greatly influenced his character.

        (1). He became crafty and deceitful.

        (2). He trusted no one, believing everyone could be bought for a price.

      b. He was well educated, intellectual, a great student, and somewhat of a poet.

      c. At the age of seventeen he became the head of the Hohenstaufens and emperor of the Holy Roman Empire.

    2. Frederick had promised Innocent III to go on a crusade.
        a. Before he undertook this mission, however, he had to make himself secure in the empire.
        b. Consequently, he kept deferring the expedition.
        c. The Pope finally lost patience and excommunicated him. Then Frederick started for the east and was again excommunicated for going while excommunicate.
        d. He met with some success in Jerusalem.
            (1). He made himself king of Jerusalem and gave the Moslems freedom of worship.
            (2). A ten-year truce was established, and Frederick agreed to prevent the west from attacking Egypt during this period.
        e. Then Frederick hurried home; made peace with the pope in 1230, and was free to administer his kingdom.

B. Frederick's policies often ran counter to the pope's.
    1. He gave much time to the affairs of Sicily.
        a. This kingdom was his home by preference.
        b. He established a centralized beaurocracy with full responsibility to the emperor.
        c. A strong state was developed and the country grew wealthy under his rule. Frederick might have united Sicily into a kingdom had not the pope opposed his policy.
    2. Frederick's policy in Germany was different.
        a. His policies in Germany were a direct contrast to those employed in Sicily.
        b. Even greater powers were granted to nobles than they already possessed, which made them almost independent.
        c. Germany was used merely to secure resources for carrying out his Italian policies.
    3. By 1235 Frederick was all-powerful.
        a. He attained this position largely through diplomacy.
        b. An alliance with the king of England helped him.
        c. His power was dreaded everywhere. He has been called the "first modern king."
    4. He struggled with the popes as had his predecessors.
        a. Frederick attempted to control Rome by placing it between strong kingdoms.
        b. Gregory IX declared against Frederick for enslaving Italy.
        c. Until this time Frederick had supported the church, but now he broke with it. Consequently, he was excommunicated by the pope in 1239.

      d. The Council of Lyons, 1245, again excommunicated him.

          (1). Innocent IV was now pope. Frederick could not win him over.

          (2). A council was called in 1245. Frederick was again excommunicated, Sicily was put under interdict, and he was deposed.

      e. Frederick was able to maintain his position in Germany, but not in Italy.

IV. The last of the Hohenstaufens and the triumph of the papacy marks the close of the Medieval Empire.

A. The death of Frederick II occurred in 1250, when he was preparing to overcome his many difficulties.

    1. Frederick had his son, Conrad, elected in 1237.

      a. Peace had been established in Germany.

      b. The cities of Italy were still causing trouble.

    2. No decisive results of the conflict between empire and papacy were evident when Frederick died, December 13, 1250, near Lucera.

B. The date 1254 marks the end of the reign of the Hohenstaufens.

    1. The struggle continued under Conrad IV.

      a. He died of fever, May 21, 1254.

      b. He left as his successor, Conradin, a child two years of age.

    2. Conradin, the last Hohenstaufen, was beheaded in Naples in 1268.

    3. The union of Italy and the empire was unsuccessful. The victory of the papacy was complete.

      a. The popes had triumphed over the Hohenstaufens politically.

      b. However, the papacy had discredited itself spiritually throughout Christendom, because of its aggressive policy in temporal affairs.

    4. The period, 1254-1273, was known as the Great Interregnum in Germany.

      a. It has been called the period of "fist-law."

      b. A new king, Rudolf of Hapsburg, was elected in 1273.

C. With the passing of the Hohenstaufens the empire had in reality come to an end.

    1. Although German kings continued to call themselves emperors, few of them were crowned by the pope.

      a. Italian territory was not reconquered.

      b. Germany was in reality divided with no real king.

2. Germany and Italy failed to develop into strong nations.
    a. In Germany many independent duchies, counties, bishoprics, and free towns appeared.
    b. In Italy the northern towns were independent: the pope controlled central Italy, and southern Italy was divided between France and Spain.

    "For the moment the pope's cause was victorious, but over against the growing individualism of nations and persons, the pope was supporting a losing cause." *

---

* *From* Thatcher and McNeal, Europe in the Middle Ages, p. 252. Copyright 1920. *Used by permission of* Charles Scribner's Sons, *publishers.*

CHAPTER XIX

THE FIRST AND SECOND CRUSADES

"The Crusades were the resultant of complex forces which had been at work for many years . . . . The roots of the Crusades go deep down into the soil of medieval history. The longest and deepest of these roots was the practice of making pilgrimages to the Holy Land, a practice which was as old as the fourth century." *

I. Toward the end of the eleventh century the West took the offensive against the foes of Christendom.

A. The two religions, Christianity and Mohammedanism, may be said to have clashed as early as the seventh century.

    1. Commercial contact had brought the East and West closer together.

        a. The Arabs acted as intermediaries between the West and the Far East.

    2. Western Europe developed as trade expanded and increased.

        a. Italian cities especially, prospered.

        b. Trade was sometimes handicapped by the conquests of the Mohammedans in the Mediterranean.

B. New conditions were introduced by the advance of the Seljuk Turks in the eleventh century.

    1. The Holy Land was first conquered by the Arabs.

        a. In the seventh century the Holy City fell into the hands of the Arabs.

        b. The Arabs, however, generally permitted Christian pilgrims to the Holy Land to worship unmolested.

    2. Pilgrims began to suffer great hardships at the hands of the intolerant Seljuk Turks.

        a. They entered the Holy Land in the eleventh century.

        b. The Turks also began to threaten the eastern empire, and encroach upon its territory.

            (1). Asia Minor was lost to them in 1071.

---

* *From* Thompson, Economic and Social History of the Middle Ages, p. 380. Copyright 1928 *Used by permission of* D. Appleton-Century Company, *publishers.*

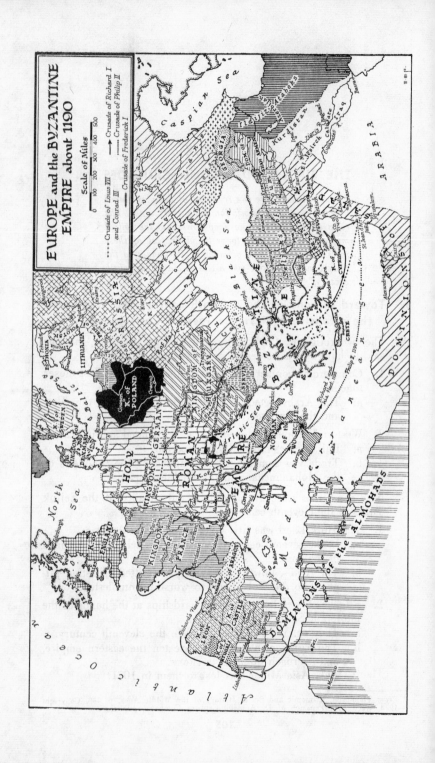

EUROPE and the BYZANTINE
EMPIRE about 1190

Scale of Miles

0   100   200   300   400   500

······· Crusade of Louis VII   ——→ Crusade of Richard I
        and Conrad III   Crusade of Philip II
——— Crusade of Frederick I

(2). They became a constant menace to the eastern empire.

(3). The emperor, Alexius, failed in his efforts to expel the Turks, and so called upon the pope for aid. He also asked for aid against the Patzinaks, located to the north of the Black Sea.

3. This was the real beginning of the great movement known as the Crusades.

II. Pope Urban II inaugurated the crusading movement at the Council of Clermont in 1095.

A. Conditions in Europe were "ripe" for the movement.
1. The policy of the papacy was definitely aggressive.
   a. Urban hoped to head the movement himself.
   b. The action might cause prestige to the papacy and unity to the church.
2. The period was one of unrest in the west.
   a. Men of Europe, especially Englishmen,[1] hoped to build up lost fortunes.
   b. The conflict between church and state had not been helpful: it had brought misery to many people.
   c. Pope Urban felt that the crusading movement would detract from the civil conflict between the princes and the popes in feudal Europe.
   d. The love of fighting and adventure was part of the spirit of the age.
      (1). Fighting was the sport of the nobles.
      (2). Conquerors were looking for more spoils.
      (3). Adventure always held a glamour for the carefree and the brave.
3. The teachings of the church gave impetus to the movement.
   a. Men were interested in a future life.
   b. Asceticism had been growing; the belief that a life of suffering would benefit them in the life to come was prevalent.
   c. Sinners were willing to undertake any pious task for forgiveness of their sins.
   d. Pilgrimages were favored as a form of penance; sinners often made a pilgrimage to the Holy Land as penance for great crimes. Many pilgrimages had been made before the organized movement of the crusades.

B. The Council of Clermont was called to lay plans for the crusades.

---

[1] Due to loss of land as a result of the Norman invasion in 1066.

1. The plan was not a new one as Gregory VII had planned to lead an army to aid Jerusalem.
2. Urban II called the council which met in Auvergne, at Clermont, 1095.
    a. After settling other important questions, Urban preached war upon the Turks, and urged the knights of the West to help their friends, the Byzantine Greeks.
    b. He praised the Franks and urged them to join the movement.
    c. He dwelt upon the suffering of the eastern Christians and the depredations of the Holy Land.
    d. Great enthusiasm was shown as the result of Urban's appeal to all Christendom.
        (1). Thousands from all over Europe took up the cross.
        (2). The problem was then to compel some of them to remain at home.

C. Several expeditions preceded the first organized crusade.
    1. Richard of Normandy, 1026, went on a pilgrimage.
        a. He was at the head of several hundred armed pilgrims.
        b. Some maintained that the Day of Judgment had come, because the number of pilgrims was so great.
        c. As the Turks were in control of the Holy Land these pilgrimages were almost impossible.

    2. Peter the Hermit became a leader in the movement and met with great success in interesting men in the crusades.
        a. He was a native of Amiens; he attempted to reach Jerusalem, but failed.
        b. He travelled throughout France mounted on a mule, preaching as Urban had done at Clermont, gathering many followers.
        c. He came to be regarded as a saint, living simply and preaching repentance.
        d. The first bands met with little success, including one led by Peter, as they were premature and unorganized.

III. The armies of the first crusade succeeded in the conquest of Jerusalem.

A. The first crusade began in 1096.
    1. Three main armies crossed Europe in different places.
        a. One led by Raymond, Count of Toulouse, went overland through Lombardy and Dalmatia.
        b. Godfrey of Lorraine and his brother, Baldwin, passed through Germany.

  c. The French and Normans under Bohemond and Tancred joined forces in Macedonia, marching on to Constantinople.

 2. These bands of enthusiasts were not real armies in any sense.

  a. Each crusader was obedient to whom he pleased.

  b. The men grouped about the leaders, but could change when they saw fit, and often did so.

  c. The leaders did not consider themselves responsible for the knights and men, as most of them were looking after their own interests.

 3. The reception at Constantinople was not entirely cordial.

  a. The march was successfully completed; the real difficulty came when Alexius, the eastern emperor, asked them for reasonable guarantees of their sincerity and honesty of purpose.

  b. He had " 'prayed' for rain, but a flood came."

   (1). He feared the crusaders would seize his capital.

   (2). The crusaders had little more in common with the Greeks than with the Turks.

   (3). The crusaders were often guilty of outrageous conduct.

  c. Alexius finally won each leader over to his cause.

   (1). This was accomplished by diplomacy, bribery, and occasional military force.

   (2). The leaders took oaths to restore conquered cities to the emperor, and Alexius promised aid to the Crusaders in return.

B. Several cities were captured from the Turks, including Jerusalem.[1]

 1. The conquest of Asia Minor was completed in 1097.

  a. The capture of Nicea, June, 1097, was the first military undertaking.

   (1). Alexius aided the expedition by furnishing boats.

   (2). The inhabitants of the city surrendered to Alexius, the emperor, to prevent sacking of the city by the crusaders.

  b. In July of the same year the successful battle of Dorylaeum completed the conquest of Asia Minor.

   (1). This battle demonstrated the weakness of armed men against the mounted Turkish archers.

   (2). In the later crusades military tactics were changed; large numbers of crossbowmen were used.

---

[1] See p. 68, Shepherd's Historical Atlas.

2.   The capture of Antioch was finally accomplished.
   a.   The march across the Tarsus was long and dangerous;
        the men were exhausted from heat and thirst.
   b.   The crusaders reached Antioch late in 1098. Baldwin
        left the army and went east to capture Edessa.
   c.   Antioch was finally captured after a long siege. It was
        then turned over to Bohemond.[1]
3.   The capture of Jerusalem was accomplished after the storm-
     ing of the city and the display of great valor.
   a.   The city was captured July 15, 1099.
   b.   There was indiscriminate massacre of the inhabitants.
   c.   With the victory at Ascalon, it seemed to the crusaders
        that the conquest of the Holy Land was complete.

C.   Forming a new government for the kingdom of Jerusalem
     proved to be a difficult problem.
   1.   The defense of the kingdom was inadequate.
      a.   The kingdom was long and narrow with few natural
           barriers.
      b.   The country was never completely conquered. Moham-
           medans held important strongholds in mountains and
           seaports.
      c.   The Western Christians needed continual reinforce-
           ments and the protection of the church to hold the
           territory. These two requirements were not adequately
           met.
   2.   The intermingling of Christian and infidel brought about
        a changed feeling; they learned to respect one another.
      a.   Close friendships were often formed; they gave mutual
           help.
      b.   Native workmen were employed by the Christians,
           which brought about closer relationships.
      c.   Eastern customs were adopted by the men from the
           west.
           (1). Western men adopted food and clothing suitable
                 to the country.
           (2). Oriental houses and doctors were preferred.
           (3). Intense feeling against heresy and schism became
                 almost non-existent; part of their worship was
                 carried on in the same temples of worship.
   3.   The setting up of a government caused many disputes.
      a.   Clergymen insisted that the city should revert to the
           church, but they had offered no real leadership; hence
           their wishes were not heeded.

---

[1] Bohemond seems to have regarded the crusades as a conquest of territory. He remained at Antioch, which he considered as his share of the spoils, refusing to go on
to Jerusalem.

  b. The nobles elected a ruler.

   (1). Raymond was offered the crown, but refused.

   (2). Godfrey was chosen as ruler, but he accepted conditionally. He did not use the title of king but took the title of "baron and defender of the Holy Sepulcher." This avoided a conflict between clergy and laity.

   (3). When Godfrey died, Baldwin inherited Godfrey's position, and took the title, "King of Jerusalem."

 4. Political organization of the kingdom of Jerusalem was faulty.

  a. Taxation fell mainly upon the peasants; the merchants, clergy, and nobles were exempt.

  b. There were sixteen "tenants in chief," each with practically independent powers. Consequently, political strife was the rule.

IV. The Fall of Edessa, 1144, caused renewed interest in the crusades.

A. The second crusade was preached by Saint Bernard.

 1. The news of the fall of Edessa dismayed Europe.

  a. A new Turkish tribe had replaced the Seljuks in Mesopotamia and Syria.

  b. First Aleppo fell, then Edessa, which was a strategic point to the Christians. Edessa guarded the mainland route from Mesopotamia to North Syria.

 2. Saint Bernard used his eloquence to enlist volunteers.

  a. He said, "The Christian who slays the unbeliever in the Holy War is sure of his reward, the more sure if he himself be slain,—".

  b. Louis VII, of France, immediately consented to go.

  c. The emperor, Conrad III, consented only after Bernard had preached before him the terrors of the Judgment Day.

  d. The mass of the men making up this expedition were largely wicked and impious. Bernard remarked that this was a double gain, for Europe to lose them and Palestine to gain them.

B. The second crusade was unsuccessful.

 1. This crusade was led by Conrad III and Louis VII.

  a. Conrad left first, 1147.

  b. Louis left in 1148.

  c. Failing to force their way through Asia Minor, they completed the journey by water.

2. The military expeditions were failures.
   a. Conrad set off for Asia Minor before Louis arrived in Constantinople, where he met only reverses.
   b. Louis' expedition into Asia Minor also met with disaster.
   c. The siege of Damascus in 1148 was also unsuccessful.
      (1). The crusaders were betrayed by their own allies.
      (2). The siege was abandoned.
3. The final result of the second crusade was to place Jerusalem itself in greater danger of attack from the Turks.
   a. Conrad left immediately for home, after the failure at Damascus; he was soon followed by Louis VII.
   b. Nothing had been accomplished of military importance.
4. The crusading movement was at a standstill until 1187, when Jerusalem was captured by Saladin, which again aroused all Christendom.

> *"The period between the first and second crusade is remarkable for the rise, at Jerusalem, of the two most distinguished orders of knighthood—the Hospitallers, and the Red-Cross Knights, or Templars. The valor of both orders became noted."* *

---

* *From* Wilson, Outlines of History, p. 284.

CHAPTER XX

LATER CRUSADES

"These misfortunes roused once more the princes of Europe, and the third crusade was undertaken by three of her sovereigns, the greatest in personal estimation as well as dignity." *

I. The capture of Jerusalem, 1187, by Saladin, led to the third crusade.

A. This crusade is often known as the "Crusade of the Three Kings."

    1. The fall of Jerusalem made a profound impression upon western Europe.

        a. Saladin destroyed the Latin army at Hattin.

        b. Then western kings made peace with each other and took the cross.

        c. The crusade was preached by the archbishop of Tyre.

    2. The three kings were aided in their purpose by the pope.

        a. They were Frederick I (Barbarossa) of Germany; Philip II, of France; and Richard the Lion Hearted, of England.

        b. The pope granted them a tax of one-tenth of all property. This was known as the "Saladin tithe." King William of Sicily supplied the fleet.

B. Unfortunately the death of Frederick Barbarossa occurred in 1190, and thus prevented the German forces from playing an effective part in this crusade.

    1. The Germans started first for the East.

    2. The eastern emperor feared Frederick and so made an alliance with Saladin, the Moslem leader.

        a. Saladin agreed to harass Frederick.

        b. Frederick threatened Constantinople so as to gain concessions from the emperor.

    3. Finally, Frederick crossed the Hellespont, but proceeded with great danger to himself and the cause.

        a. Iconium was captured by the Germans.

---

* *From* Hallam, View of the State of Europe During the Middle Ages, p. 35. Copyright 1876. *Used by permission of* Harper and Brothers, *publishers.*

      b. Then, crossing the mountains, they reached the river Chalycadnus where Frederic was drowned.

    4. His untimely death caused most of the German army to return home, only a few thousand continuing on to Acre.

C. Practically all forces in the Holy Land were engaged in the siege and capture of Acre, 1191.

    1. Acre was captured by the crusaders in 1191.

      a. The siege had been going on for many months.

      b. Philip and Richard were enemies, but furnished the necessary reinforcements.

      c. The siege began in August, 1189, and the city was captured in July, 1191.

      d. Twenty-five thousand Mussulmans were put to death by Richard; more cruelty was shown than by Saladin at Jerusalem.

    2. After the battle of Acre Richard remained in Palastine, while Philip left for home, and started a series of intrigues which endangered Richard's throne.

      a. Richard fought bravely.

        (1). Recaptured Jaffa and Ascalon, then marched on to Jerusalem.

        (2). When Saladin took the offensive, Richard sued for peace.

      b. Truce was finally established.

        (1). It was concluded for three years, three months, and three days.

        (2). Christians were allowed to enter Jerusalem freely. They retained the coast from Tyre to Jaffa.

      c. Richard was captured on his return home, but was freed by paying a huge ransom.

        (1). He was captured by Duke Leopold of Austria.

        (2). He was turned over to the Emperor, Henry VI, thrown into prison, and held for £100,000 ransom. All of Richard's subjects contributed to pay his ransom.

C. The third crusade may be said to have resulted in failure.

    1. Richard accomplished nothing of importance.

      a. His time was wasted in quest of knightly adventure.

      b. On several occasions he could, by diplomacy, have secured the whole kingdom.

      c. However, this crusade has become the theme of romance.

    2. This was the last crusade carried on upon a large scale.

      a. It is estimated that this crusade took a toll of 300,000 lives.

  b. The only important accomplishment was the capture
      of Acre.
  c. It was the last great effort to destroy the power of the
      Mohammedan. Other interests attracted the West in the
      future.
  3. Henry VI planned a crusade in 1195 in which he hoped to
      extend his power to the East.
  a. Several thousand crusaders were sent in advance.
  b. An end was put to preparations in 1197 when death
      overtook the emperor.

II. The Eastern Capital was captured by western knights during the fourth crusade.

A. A number of French knights took the cross in 1201.
  1. It was in the nature of a free-booting undertaking.[1]
  a. As the knights lacked money for the undertaking,
      vessels were furnished by the Venetians.
  b. Venice, eager to increase its possessions in the East,
      proposed that the crusaders capture the city of Zara to
      pay for their transportation.
  c. In 1202 the Christian cities of Zara, Trieste, and Muglia
      were captured.
  2. Later, Constantinople was captured.
  a. Fresh plots were promulgated by the Venetians and the
      leaders.
  b. It was proposed that the crusaders capture Constanti-
      nople in payment for the remainder of their journey
      and their provisions.
  c. The empire had been taken from Isaac Angelus; this
      was a good excuse to capture the city.
  d. Constantinople was taken and Alexius Angelus placed
      on the throne.
  3. Constantinople was sacked following Alexius' inability to
      pay the promised money to the crusaders.
  a. A quarrel followed and Constantinople was sacked.
      Many crusaders helped in the wanton destruction.
  b. The Venetians were excommunicated for their part in
      the destruction.

B. The capture of Constantinople resulted in a division of the
    empire.
  1. The division of the spoils had been provided for before the
      capture.

---

[1] The leaders of this crusade probably never intended to enter the Holy Land, but had
in mind the conquest of the eastern empire, and perhaps Egypt.

a. An emperor, who was to receive one-fourth of the empire, was to be elected.

b. The remainder was to be divided between the Venetians and the crusaders.

2. The Latin Empire was destined to have a short life.

a. The pope ordered the crusaders to remain for one year to protect the empire. Baldwin of Flanders was chosen emperor.

b. This empire lasted only until 1261; the Greeks then reconquered the city, re-establishing the Greek empire.

3. Results of this crusade were important, but detracted from the cause of the crusades.

a. The chief result was the increase in the power and wealth of Venice.

b. Constantinople was weakened; in fact, it never fully recovered.

c. The depredations hurt the cause of the crusades.

III. The remaining crusades were of relatively little importance.

A. The Children's Crusade was attempted in 1212.

1. Innocent III was always eager for a new crusade.

a. Preachers were sent through the West urging the people to take the cross.

b. People were disgusted with the failures thus far, and did not respond readily.

c. It was argued that if a group of truly good and innocent people took the cross that God would deliver the Mohammedans into their hands.

2. Under the leadership of boys a strange movement took place in France and Germany called the Children's Crusade.

a. It was preached that God would give them dry passage through the Mediterranean, as the Children of Israel had passed through the Red Sea.

b. The idea was accepted and many followers were secured in France and Germany, especially in the latter country.

c. The children assembled for the start, but were preyed upon by unscrupulous slave-traders.

d. Most of the children lost their freedom or their lives in their enthusiasm; only a few returned home.

e. The whole expedition was a total failure, but illustrates the spirit of the age.

B. The fifth crusade was also disastrous, 1219-1221.

1. It had been ordered by Innocent III.

a. The army succeeded in taking Damietta, in Egypt, the key to the Nile.

    b. The crusaders fought among themselves over the divi-
       sion of the booty. The incompetency of the leaders lead
       to the recapture of Damietta by the Mohammedans.
    c. The sultan offered to exchange Jerusalem for Damietta,
       but the offer was refused.
  2. This crusade ended in complete failure.
C. Frederick II gained diplomatic advantage in the sixth crusade,
   1229, when a promise to the pope forced him to embark upon
   the mission.
  1. Frederick had promised to go on a crusade before the death
     of Innocent III.
    a. He repeatedly postponed the expedition.
    b. Finally, Gregory IX excommunicated him, and he
       started the long delayed crusade.
  2. This crusade is remarkable because of the gain without
     actual fighting.
    a. Frederick took advantage of civil strife among the
       Mohammedans.
    b. He acquired, by diplomacy, Jerusalem, Bethlehem,
       Nazareth, and a considerable strip of territory for the
       Christians.
  3. Frederick secured a truce and treaties of commerce and
     alliance.
    a. Hostilities were again renewed when the ten-year truce
       expired.
    b. The Christians were defeated at Gaza.
    c. In 1244 Jerusalem was captured and sacked.
    d. The Holy City remained in the hands of the Turks from
       this date down until the World War, 1917.
D. The last two crusades were carried on largely by Louis IX of
   France, 1226-1270.
  1. The seventh crusade, 1248, was undertaken by Louis, and
     resulted in an unsuccessful invasion of Egypt.
  2. The eighth and last crusade, 1270, was equally a failure.
    a. Louis again set out for Egypt.
    b. The plague was largely responsible for stopping his
       troops.
    c. Louis' death from the plague in 1279 ended the whole
       crusading movement.

IV. Various influences of the East on the West were the most important results of the crusades.

A. The causes for the failure of the crusades were many.
  1. The crusades were carried on at a great sacrifice of men
     and money.

      a. These expenditures, from the standpoint of winning back the Holy Land, were in vain.

      b. Europe was bankrupt as a result, especially France.

  2. Causes of failure were numerous and understandable.

      a. A great variety of people made up the crusading army. The horde of pilgrims in the army was a liability.

      b. Effective leadership was usually lacking.

      c. The pretensions of the Greek empire in Syria was a factor contributing to failure.

      d. Rivalry between popes, emperors, rulers, and the cities, plus lack of proper motives, were important causes of failure.

B. Nevertheless, the crusades greatly affected the peoples of Europe.

  1. People of different nationalities were brought together.

      a. An interchange of ideas and customs resulted.

      b. Perhaps many of the great changes in western Europe after the crusades were due to other causes, but undoubtedly the crusades had important effects.

  2. The crusades effected a change in almost every phase of western European life.

      a. There followed a period of general intellectual stimulus.

         (1). Western Europe contacted a civilization higher than its own.

         (2). This helped to bring about an intellectual and scientific awakening.

      b. Transportation improved.

      c. New tastes were created and developed.

      d. Commerce was stimulated.

      e. Increased manufacturing resulted.

      f. Many of our modern financial institutions find their origin in this period.

  3. The political results of the crusades were far-reaching.

      a. New cities were built, old cities grew, and a third estate came into being.

         (1). Large population of cities brought large accumulations of wealth, and the rise of a new class.

         (2). This merchant and manufacturing class developed power to force its demands.

      b. The new industry demanded protection.

         (1). This condition called for better government.

         (2). Better systems of law developed.

         (3). More general and uniform government resulted.

      c. The rise of industry brought about the fall of the feudal system.

(1). Taxation began to support the state. Barter was no longer necessary because of the increased use of money.

(2). The demand for labor in the cities raised the standard of living of the serfs; they became free laborers as their conditions were bettered.

(3). Feudalism ceased to be so important, but, of course, greatly influenced the later history of Europe.

"The crusades had occupied a period of nearly two centuries, and had, led two millions of Europeans to find their graves in Eastern lands; and yet none of the objects of these expeditions had been accomplished;—a sad commentary upon the folly and fanaticism of the age." *

---

* *From* Wilson, Outline of History, p. 288.

CHAPTER XXI

ENGLAND FROM THE NORMAN CONQUEST TO 1272

*"The claim to be heir to the Confessor and guardian
of his 'good laws' thinly covered over the brute facts
of conquest, and seemed of little avail to protect the
country against French robbery and violence . . . Nor
was the yoke of Norman king or Norman baron like
the easy yoke of Canute and his Earls. The new
monarchy and the new feudalism were riveted on
the land by the new military system."* *

I. The Norman conquest put an end to the Saxon kings and established William, Duke of Normandy, on the English throne.

A. William of Normandy claimed the English throne, based on
Edward the Confessor's relationship and promise.

1. William had been promised succession to the throne.
   a. He was the first cousin of Edward the Confessor.
   b. As the result of his visit to Edward, who had grown up
      in Normandy and preferred Norman ways, he was
      promised succession to the throne.
   c. But English nobles objected to Edward's favoritism to
      Normans.

2. Harold, who was to be the last of the Saxons, was duly
   elected and crowned at Edward's death.
   a. Harold was head of the Godwin family, one of the most
      powerful in England.
   b. He was favored by the nobles, and was elected in pre-
      ference to William by the *witan*.

3. Nevertheless, William's claim was two-fold.
   a. He based his claims on Edward's promise and also up-
      on his relationship to the old line.
   b. Furthermore, he accused Harold of perjury, as he
      claimed Harold had taken an oath to respect his rights
      of inheritance.
   c. William appealed to the pope and was supported by
      him.

---

* *From* Trevelyan, History of England, pp. 118-119. Copyright 1926. *Used by permission of* Longmans, Green and Company, *publishers.*

B. In order to gain the English throne, William prepared to invade England at a time when Harold was warding off the attacks of the Swedish king in the North.

   1. William's preparations were elaborate and extensive.
     a. First he built a fleet.
     b. Then, he assembled at Lilleboune a large force of adventurers from France, Flanders, Brittany, Aquitaine, Burgundy, and Sicily.
     c. Further, great inducements were offered to those taking part in the venture.

   2. The Battle of Hastings in 1066 was hard fought by both sides, but proved decisive when Harold was killed.
     a. Unfortunately for the Saxons, Harold was engaged in crushing a revolt at Stamford Bridge on the same day the Norman fleet landed.
     b. However, he hurried south to give battle a few miles north of Hastings, even though many of his troops were yet in the North.
     c. Largely because he lacked reinforcements, he was defeated and killed at Senlac, near Hastings, October 14, 1066, after fighting a brave and hard battle.

   3. With but little difficulty, following his victory, William succeeded to the crown of Edward the Confessor, successfully claiming to be king of all England.
     a. He was crowned in London on December 25.
     b. He was consecrated by the church, so became the legitimate sovereign.

C. William proved to be an organizer of much ability, as well as a politician and soldier.

   1. Completion of the conquest was brought about with little regard to the rights of the Saxon lords.
     a. He confiscated the property of most of the Saxons and gave it to his Norman followers.
     b. The struggle with revolting subjects lasted until 1071, when the conquest was complete.
     c. It is true that some of the seized land was returned to the owners as a fief from the king.

   2. At first William interfered but little with the old order, but his policies gradually brought about many changes.
     a. He declared he would rule according to the laws of Edward the Confessor.
     b. He continued the royal agents of the local divisions of government.

    c. The power of the Norman nobles was restricted in a great many ways, and their holdings were widely scattered.[1]

3. William dealt intelligently with finances.
    a. All property was registered in a land register called the Domesday Book. This is the most valuable record of the time.
    b. An account was taken of all property of the citizens.
    c. The creation of the New Forest, a section William reserved for hunting, was unpopular; but in general, his actions were not objected to seriously.

4. "The changes in the church were many and far-reaching."
    a. William substituted for the native bishops those who owed their position to him.
    b. Lanfranc, who supported William's policy, was made Archbishop of Canterbury.
    c. William controlled the legates of the church, and steadfastly refused to pay homage to the pope.

D. As a result of the conquest, England became Normanized.
1. The Norman Conquest resulted in a great cultural influence on England.
    a. Norman legal and political practices supplanted those of the Saxon. Norman ideas, language, and architecture became common in England.
    b. Many Norman merchants and artisans took up their work across the channel.

2. Normans were elevated to the most important offices, and England came to have much in common with the mainland.
    a. The civilization gradually became more Norman than Saxon.
    b. Most of the land was owned by Normans.

3. William left three sons to succeed to his lands and wealth.
    a. He died in 1087, in France, as the result of a fall from his horse.
    b. His three sons were:
        (1). Robert, the oldest, to whom he left the Duchy of Normandy.
        (2). William Rufus, the second, received the English crown.
        (3). Henry Beauclere inherited 5000 pounds of silver.

[1] William forced every landowner to take oath of fidelity directly to him. This gave him direct control of vassals instead of indirect control through a few great landholders.

II.   William the Conqueror was succeeded by his two sons, William Rufus and Henry I.

A.   Under the Norman kings England became an absolute monarchy.
   1.   The king's main interest was in Normandy.
      a.   Two languages were used throughout the realm: Norman became the court language, while English remained the language of the people.
      b.   At first the church was subservient to the king, but later it became the champion of the people.
   2.   There seemed little likelihood of a united nation, free from foreign entanglements. However, in the thirteenth century, united England became a powerful influence in Europe.

B.   By 1154 England had gradually drifted into misery and feudal anarchy.
   1.   William Rufus, 1087-1100, was both disliked and incompetent.
      a.   Although he was crowned, the nobles preferred his brother Robert, who had been left the Duchy of Normandy.
      b.   His harsh rule made him detested; consequently, the people were much relieved when he was shot while hunting.
   2.   Henry I, the youngest son of William, had himself crowned and ruled from 1100 to 1135.
      a.   He promised better government, and, to a degree, refrained from acts which had made William unpopular.
      b.   He married the English Edith, a descendant of Alfred the Great, in order to please the English people.
      c.   Henry, after a somewhat extended struggle with Robert, whom he captured and imprisoned, obtained Normandy.
   3.   Stephen, the nephew of Henry I, 1135-1154, was weak, and the country drifted into anarchy.
      a.   He was forced to issue a charter of liberties, as his position was somewhat insecure.
      b.   The church became more independent under his rule.

III.   Henry II, 1154-1189, brought about many reforms in government, ruling wisely and well.

A.   Henry experienced many difficulties.
   1.   The kingdom was in a melancholy state.
      a.   Nobles had erected castles without royal permission, setting themselves up as independent rulers.
      b.   Mercenaries had been called in by the king's rivals, which added to the chaos.

     2. He adopted vigorous measures.
        a. The illegal castles were destroyed and mercenaries were no longer used.
        b. Although a great amount of his time was spent in Normandy, he became one of England's greatest rulers.

B. Both the finances and the judicial system of the nation were reformed.

     1. The exchequer[1] came into being.
        a. The *curia regis* sat twice each year to receive accounts of the sheriffs and of the money owed the king.
        b. All business was transacted on parchments, which were rolled up as permanent records. These give us much information about the period.

     2. Reforms in the judicial system were notable and lasting. Among the most important were:
        a. Circuit judges made regular circuits, trying cases twice each year in the different localities.
        b. The Court of the King's Bench tried cases coming under the king's jurisdiction.
        c. The grand jury, consisting of a group of men to bring accusations, developed.
        d. Trial by jury was generally adopted.
            (1). This institution did not originate with Henry II.[2]
            (2). It became the usual custom, rather than a special favor, as previously.
        e. Common law, based on the decision of judges, developed, as contrasted with Roman law on the continent.
        f. In many cases the power of the sheriffs was taken over by Henry's judges.

     3. Henry's military reforms resulted in a more efficient army.
        a. In 1181 every freeman was required to bear arms appropriate to his status.
        b. He collected fines and hired mercenary troops for foreign wars.

     4. Henry's conflict with Thomas Becket developed over the question of "criminous clerks," for Henry demanded that criminals be handed over to the secular courts for trial and punishments; and Becket refused.
        a. Becket's career was noteworthy.
            (1). At first he held low office in the church, but grew in the service of the crown.
            (2). Finally, he was recommended by the Archbishop of Canterbury to Henry, and was made Chancel-

---

[1] Tables on which money was counted were marked off into squares, resembling a checker-board. From this comes the name, Exchequer.

[2] Authorities disagree as to the origin of Trial by Jury, but certainly it was introduced into Norman England by Henry II.

lor, which office he carried out in the interests of Henry, resulting in a great friendship.

(3). Then, when the Archbishop of Canterbury died, Henry had his favorite elected by the monks.

b. When appointed archbishop he gave up his gay life, and opposed the king in the interests of the church.

c. The first serious break was the quarrel in 1164, when Becket refused to sign the Constitutions of Clarendon, as they made the church subservient to the king.[1]

(1). Thomas, fearing for his life, fled to France to seek aid from France and the pope.

(2). Becket and the king reached a reconciliation, but later Becket suspended some of the English prelates.

(3). Rash words uttered by Henry were taken by his knights as authority for action, and Becket was murdered in Canterbury Cathedral.

(4). The murder of Becket made of him a martyr.

(5). Thereafter, Henry lived a life of remorse. He had not meant to resort to violence, and honestly grieved at Becket's untimely death.

C. Henry II had vast realms abroad which were greater in extent than all his English territory.

1. This territory was acquired mostly through marriage and inheritance.

a. He inherited Normandy and Brittany from William the Conqueror.

b. His mother married Geoffrey Plantaganet, Count of Anjou; and Henry himself married Eleanor of Aquitaine, heiress of the vast realms of the Dukes of Guienne.

2. These foreign possessions greatly influenced the history of England for centuries to come.

a. Philip Augustus, of France, promoted many treasonable plans among Henry's sons to further his own ends.

b. The expulsion of the English from France was the main policy of Philip.

IV. The greatest event of the first part of the thirteenth century was the signing of the Magna Carta.

A. Richard the Lion Hearted, 1189-1199, succeeded Henry II.

1. Henry's good government continued throughout Richard's reign.

a. Richard was one of the most romantic figures of the middle ages, but a very poor ruler.

---

1 This demonstrates how the medieval king was dependent on churchmen. The chief issue at this particular time was whether criminous clerks—not true clergy—were to be tried in civil as well as church courts.

        b. He spent very little time in England, although king for ten years.

    2. John, Richard's brother, a detestable ruler, succeeded to the throne, 1199-1216, and lost much of the crown's heritage.

        a. He lost most of his possessions on the continent.

        b. His reign is notable for his forced signing of the Great Charter (Magna Carta), 1215.

        c. Furthermore, John handed England over to the pope, and received it back as a fief in 1213.

B. The signing of the Great Charter has been of great importance to posterity.

    1. John's foreign expedition had been a failure.

        a. He wished to reconquer his lost possessions on the continent, but the nobles did not support him.

        b. Philip of France defeated John at Bouvines in 1214. This is of great importance for it greatly increased the realm of the king of France, creating a powerful rival for the English on the continent.

        c. John being weakened, the nobles pressed their claim.

    2. In 1214 the nobles met and took an oath to compel John to sign a charter, containing the things which an English king might not do.

        a. At first, John refused, so the nobles marched against him and defeated him at Runnymede. Prince Louis of France invaded England to assist the barons and to embarrass John.

        b. Therefore, in June, 1215, John was compelled to confirm the rights of the nation.

    3. The charter was the great landmark in the development of English liberties, although much has been read into it since.

        a. The rights and duties of the commoner as well as the noble were outlined and protected.

        b. The power of the king, especially his power of taxation, was greatly restricted.

        c. It begins a new period in English history.

        d. John and certain later kings attempted to evade the provisions of the charter, but it withstood all attempts, and today is one of the most important parts of the written and unwritten constitutions of England.

V. During the reign of Henry III, 1216-1272, the English parliament began to be an important influence in government.

A. The rule of Henry may better be called the "Misrule of Henry III."

1. During Henry's minority, England was ruled by a regent, but he assumed full power when he became of age.
    a. He surrounded himself with foreign favorites, giving them great amounts of money.
    b. He allowed the pope to collect heavy taxes in England.
    c. He added to his unpopularity by engaging in costly foreign wars.

2. The Provisions of Oxford, 1258, resulted from Henry's demand for money.
    a. The barons, demanding government reform, drew up the "provisions."
    b. They provided for ridding the country of foreigners, and a council of twenty-four was chosen to advise the king.
    c. For a few years a council governed England.
    d. Simon de Montfort was the leader in the council.

B. Simon de Montfort's famous parliament met in 1265.

1. A new class, the knights and burgesses, was represented.
    a. Simon's position as leader was not secure.
    b. To make his position more secure he included, besides the barons and clergy, representatives of the boroughs, and two knights from each shire.
    c. This precedent led to Edward's Model Parliament, 1295.

2. The rise of the third estate became imminent.
    a. Although Henry's reign had been spent largely in civil and foreign wars, great gains had been made by the people toward greater self-determination of their government and laws.
    b. Trade and industry revived, and the third estate was destined to play an increasing part in English government.

> *"In less than a generation after the loss of Normandy and Anjou the more ancient of the English baronage . . . . had become as national in spirit as the mass of the people; and the larger part of the nobility, which had been raised to the ranks of the aristocracy only within the last century, had always been English in spirit . . . The English were rapidly being welded into a powerful nation. The mass of the English people 'desired nothing more than peace, quietness, and good governance.'"* *

---

* *From* Hulme, History of the British People, pp. 99-100. Copyright 1924. *Used by permission of* D. Appleton-Century Company, *publishers.*

CHAPTER XXII

FRANCE FROM 1108 TO 1328

"There were reasons for the growth of royal power in France . . . First . . . a superior title . . . Second, . . . unbroken succession . . . with few minorities and regencies from 987 to 1328 . . . Third, the evolution of an efficient and centralized administration . . . . Fourth, . . . energetic reigns of several kings after Louis VI . . . Fifth, the many opportunities . . . for alliances with the pope, clergy, communes, or sub-vassals against the great feudal lords—or with the nobility of one part of France against those of another." *

I. **The reign of Louis VI, the Fat, marks the beginning of consolidation of the French lands and the French monarchy.**

A. The process of development was beset with many difficulties.

    1. The Capetian line of kings proved strong and important.

        a. During this period France held undisputed leadership in western Europe.

        b. For over three hundred years the direct male line of Capetians never failed.

        c. By the fourteenth century it was evident that the king was to prevail over the feudal lords.

        d. Capetian rulers were strengthened by the church lands which they controlled; the revenue was used to combat the feudal lords.

    2. The king's position was maintained, however, in the face of many difficulties.

        a. The doctrine of feudalism gave rights to the feudal lords as well as to the kings.

        b. There was a lack of geographical unity, and a diversity of peoples, languages, customs, and laws.

        c. Until the twelfth century the French king was actual ruler only of Paris and the surrounding countryside, and even here, he was not without opposition.

---

* *From* Thorndike, The History of Medieval Europe, p. 491. Copyright 1917. *Used by permission of* Houghton, Mifflin Company, *publishers.*

B. Louis the Fat was the first king to undertake the complete mastery of his own duchy.

  1. He was an active soldier and in spite of his corpulence was indefatigable.

      a. He kept the means of communication free between the different centers of his scattered domains.

      b. He attempted to destroy the power of feudal lords.

  2. Louis was fairly successful in putting down disorder, and making his power effective.

      a. He succeeded in increasing royal prestige throughout the kingdom.

      b. His popularity and success were due largely to his liberal economic policy, and even the great lords rallied to his support when invasion threatened.

C. There was little development under Louis VII, 1137-1180.

  1. He was not endowed with strong character or particular ability.

      a. He is often represented as weak and over-pious, although the latter was not true in his younger days.

      b. The promise of a strong and successful government was lost by the disastrous second crusade of 1145.

  2. Louis had much trouble with Henry II of England after Henry's marriage to Eleanor, Louis' divorced wife.

      a. Louis VII had married Eleanor, heiress of Poitou and the duchy of Aquitaine, the largest feudal state of France.

      b. Louis quarreled with his queen and divorced her, honestly returning to her the great dowery she brought to him at her marriage. Then Eleanor married Henry II, King of England, a man of energy and ability.

      c. The marriage greatly increased the power of Henry Plantagenet, and gave him lordship over much of France.

II. France advanced rapidly under Philip II, or Philip Augustus, 1180—1223.

A. Philip ruled exactly as long as his father Louis, but with greater ability.

  1. He was crowned about a year before his father's death.

      a. Louis became paralyzed; consequently, was unable to rule.

      b. Philip was only fifteen, but was determined to rule.

  2. At an early age Philip was mature enough to reign, ruling under the guardianship of his uncle, the Count of Flanders.

B. Philip had a very difficult problem to face in his conflict with
    Henry II of England and Henry's sons.
    1. Philip's chief purpose was to wage incessant war against
        the Plantagenet kings.
        a. He was aided by intrigue among his enemies.
        b. He took advantage of the quarrels of the brothers
            among themselves and with their father, Henry II.
        c. With cooperation, the English could easily have an-
            nihilated Philip and his kingdom.
    2. The situation changed at the death of Henry.
        a. Philip and Richard the Lion Hearted, who succeeded
            Henry, were at first on friendly terms.
        b. They set out together on the third crusade, but soon be-
            came bitter enemies.
        c. Philip soon returned from the crusade and planned the
            conquest of Richard's territories.
        d. In the war which followed, Philip was forced to give
            up most of his conquests.
    3. The battle of Bouvines, 1214, made Philip still stronger.
        a. John had become king of England.
        b. A coalition was formed against France which included
            the emperor, Otto, the Count of Flanders, the lords of
            Lorraine and Holland, and England.
        c. Philip defeated the allies at the battle of Bouvines.
        d. This battle crushed all of John's hopes, and left Philip
            in possession of the greater part of France.

C. Philip increased the extent of his domain and increased his con-
    trol over his subjects until he was the real power in France.
    1. The king now had more actual authority than any of his
        vassals.
    2. He checked the power of nobility and clergy by favoring
        the third estate.
        a. He realized the importance of the towns, treating them
            with consideration.
        b. Frequently he employed burgesses as officials.
        c. Merchants were protected, and in this way he increased
            his revenues.
    3. Philip's administrative changes are noteworthy.
        a. He reduced the number of feudal lords serving as offi-
            cials, especially the *curia regis*. The jurisdiction of
            this body was greatly extended.
        b. The "inquests," fact-finding organizations, were de-
            veloped.

    c. He also inaugurated the system of "bailiffs," which were responsible to the "King's Council." Expenses of these officials were paid out of the royal treasury.

D. There were no great changes under Louis VIII, 1223-1226. He had been an aid to his father, having real ability.

    1. Louis VIII created appanages.
        a. He assigned fiefs to his three younger sons.
        b. This policy worked counter to consolidation, resulting in strife among the royal family.

    2. During his short reign he waged war against the Albigenses, and paved the way for territorial gains.

    3. He was succeeded by Louis, a boy of thirteen, who was destined to be one of France's greatest kings. His mother held the regency during his minority.

III. France stood at the height of her medieval glory under Louis IX (Saint Louis) 1226-1270.

A. Louis IX's great reputation for justice, acknowledged even beyond the frontiers of his own realm, made him a very popular monarch.

    1. His character was noteworthy, and he has been called "a justiciary in ermine."
        a. He insisted on exact justice to all, regardless of rank.
        b. He was religious, but remarkably independent for so pious a ruler.
        c. He was endowed with great ability, moderation, and good sense.
        d. He won the respect and love of all his people by "constantly seeking to make the government serve its purpose to both king and people."

    2. He was the strongest monarch of his age.
        a. He had ample income, and his finances were usually in excellent shape. Taxation was resorted to only for special undertakings.
        b. The work of the consolidation of the French monarchy was carried on with great skill and ability.

B. He settled the question of English possessions in France very skillfully.

    1. The revolt of the barons resulted in misfortune for them.
        a. The barons formed a coalition with the king of England.
        b. The revolts were easily put down by Louis.

2. The final settlement was most reasonable.
   a. The English king retained Poitou, Gascony, and Guienne, but was forced to do homage to Louis.
   b. English claims to the rest of French territory on the continent were relinquished.

C. Louis undertook two crusades; both were failures.
   1. Cyprus was his first destination, setting sail in 1248.
      a. The expedition resulted in failure.
      b. He returned to France in 1254 after many disasters.
   2. The second crusade was equally unsuccessful, and resulted in his death.
      a. Louis was not able to arrange another expedition until 1270.
      b. As a result of his trip to Tunis he was stricken with plague and died at Carthage in 1270.

D. Louis introduced many improvements in governmental machinery, making for greater centralization.
   1. Three bodies of the assembly were established, and so divided the powers of government.
      a. The king's council aided in conducting general affairs of the kingdom.
      b. The chamber of accounts attended to the revenue.
      c. The parlement—judicial body, supreme court, was the third division.
   2. A regular system of appeals was established.
      a. The parlement sat in the great court-house at Paris.
      b. It greatly increased the king's power in the various parts of the realm, especially in the more remote sections.
   3. Only royal coins were used and they came to be acceptable everywhere in the realm.

E. France in 1270 was the strongest power in Europe.
   1. The position of the king was supreme. Feudal lords and the churchmen had been shorn of much of their power.
   2. A spirit of nationality was gradually developing.
      a. Cities were growing and virtually all of them were loyal to the crown.
      b. The inhabitants became known as Frenchmen.
      c. Local differences were still present, but a feeling of nationality was evident even in some of the more remote parts of the realm.

IV. France, under the later Capetian rulers, witnessed rapid progress in institution-making.

A. Philip III, the Bold, added to the French territory.

    1. His wars with Spain led to the acquisition of Navarre.

    2. He added Toulouse and other territory in the south of France.

    3. Rebellious vassals and the church were rendered subservient to him.

B. Consolidation of the French absolute monarchy was largely brought about under Philip IV, the Fair, 1285-1314.

    1. He had both the will and the means to set up an absolute monarchy.
        a. Having inherited a well organized government, he extended his power to an even greater extent.
        b. His advisors and lawyers encouraged a centralized government.
        c. Roman law was the model of the monarchy.

    2. The meeting of the Estates General, 1302, was called to gain the support of the whole nation in his conflict with the church.
        a. This was the first time representatives of the towns had been called with the nobles and clergy.
        b. It coincided with the movement in England.

    3. Philip's relations with Pope Boniface VIII were not cordial.
        a. Philip and the pope entered into conflict over the question of taxation—the clergy were being exploited.
        b. The pope issued the *clericis laicos* in 1296.
            (1). This was a papal bull issued by Boniface.
            (2). It stated that all powers over the clergy were forbidden to laity, and that whoever taxed the clergy would be considered excommunicated.
        c. *Unam sanctam*—the second papal bull.
            (1). Philip renounced the pope's authority.
            (2). Then Boniface issued the statement that subjugation to the pope was necessary to salvation for every human creature.
        d. Philip established his supremacy over the pope, and from this time the papal power collapsed.

    4. The "Babylonian Captivity" of the papacy, 1309-1377, brought the papacy under French influence.
        a. Philip was exonerated by Clement V, one of Philip's councillors who was elected pope.

    b. Clement established himself at Avignon, and the papacy came directly under the influence of the French monarch.

C. The Capetian line came to an end with the reign of Charles IV in 1328.

    1. Philip was succeeded by his three sons in turn.
        a. Louis X, 1314-1316.
        b. Philip V, 1316-1322.
        c. Charles IV, 1322-1328.

    2. Charles IV was the last male descendant of Philip IV, and with his death the house of Valois was established upon the French throne.

> *"In 1270, St. Louis . . . . left a solid dominion, spreading from sea to sea, with great revenues and a formidable fighting power, to his son, Philip III. France had reached a high estate in Europe, from which, notwithstanding many hours of sore trial, she was never really to fall."* *

---

* *From* Davis, A History of France, p. 63. Copyright 1919. *Used by permission of* Houghton, Mifflin Company, *publishers.*

CHAPTER XXIII

CULTURE OF THE MIDDLE AGES

"The Middle Ages, with all their roughness, were far from remaining in a state of intellectual stagnation, or even of intellectual darkness. There is not a generation from the sixth to the sixteenth century which failed to produce a man of scholarship." *

I. **The two most important factors in the change from ancient to medieval culture were the barbarian invaders and the forces of Christianity.**

A. Europe in the middle ages was far behind the classic civilizations of ancient Greece and Rome.

   1. Many have called the period the "Dark Ages."

      a. Much of the ancient learning had been lost or forgotten.

      b. The barbarians were little more than children, intellectually.

   2. The change from the older to the medieval culture evolved gradually.

      a. Many Roman customs were adopted by the Germans, and the Romans likewise adopted German customs.

      b. However, the barbarians were not mature enough in mind to take advantage of Roman culture, art, and science.

B. The Europeans were destined to equal and even excel the ancients in cultural development.

   1. The barbarians were a strong race of people.

      a. They surpassed the Romans in physical characteristics.

      b. Later their mental faculties were developed.

   2. Charlemagne succeeded in combining the best characteristics of the two people, bringing about the development of a superior race.

---

* *From* Brown, Medieval Europe, p. 315. Copyright 1932. *Used by permission of* Harcourt, Brace and Company, *publishers.*

II.   In a broad general way, the languages of western Europe may be divided into two great families, Romanic and Germanic.

A.   During the middle ages Latin was in general use.
  1.   Latin was the language of the learned, and most books were written in it.
    a.   Latin was the language of the professors in the universities.
    b.   The educated wrote their personal letters in Latin.
  2.   It was the language of the church and state.
    a.   State papers and legal documents were drawn up in Latin.
    b.   It was the universal language of the church.
    c.   The use of Latin had a unifying influence, making travel and study in foreign countries possible.
B.   Gradually Latin was supplanted by the vernacular.
  1.   As time went on Latin was used less in speech than in writing.
    a.   The spoken Latin differed from the written.
    b.   Finally, common people could not understand Latin.
    c.   There grew up distinct languages in each country, and Latin ceased to be used, even in writing.
  2.   The Romance languages, those based on Latin, gradually took form.
    a.   Five languages are commonly classified as Romance.
      (1). Spanish,   (3). Italian,
      (2). French,   (4). Portuguese,
              (5). Roumanian.
    b.   These languages, all based on Latin, are distinct but they resemble one another in many ways.
  3.   The Germanic or Teutonic languages (those based on the dialects of the people of Northern Europe) became more developed.
    a.   These languages are used today by the peoples of northern Europe, namely:
      (1). German,   (5). Danish,
      (2). Dutch,   (6). Norwegian,
      (3). English,   (7). Icelandic,
      (4). Swedish,   (8). Flemish.
    b.   The above peoples, for the most part, had been either completely outside the old Roman Empire, or were within for too short a time to become Romanized, hence they continued to use their old language.
  4.   The languages of the people of eastern Europe are classified as Slavic: Russian, Polish, Bulgarian, Czech, etc.

III. The development of the different languages was a fore-runner to the development of different literatures.

A. Most of the countries of Europe developed a literature distinctly their own.

    1. Before the twelfth century books were still written in Latin.

        a. The different languages were spoken several hundred years before they were written.

        b. The written Latin of the middle ages differed, however, from the purely classical language of ancient times.

        c. The church complained that the writing of the time was a very inferior product.

        d. Beginning with the twelfth and thirteenth centuries songs and poems began to be written in the peoples' language.

    2. The earlier writings in the vernacular were mostly lyrical songs and legendary romances.

        a. Songs of the troubadours were written by those of the knightly class.

            (1). They sang the songs to the accompaniment of the lute, carrying them from court to court.

            (2). Our best idea of chivalry comes from these songs.

        b. Roland was the hero of the national epic of France.

            (1). Probably it was written just before the first crusade.

            (2). It tells of Charlemagne's retreat from Spain, during which Roland lost his life in the Pyrenees.

        c. The romances of King Arthur and the Knights of the Round Table appeared in the latter part of the twelfth century.

            (1). They enjoyed popularity in all western Europe.

            (2). Arthur was supposed to have been king of Britain shortly after the coming of the Saxons.

            (3). In these romances there was almost absolute disregard for historical fact.

        d. Germany developed many lyrical songs. The most famous was the epic telling of Siegfried.

        e. Spain's greatest epic was the story of the Cid. He was made a national hero, although in real life he was given to plunder, and ill deserved the fame acquired.

B. Other medieval literature was of a more enduring character.

    1. This was true of all European countries, but England and Italy were the leaders.

    2. Dante was the greatest of all Italian poets, and "The Divine Comedy," his greatest poem, occupies an important place in the world's literature.

3. England produced Chaucer—the first of the great English poets.
    a. He has been called the "Father of English Poetry."
    b. His greatest work is his "Canterbury Tales."

IV. Education during the middle ages was of a very elementary character.

A. Before the eleventh century there was nothing in western Europe which resembled the later universities.
    1. During the "dark ages" civilization declined definitely.
        a. Ancient culture and learning were lost.
        b. Education was confined to the monasteries.
    2. The church was the greatest civilizing agency.
        a. Its influence bettered the crude people.
        b. It was the guardian of learning and promoter of the arts.
        c. The church developed most of the great men of the period.
    3. Learning may be said to have revived in the ninth century as a result of the influence of Charlemagne and Alfred the Great.
        a. Charlemagne endeavored to raise the clergy to a higher level.
        b. He sought learned men throughout Europe, such as Alcuin of York, Peter of Pisa, and Paul the Deacon, of Italy.
        c. Their success was slight, but paved the way for a general system of education in the liberal arts.
        d. From the time of Charlemagne knowledge increased and the quality of instruction improved. This period was the forerunner of the great university period of the thirteenth century.

B. The culture and education of the later middle ages are known as Scholasticism.[1]
    1. Scholasticism emphasized logic. It was based on the teachings of Aristotle, employing the deductive method.
        a. Reasoning was often false; students were slaves to their books; there was no experimentation.
        b. The emphasis placed upon religion made this culture narrow and intellectually sterile, as practical study was avoided.
        c. St. Thomas Aquinas, Abelard, and Peter Lombard were among the greatest scholastics.

---

[1] This subject will be discussed more fully in Chapter XXVIII-Education and the Beginning of the Universities.

2. Roger Bacon, an English Franciscan monk of the thirteenth century, was the chief opponent of scholasticism. He used the inductive method, reasoning from observation and experiment.

C. A revival of learning and art took place in the twelfth century.[1]
   1. There was progress in the arts and a beginning in experimental science.
      a. Magnificent churches were built.
      b. There developed a group of scientific investigators who paved the way for later development.
   2. About 1100 students began to study law, as well as theology and philosophy.
      a. The method of study was through lectures delivered by the masters.
      b. Thus, the first modern universities had their beginning.
   3. Learning was no longer limited to the clergy.
      a. Books were written in the language of the people.
      b. Laymen began to write books as well as to read them.
      c. This was the period of the appearance of the third estate—merchants and artisans rose to wealth and importance everywhere.

V. Architecture was the dominant art of the middle ages.

A. The art of the middle ages reflected the life of the people much in the same manner as did their literature.
   1. Illuminations by the monks were fairly common.
      a. These were chiefly illustrations in books, painted by hand on parchment in brilliant colors.
      b. They were chiefly found in religious books used in church services.
      c. Some secular books illustrated everyday scenes.
   2. The artist of the time was bound by custom.
      a. Individuality was lacking.
      b. Established practices were used generation after generation.
   3. Sculpture concerned itself mostly with decorative carving.
      a. This art was more widely used than painting, but it did not represent the human figure.
      b. The dominant art, however, was architecture.

B. The greatest achievements in medieval architecture are found in the churches of western Europe.
   1. The church was the all important factor throughout the middle ages.

---

[1] Most authorities feel that the crusades gave a definite impetus to this movement.

    a. The building and beautifying of churches was a matter of interest to all, as everyone belonged to the church.

    b. The churches represented religious sentiments, local pride, and artistic craving, taking the place of the modern art museum.

2. There were several different styles of architecture used during the middle ages.

    a. Byzantine style developed.

        (1). Roman architecture declined after the barbarian invasions.

        (2). From the fifth to the tenth centuries most buildings were built of wood. We know little of them.

        (3). Charlemagne introduced the Byzantine style in the building of his church at Aachen.

    b. Romanesque style began early in the eleventh century.

        (1). About the year 1000 most of the churches were rebuilt in this new style.

        (2). It is characterized by its round arches, horizontal lines and thick walls. The result was dark and gloomy churches.

    c. Gothic style developed in the twelfth century.

        (1). It was characterized mainly by the pointed arch or flying buttress, capable of supporting immense weight.

        (2). The result was many windows, adequate light, and tall buildings with thin walls.

        (3). It predominated until the sixteenth century when the Gothic gave way to the architecture of the Renaissance.

*"The Gothic cathedral is not only a masterpiece of art, but is perhaps the greatest social achievement which art has yet attained." ***

---

* *From* Sellery and Krey, Medieval Foundations of Western Civilization, p. 273. Copyright 1929. *Used by permission of* Harper and Brothers, *publishers.*

CHAPTER XXIV

LIFE OF THE NOBLES—THE AGE OF CHIVALRY

"A great lord was a busy man . . . . In addition to the administration of the fiefs and holding courts of justice, the lord directed the education of the young nobles in the castle. His chief amusement was hunting . . . Next in importance among his amusements were possibly the banquets . . . Other diversions were bearbaiting . . . jousting or watching others fight, receiving guests, making love, playing chess or checkers, and dancing. His wife shared in all of these amusements and had many duties in addition." *

I. There were three important classes in the middle ages.

A. First, there were the clergy.

    1. These were either secular or regular.

        a. The secular clergy were those not bound by rule— that is, they were not members of one of the monastic orders. Some of these clergymen were worldly and wealthy.

        b. The regular clergy[1] confined their activities to religious matters.

    2. They were of two classes: noble and non-noble.

        a. Bishops were frequently great military leaders who lived the life of other high nobility.

        b. Other clerics held a lower position in the feudal system and were not nobles.

B. Second, there were the lay nobles.

    1. The wealthier nobles lived in castles.

        a. Sometimes they had many castles to aid in the defense of their many scattered fiefs.

        b. In the earlier middle ages castles were usually located in quite inaccessible places; often surrounded by high walls and moats.

    2. Before the twelfth century the members of the nobility were largely determined by the size of their income.

---

* *From* Munro, The Middle Ages, pp. 312-313. Copyright 1922. *Used by permission of* D. Appleton-Century Company, *publishers.*
1 The regular clergy lived by rule (regulus). Hence the various monastic orders.

      a.   Anyone holding sufficient land was classified as a noble.

      b.   Later the nobility became a distinct class, and enjoyed many privileges denied others.

C.   Third, there were the Commoners who made up the great bulk of the population.

   1.   At first all of this class were peasants or tillers of the soil.

      a.   The nobles lived from the labor of this peasant class.

      b.   This class was looked down upon by the nobles.

   2.   Later the third estate developed from this group.

      a.   The burgher class became wealthy and powerful.

      b.   They developed into bankers, merchants, and financial leaders.

      c.   Finally, they were given a voice in government.

II. By the middle of the twelfth century these classifications became more distinct and the importance of the nobility grew.

A.   The title of nobility became hereditary.

   1.   Knighthood and the possession of a fief constituted the dividing line between nobles and the commoners.

      a.   The nobles were the ruling and fighting class.

      b.   This distinction became more marked as society developed.

   2.   The lay nobles differed from the rest in two ways: their possession of complete fighting equipment, and their abstinence from manual labor.

   3.   The nobles were tenants-in-chief, holding their titles directly from the king.

      a.   These titles had become firmly established, especially in France.

      b.   In Germany the nobility divided their holdings among their sons. This led to many small holdings, and the distinction was less marked.

      c.   In Italy the nobility were chiefly of German blood; hence they were not only a different class, but a different race.

      d.   While the practices were not uniform in the different countries, the tendency in all countries was to establish an upper or noble class.[1]

B.   Royal power in Europe almost completely collapsed during this period; especially was this true in France.

---

[1] Chivalry was essentially aristocratic, increasing social stratification. The code of chivalry applied mostly to people of noble birth, hence little of its humanitarianism ever reached the lower classes.

1. The nobles gradually, but surely, had usurped authority from the king as he no longer was able to make his power felt.
    a. Anyone strong enough might become a ruler, and the result was many small independent holdings.
    b. Finally, the stronger families established recognized authority over lesser feudal lords.
2. When Hugh Capet received the title of King of France in 987 there was a slight improvement in the position of king for a time.
    a. There was a desire for peace and order, and the people would accept almost any ruler who promoted these.
    b. Some of the Capetian line were weak, but by the middle of the twelfth century the king of France had become one of the most powerful nobles in the country.
    c. The church during this period was a unifying influence, and so greatly aided the French kings' efforts to establish their position.

III. The occupations and education of the nobles showed a life of varied activity.

A. The nobles' chief occupation was maintaining and governing their castles and fiefs.
1. A great lord was a busy man for he usually had several castles to watch over.
    a. Much of his time was spent in traveling.
        (1). Transportation of commodities was difficult.
        (2). So he usually ate the food where it was grown.
    b. He directed the education of the young nobles.
2. His chief amusement was hunting,[1] but it was also a necessity, for his supply of fresh meat depended upon it.
    a. In addition, the banquet served as a most important part of his social life, and was always accompanied by gluttonous eating and drinking.
    b. Other favorite pastimes of the nobles consisted of bear-baiting, checkers, dice, chess, and dancing.
3. The position of women was raised in feudal society.
    a. The wife joined in the amusements.
    b. She superintended the household and directed the education of the girls.

B. The education of the young nobles was a very important duty of the lay lords.

---

1 In 1000 a decree was promulgated which stated that no one should kill or steal "colts, asses, oxen, sheep, goats, or pigs." This would indicate extensive cattle raising.

1. The son was usually sent to the castle of the suzerain when very young.
   a. Here he began his training as a page.
   b. His duties were to wait upon the ladies, run errands, and begin his education for knighthood.
   c. Next, he became a squire.
      (1). Now he served his lord, looking after his lord's horses, his armor, and his dress.
      (2). Furthermore, the squire learned the use of implements of warfare, and was taught the art of being an agreeable "companion."
2. In addition, the young noble was taught various languages. Some learned not only the different dialects, but also the Latin of the church.

IV. Upon proving his ability the squire might become a knight.[1]

A. No one was born a knight.

1. Even the king's son had to achieve knighthood.
2. The ceremony might be very simple, but was usually quite elaborate.
   a. The only essential was that some knight should give the accolade (a stroke on the neck or shoulders) and declare him a knight.
   b. This part of the ceremony was inherited from the old German custom of bestowing the arms of manhood upon a young warrior.

B. In the twelfth century the church shared in the ceremony.

1. The church taught that knighthood and priesthood had much in common.
   a. Oaths were taken to observe the Peace and Truce of God; and to protect the weak, the needy, and the church.
   b. The crusades also had their influence.
2. The ceremony further included:
   a. Prayers and fasting.
   b. The blessing of the weapons.
   c. A bath of purification.
   d. And, finally, a test of skill in horsemanship and handling weapons.

---

[1] Meyers attributes the rise of chivalry to three factors:
1. The reverence of the Teuton for womanhood.
2. The warlike nature of the people.
3. The gentle influence of the church.

3. The cost of the ceremony was usually great as it often lasted several days, and was attended by many guests and hired entertainers; hence younger sons frequently had to do without this initiation.

V. Private warfare threw feudal Europe into anarchy much of the time.

A. The castle was of first importance in feudal warfare.

1. The castle site was chosen for its inaccessibility.
   a. The ideal situation was to be surrounded by water, on the spur of a hill, or on firm ground in the midst of a bog. If so located, the castle was safe from the siege-machines.
   b. In the open country safety was insured by surrounding the castle by moats or ditches.

2. Castles were first made of wood, later of stone. The stone wall and the moat were developed in the twelfth and thirteenth centuries.
   a. In the later middle ages castles were often quite large.
   b. The crusades helped in the development of castles, for the ideas of the East caused the nobles of Europe to want stronger and better homes.
   c. Garrisons were increased and life was more elaborate.

3. With the development of better communications there were many changes in castle life.
   a. Formerly the knight was isolated; he had no education, and was often a cruel tyrant. However, contact with other people brought advance and progress, and life became more genteel.

4. With the introduction of gunpowder, however, the importance of the castle diminished.
   a. With the changed methods of warfare castle walls would no longer withstand the improved implements of war.
   b. The common footsoldier became as efficient as the knight in mailed armor.

B. Private warfare, a chief occupation for many knights, was often constant and long protracted.

1. The lords suffered little, but the peasants suffered much; for the lords were seldom killed, and when captured, the peasants bore the expense of ransom.

2. The Truce and Peace of God reduced private warfare considerably.

    a. The number of days when fighting was outlawed steadily increased until there were only eighty days on which it was lawful to fight.

    b. Unfortunately, these laws were not strictly enforced.

    c. Private warfare continued until checked by the monarchs when the "King's Peace" was extended over the whole kingdom.

VI. The many changes in Western Europe brought about the decline of chivalry.

A. Gradually, the monarchs became more powerful, and so wielded greater influence than they did in the period known as "the Dark Ages."

    1. The church supported royal power, and became closely associated with the government.

       a. The clergy provided the king with educated counsellors.

       b. The church was the natural enemy of feudal anarchy, and helped break it up.

    2. The church realized that bringing order out of chaos by force was not its business, so instituted the Peace and Truce of God.

B. There were several other influences contributing to the decline of chivalry.

    1. The gradual disappearance of serfdom was a factor.

    2. The change in methods of warfare weakened the knightly class.

    3. The extension of the universities and the rise of the intellectual class hastened its end.

    4. With the rise of a rich merchant, and a comfortable artisan class, feudal life and its complement, chivalry, was no longer impregnable.

    5. As public opinion grew in importance, ridicule and satire were sometimes directed against the nobles.

> *"The sun of chivalry set on the fields of Crécy, Poitiers, and Agincourt. From that time its period of twilight began. It became a strange, unreal, fantastic, and mystical thing, unlike anything the world will see again. Its men and women were natural only in those things to which the hot and fierce passions of their uncultured souls compelled them, in lust, in blood, and in cruelty . . . In time, as all such phases of life do, chivalry passed into literature."* *

---

* *From* Hulme, History of the British People, p. 116. Copyright 1921. *Used by permission* of D. Appleton Company, *publishers.*

CHAPTER XXV

PEASANT LIFE IN THE MIDDLE AGES

"The villein has been described as 'the meanest of freemen.' He might, too, be described as the most fortunate of serfs." *

I. Comparatively little was known of peasant life prior to the thirteenth century.

A. It is difficult to get accurate information about peasant life before the thirteenth century.

    1. The peasant was seldom mentioned in early literature.

        a. Either he was not mentioned at all, or he was named with scorn.

        b. As time passed, the gulf between classes grew greater.

    2. However, the importance of the peasant was real as he furnished the lords' income, and made up the greater part of the population.

    3. A bishop of the eleventh century mentions the three classes as:

        a. The nobles—who do the fighting.

        b. The clergy—who do the praying.

        c. The others—who do the work.

    4. After the thirteenth century a great amount of material became available which has thrown much light upon peasant life and customs.

        a. This is especially true in England.

        b. The Lords' records of the manor have been good sources of information.

B. The laboring classes were divided into several classes which in turn were subdivided into various degrees, conditioned largely by the sort of land tenure held.

    1. The largest group was known as villeins.

        a. They were feudal-serfs "who as regards their lord were slaves, but were free in their legal relations with respect to all others."

        (1). Men might be born to this condition.

---

* *From* Thompson, Economic and Social History of the Middle Ages, p. 746. Copyright 1928. *Used by permission of* D. Appleton-Century Company, *publishers.*

(2). They might agree to accept feudatory obligations in return for protection, etc.

   b. They lived on the lord's land, performed work for him, and turned over part of the produce to him.

   c. They were tillers of the soil for the most part.

2. However, there were numerous other classes.

   a. The "Bordars" or "Cotters" were a numerous class of free peasants somewhat lower in rank than the villein.

    (1). These held smaller amounts of land.

    (2). They had to work for the more prosperous villeins, or the lord, in order to make a living.

    (3). It is well to remember that there was a group of wage earners in all feudal estates in all periods.

   b. The tradesmen and the priests were the most important classes.

    (1). There was usually a miller, a smith, and a carpenter on each manor.

    (2). Furthermore, each village had its own priest who not only looked after the religious and social needs of the community, but oftentimes engaged in manual labor.

   c. The Freemen[1] were very limited in number, holding land by making an annual payment to the neighboring lord as a political ruler.

   d. The slaves were very few in number, and usually of foreign birth.

II. Most of the people lived in the village or manor.

A. The origin of the manor is not certain, but it resembled both the Roman villa and the German village communities (the Mark).

1. It had some indication of German influence, and many manors of the thirteenth century resembled many villages of central Europe today.

2. Because of different geographical conditions the manors were not the same in all sections of western Europe.

   a. In some sections there was much waste land, and the manors were mostly in the valleys and on edges of this waste land.

   b. In other sections the houses were more concentrated.

---

[1] "But not even in the depth of the feudal age was the freeman wholly extinguished, and where he survived he was the freest of men. His land was non-noble, but it was also non-servile." *From* Thompson, Economic and Social History of the Middle Ages, p. 752. Copyright 1928. *Used by permission of* D. Appleton-Century Company. *publishers.*

    c. Feudal obligations varied greatly: in the lowlands they were many, in the hills they were few, and in the mountainous area they were sometimes not recognized at all.

  3. The term, manor, was not universal, for other names were used in different sections.

B. The manor was principally an agricultural unit.

  1. It was laid out along a single street with houses on either side.

    a. Usually they were located on a stream which furnished water and power for the mill.

    b. Away from the houses extended the fields.

    c. At a further distance was usually found the pasture and meadow land.

    d. Beyond the fields and meadows were the waste lands and woods used for hunting and the fattening of pigs.

    e. The country was virtually dotted with these agricultural units.

  2. The buildings of the manor were:

    a. The church—located a short distance back from the street, usually surrounded by an open space.

    b. The manor house was usually back from the street some distance.

      (1). Here lived the lord or the provost.

      (2). Generally the manor house contained three rooms: the hall, used as the dining room and a place for the manor court; the parlor; and the bedroom.

      (3). Even in the manor house there was to be found little furniture.

    c. The peasant's home consisted of one room and a cellar and attic.

      (1). It was constructed of wood with a thatched roof.

      (2). This hut was used to shelter live stock and poultry as well as the family.

      (3). The cellar or pit was used to store grain and vegetables.

      (4). There was little furniture; but there were usually such articles as a spinning wheel, a loom, cooking utensils, and tools.

    d. Other important manor structures were:

      (1). A shop, for the village smithy.

      (2). A mill, in which grain was ground.

(3). A bake-oven, built of rock or stone, located near the mill, serving the whole community.

(4). These were the property of the lord and a fee was charged for their use.

III. Agriculture was the chief occupation of the peasants.

A. The land was cultivated either by the two or three field system.

1. The three field system was more common in the later Middle Ages.

   a. One field was planted in the fall with rye or wheat for the supply of bread.

   b. The second was planted in the spring with barley for beer, or with forage crops for the cattle.

   c. The third was allowed to lie fallow (necessary because they did not know the use of fertilizer).

2. Cultivation was regular, but brought poor returns as the implements were crude.

   a. Each field was divided into acre strips, forty rods long and four rods wide; or half acre strips, forty rods long and two rods wide.

   b. The strips were separated from one another by uncultivated strips.

   c. Usually the villein's land did not all lie together. He might have thirty acres located in three different fields.

   d. Part of the land was cultivated by the peasants for the lord's use.

   e. A four-fold return was considered a good crop.

B. The social life of the manor was necessarily limited, but not entirely lacking as some writers have indicated.

1. There was little time for other than work.

   a. The peasant's wife cared for the house and children, helped care for the cattle, and often assisted in the fields as well.

   b. In addition, she prepared the food for the family, and made all of their clothing.

   c. The children also assisted in the work.

2. What little social life existed revolved chiefly around the church, but the gatherings at the manor house for work were accompanied by merry-making and feasts.

   a. There were festivals, feudal ceremonies, and sacramental services, which were accompanied by merry-making and manor gossip.

   b. Relatively, there was little contact with the outside world, although occasional visits were made by friars and wayfaring minstrels or entertainers.

IV. The self-sufficiency of the manor made for little contact with the outside world.

A. The prosperity of each inhabitant of the manor depended upon the prosperity of all, as all did practically the same work.

　1. Local famines were frequent, for poor roads often made the sale of goods from one manor to another impossible.

　2. The diet was universally simple.
　　a. Pork was the principal meat; bread, made from coarse grain, was used extensively, and vegetables were available in season.
　　b. Dairy products played a part, but cattle were few and of poor quality.
　　c. Honey was used for sweetening, but was a luxury.

　3. Shoes, clothing, fuel, material for building, and implements were usually produced in the manor, but even as early as the twelfth century, certain well-defined market organizations were developing.

　4. Each manor had its own priest and its own court, which tried offenders and transacted public business.

B. However, the isolation of the peasants has often been exaggerated, for some commodities had to be supplied from outside.

　1. Iron was needed for plowshares and tools; millstones were obtained from the sea coast; tar was needed to check disease among sheep. These articles were usually obtained at the fairs, held from time to time in almost every population center.

　2. There was some travel by the peasants from manor to manor.
　　a. Many engaged in "carrying," for there was a great amount of land owned by the church, and produce had to be carried to the monastery.
　　b. Many went on one of the crusades.
　　c. An increasing number left the manor to better themselves in the towns which were developing rapidly all over Europe.

　3. There was a considerable number of communities engaged in other than agricultural pursuits.
　　a. Mining centers existed where salt, iron, and other metals were produced.
　　b. Some villages along the seacoast were engaged primarily in fishing.
　　c. However, even these communities engaged in agriculture sufficiently to meet their own needs.

C. Progress of peasant life was slow, but the industrial development beginning in the twelfth century had important consequences.

    1. New villages appeared; old villages grew into towns; and certain towns grew into cities.

        a. The twelfth and thirteenth centuries witnessed great economic expansion.

        b. Agriculture was no longer the only important occupation.

        c. The rural districts were affected by three movements:

            (1). The rise of towns.

            (2). The impulse to colonization.

            (3). The disintegration of the manor.

    2. This industrial development brought many changes.

        a. Money came into common use.

        b. The peasants enjoyed greater freedom.

        c. The opportunity to get lands in eastern Europe caused many desertions.

        d. There was now a new avenue out of serfdom other than the church.

    3. The underlying cause of all these changes was the increase in population.

    4. The peasantry were not altogether discontented with their lot, for they were not greatly conscious of the limitations on their freedom.

        a. They felt a certain confidence in their occupations as villeins.

        b. The more enterprising and venturesome could seek advancement.

        c. Before the close of the twelfth century it was possible for peasants to gain wealth, distinction, and even power, if industrious and capable.

"Villein tenure, while it seems analogous to the fief, must be sharply distinguished from it. The manorial world was the lower side of the feudal world. Politically a fief was a territory ruled by a noble . . . . Economically a fief was an aggregation of 'domains,' and a domain was an aggregation of 'manors.' Every manor was a unit in a domain, and every domain was an entity in a fief. The lord was a noble of some degree, lower or higher; his tenantry on each and every manor were serfs and villeins." *

---

* *From* Thompson, Economic and Social History of the Middle Ages, p. 747. Copyright 1928. *Used by permission of* D. Appleton-Century Company, *publishers.*

CHAPTER XXVI

THE CHURCH IN THE LATER MIDDLE AGES

"The noonday of papal dominion extends from the pontificate of Innocent III inclusively to that of Boniface VIII; or, in other words, through the thirteenth century." *

I. This period is marked by a conflict between the popes and the national monarchs.

A. The papacy in the time of Innocent III triumphed over the state, but by the middle of the fourteenth century lost much of its power to the national monarchs.

   1. The Lateran Council, 1215, was convoked by Innocent III, who succeeded in continuing papal power for a time.

     a. The power of the house of Hohenstaufen was broken.

     b. Franciscan and Dominican friars continued to work for the church.

   2. Nevertheless, temporal power of the papacy declined and never again recovered its former strength.

     a. The pope was no longer the arbiter of Europe, which was shown by his lack of influence during the Hundred Years' War.

     b. Rulers and peoples came to resent papal interference in political affairs.

   3. There were several causes for the decline of the pope's temporal power.

     a. The rise of national monarchs and the breakdown of feudalism were among the most important.

     b. The dominating influence of political and commercial interests contributed.

     c. The developing sense of nationality and the increased loyalty of the people to their rulers was a major factor.

     d. Furthermore, there were several inherent weaknesses in the church such as:

       (1). Methods of procuring money and high taxes.

       (2). Sale of offices and indulgences.

       (3). Laxity of churchmen.

---

* *From* Hallam, View of the State of Europe During the Middle Ages, p. 289. Copyright 1876. *Used by permission of* Harper and Brothers, *publishers.*

B. Pope Boniface VIII was definitely humbled by Philip IV, the Fair, of France.

    1. Edward I, of England, and Philip IV, of France, both taxed the clergy.

        a. Expenses of these monarchs were heavy, so these kings resorted to taxing the rich estates of the clergy.

        b. The clergy claimed their property was exempt.

        c. Edward I demanded one-fifth of the personal property of the clergy; Philip IV one hundredth and then one fiftieth of the property of both clergy and laity.

    2. Boniface issued the bull, *clericis laicos*, 1296, against Edward and Philip.

        a. He resented their taxing the clergy, and furthermore he insisted that Edward and Philip submit to arbitration in their dispute over the possession of Guienne.

        b. They refused and Boniface issued the bull, *clericis laicos*, which forbade the clergy to pay taxes without papal consent.

        c. Philip and Edward replied with retaliatory measures.

    3. In spite of conditions the papal jubilee of 1300 was successful.

        a. Boniface conceded a limited right to tax churchmen.

            (1). Philip forbade all exportation of gold and silver, which cut off an important part of the pope's revenue.

            (2). Boniface gave up his extreme claims, saying he had not meant to interfere with the clergy's payment of customary feudal dues nor with their loans to the king.

        b. Nevertheless, Boniface seemed the recognized head of the western world.

            (1). All Christendom met at Rome to celebrate the opening of a new century.

            (2). People came from all parts of Europe, paying respects to Boniface and heaping offerings of money at the tomb of St. Peter.

        c. However, Boniface did not read the signs of the time and failed to appreciate the growing sense of nationality.

    4. The struggle with the monarchs continued. Other decrees were issued by the pope.

        a. *Ausculta fili*, 1301.

            (1). To the French people Philip was the champion of their nationality.

   (2). During the controversy the papal legate was imprisoned and brought to trial.

   (3). Boniface's reply was the bull, *Ausculta fili*, which reasserted papal power over kings and kingdoms.

   (4). The bull was burned in public.

  b. *Unam Sanctam*, 1302.

   (1). Boniface claimed both spiritual and temporal power.

   (2). He decreed that salvation was possible only through the church.

 5. The States General of France, 1302, voiced its protest against the pope's demands.

  a. The pope was accused of heresy, tyranny, and unchastity.

  b. An appeal was made to a general council of the church to try the pope.

 6. The outrage of Anagni was indicative of the pope's loss of power and prestige.

  a. Boniface pronounced excommunication against Philip.

  b. Aided by Italians, Boniface was seized by the French emissary.

  c. The conspirators were driven from the town and Boniface was released.

 7. The death of Boniface was also the death of the political power of the medieval papacy.

II. From 1309 to 1377 the papacy was greatly under the influence of French interests and is usually termed: "The Babylonian Captivity."

A. Soon after the death of Boniface, the papacy was moved to Avignon.

 1. There were several popes within comparatively few years.

  a. Benedict XI succeeded Boniface, but died within a year.

  b. After nine months, Clement V, a Frenchman, was elected, and after his coronation never set foot in Italy.

  c. Thereafter for about seventy years, seven successive popes resided at Avignon.

 2. The popes were brought into discredit with other nations, although they were probably less under French influence than has been commonly supposed.

  a. Their place of residence led to natural suspicion.

  b. For the most part they were all good men, but they were all Frenchmen.

B. The absence of the papacy from Rome had many evil effects.

   1. Rome became a city of lawlessness and license.
       a. It was a difficult city to govern, and now lapsed into
           anarchy.
       b. The papal states had never been efficiently governed,
           but order was generally maintained.
   2. The church lost, to a great extent, the respect and support
       of other countries, resulting in decreased revenues and ir-
       regular practices.
   3. Religion suffered, as corruption permeated both regular
       and secular clergy.
       a. Many were still devout, but immorality was increasing.
       b. Avignon was a city of worldly affairs, pleasures, and
           corrupt politics.
   4. Dissatisfaction with the Avignon papacy was largely eco-
       nomic.
       a. Having lost most of its lay subjects, the papacy had to
           resort to increased church taxes to support its immense
           bureaucracy.
       b. This condition resulted in a vicious circle, for it intro-
           duced further corruption.

III. Before the papacy was again definitely established in Rome there was a division in the church known as the Great Schism, 1378-1418.

A. St. Catherine of Siena succeeded in bringing the papacy back to
    Rome, 1376.

   1. Catherine determined to restore the papacy to Rome and
       to initiate moral reform.
       a. She had great religious enthusiasm.
       b. Throughout Italy she traveled preaching peace and re-
           form, and finally interviewed Pope Gregory at Avignon.
       c. Through 'her influence Gregory returned to Rome.
   2. Urban VI, an Italian, was elected pope after the death of
       Gregory.
       a. Most modern scholars agree that this election was
           canonical.
       b. Urban immediately began reform, but by tactless and
           brutal methods offended the Cardinals.
       c. Led by the French Cardinals, Roger, of Geneva, was
           elected pope, and assumed the name of Clement VII.
           He immediately took up residence at Avignon and pre-
           cipitated a great crisis.

B. This double election resulted in the Great Schism.

   1. All the circumstances, or exact truth, have never been known definitely.

      a. Political motives caused a division in various nations, both popes receiving some support.

      b. Church officials and the people followed the rulers in their allegiance, so the schism was final.

   2. The nations were divided in their allegiance.

      a. Germany and Italy were divided between Urban VI and Clement VII.

      b. France, Scotland, Castile, Aragon, and Navarre supported Clement, the French pope.

      c. England, Portugal, Flanders, Hungary, and Poland supported Urban, the Italian pope.

IV.   The plan for the settlement of the Schism was a general council of the church.

A. There were many difficulties in the way of any such council.

   1. Where would the council be held?
   2. Who would call the council?
   3. Who should be summoned?
   4. How could decrees of the council be enforced?
   5. However, cardinals representing both popes finally invited all bishops to attend a council to be held at Pisa.

B. The council of Pisa met in 1409, but really failed in its mission.

   1. Instead of removing one of the rival popes, the council elected a third, Alexander V, and deposed both of the rivals.

      a. A great number of bishops were present, but the two rival popes did not appear.

      b. Furthermore, it failed to reform the church or its morals.

   2. Alexander V proved inefficient and was soon succeeded by John XXIII, a great politician, but in no respect a churchman.

C. A second council was inevitable, and met at Constance in 1414.[1]

   1. The work of this council was threefold:

      a. To deal with heresy.
      b. To consider general reform of the church.
      c. To heal the schism.

---

[1] This council may be regarded as a great international congress, and, as such, was an important precedent in international affairs.

2. The question of heresy was soon disposed of when John Huss of Bohemia was condemned and burned, 1415.

3. The reform of the church was a more difficult problem.
    a. There were three years of deliberation with but little results.
    b. The council passed a decree calling for a general council at least every ten years.
    c. Then the council drew up a list of abuses which the new pope was to consider.

4. However, the ending of the schism was the most important work of the council.
    a. John XXIII was deposed by decree, Gregory XII readily resigned, and Benedict XIII was deposed after the Spanish withdrew their support.
    b. In November, 1417, the council elected a new pope, Martin V, which brought the Great Schism to an end.

5. The results of the Council of Constance were important.
    a. It healed the schism.
    b. It tried to stem the tide of heresy, and so disposed of Huss; but heresy continued.
    c. It made a futile effort to reform the church.

D. Later councils were called to deal with heresy and to consolidate the eastern and western churches.

1. The Council of Basel, 1431-1449, was called by Eugenius IV to deal with heresy.
    a. At first the council dominated the pope; in fact, it reached so great an authority that it elected an antipope, but finally acknowledged the legitimate pope.
    b. Efforts were futile in dealing with heresy, especially the beliefs of the Bohemians.
    c. Eugenius finally dealt a death blow to the theory of counciliar supremacy.

2. The Council of Ferrara, 1438-1439, met to consolidate the eastern and western churches.
    a. It brought about an ineffective union.
    b. The eastern church conditionally accepted the headship of the pope.

E. In conclusion it may be said that the results of the schism were:
1. The captivity was concluded, and the schism was brought to an end.
2. The papacy was given new life, but was not restored to its former power and prestige.

3. It seemed there was to be a period of peace, but there
    loomed on the not far distant horizon a greater conflict, the
    Protestant Reformation.

    > *"It is a natural subject of speculation, what would
    > have been the effects of these universal councils,
    > which were so popular in the fifteenth century, if
    > the decree passed at Constance for their periodical
    > assembly had been regularly observed."* *

    ---

    * *From* Hallam, View of the State of Europe During the Middle Ages. p. 311 Copy
    right 1876. *Used by permission of* Harper and Brothers, *publishers.*

CHAPTER XXVII

THE DEVELOPMENT OF TOWNS AND COMMERCE

*"Commerce promoted industry and industry promoted
commerce and both centered in the towns."* *

**I. During the eleventh, twelfth, and thirteenth centuries
many new towns were founded.**

A. There had been many prosperous cities in the old Roman
Empire.

    1. These Roman cities had a vigorous industrial life, and pro-
duced many and varied articles of commerce.

    2. The Roman cities declined when the people lost their eco-
nomic independence, their powers of production, and their
purchasing power.

        a. With the disintegration of the empire, commerce suf-
fered and the cities declined.

        b. Heavy taxes, paid to ward off the invading barbarians,
completed their ruin.

    3. Some of the cities survived in spite of their many difficulties
because, for one reason or another, they were easily de-
fensible.

B. New towns were often founded to afford needed protection.

    1. Sometimes they were founded on sites of old Roman towns,
or other locations that might be advantageous, such as on
the manors of feudal lords, or about castles or monasteries.

    2. Medieval towns were compact and enclosed by walls for
safety from attack.

        a. The market and the church were about the only open
spaces.

        b. There were no amphitheaters or public baths as in the
old Roman cities.

    3. The towns, surrounded by walls, were strengthened by
moats, towers, and fortresses. The streets were narrow and
the houses were tall, frequently five or six stories.

        a. The houses were usually built of wood.

---

* *From* Sellery and Krey, Medieval Foundations of Western Civilization, p. 333. copyright 1929. *Used by permission of* Harper and Brothers, *publishers.*

      b. Each upper story jutted out and beyond the one below, until the highest stories almost met over the street.

      c. There was complete lack of sanitation, for there were no sewers, and the streets were unpaved; usually they were muddy and filthy.

   4. The churches afforded open places where markets were often established.

      a. The churches also provided hospitals and schools.

      b. In the larger towns there were many churches.

C. These new towns increased in population as they were able to offer many special privileges to their inhabitants.

   1. Many of the towns were founded by the clerics and the nobles, who saw the advantage of the plan, but others were founded by merchant guilds for purely commercial reasons, while still other towns grew from the custom of tradesmen meeting from time to time at certain convenient intersections.

      a. The purpose of the clerics was to increase the value of the church lands.

      b. The nobles frequently founded towns in order to benefit by the trade and industries of town life.

      c. These towns were called *villes neuves*.

   2. At first these cities offered new freedom and privileges to their **residents.**

      a. There were many attractions:

         (1). Association of workmen and families.

         (2). Many festivals and games.

         (3). Street criers gave the news.

         (4). Life was broadened. Social impulses were given more scope.

         (5). In short, town life was interesting.

      b. The towns offered greater freedom.

         (1). There was an emancipation of the peasants.

         (2). The citizens demanded the right of self-government, and charters were obtained from the lords.

         (3). For a time more freedom was the rule, but there were certain exceptions.

II. The medieval towns gained and developed self-government.

A. In the time of Charlemagne local self-government was unknown, for each town formed a part of the country in which it was situated, and this was governed by the king's official.

   1. Bishops performed the count's duties, the inhabitants having no voice in the management of public affairs.

   2. In many instances, however, the count became the lord of the town, and the independence of the town was largely forfeited.

       a. Inhabitants lost their personal freedom for they bore the same relation to their lord as did the serfs in the country.

       b. Gradually the towns separated from the rest of the country, and inhabitants of towns (citizens) became distinct from the residents of the country, (peasants and serfs).

B. The Communal movement succeeded, for a time, in its resistance to the arbitrary rule of the lords.

    1. The Communal movement had its origin in the banding together of French citizens into unions or communes.

       a. Occasionally the insurrections of the townspeople were put down with great cruelty by the lords.

       b. Sometimes, however, the lords realized their prosperity would be enhanced by granting freedom from arbitrary taxation and by granting a degree of self-government.

    2. The town charter, a written contract between the lord and commune, created the town and also served as its constitution.

       a. It recognized the existence of the various merchant guilds.

       b. It limited the rights of the lord and increased the privileges of the people.

    3. This form of government was at first quite democratic.

       a. The usual officials were a mayor, or burgomaster, and the town council.

       b. Suffrage was limited for the most part to members of the larger guilds.

       c. This limited suffrage often led to civil strife between the greater and the lesser guilds. In the course of time many of the lesser guilds obtained a voice in government.

    4. This experiment in government failed, as officials became dishonest and the Communal government was all too often unable to cope with the problems of the city.

III. The guild system was an integral part of the economic organization.

A. The merchant guilds were composed of merchants and bankers.

    1. This was the aristocracy, and they became monopolistic.

       a. Non-members could not buy and sell except under certain restrictions.

       b. The guilds performed several functions in addition to regulating trade, such as:

            (1). Settling quarrels among members.

            (2). Providing charity for widows and the poor.

            (3). Establishing benefits of a fraternal nature to their members.

            (4). Creating definite standards of quality for manufactures.

    2. Craft guilds superseded the guild merchant.

        a. Tradesmen became both artisan and merchant, selling articles produced in their shops.

        b. These new corporations of guilds were called craft guilds.

        c. The system of apprentice, journeyman, and master was established early.

            (1). There were really no classes of capital and labor in the artisan guilds.

            (2). The employers were also members of the laboring class; that is, they worked in their own homes, with their journeymen and apprentices, having worked their way up through these two classes.

            (3). There was little capital involved.

        d. Among some guilds there was a marked division of labor in the manufacture of an article of commerce. This was particularly true of the metal workers (armorers, etc.).

B. Commerce, which had been preserved in the Italian cities, now spread rapidly throughout Europe.

    1. Italian cities had developed considerable commerce, even before the crusades.

        a. Their merchants supplied the needs of the crusaders.

        b. Luxuries of the east were introduced into western Europe by them.

    2. Commerce stimulated and revolutionized industry until western Europe began producing a surplus of goods to pay for the luxuries of the east.

IV. There were many obstacles in the development of medieval trade and commerce.

A. Restrictions on trade were many.

    1. The idea of a "just" price became established.

        a. A "just" price was merely enough to cover cost of materials and wages.

        b. Speculators were branded "forestallers."

        c. There were no wholesalers.

        d. Raw materials were bought in common by the organization.

2. Interest on money was forbidden and capital was thought unproductive.
    a. Usury, a term used even for moderate rates of interest, was forbidden by church law.
    b. Money lending was left to the Jews who played an important part in economic development, but were maltreated by the Christians.
    c. However, the southern part of Europe was more liberal in this respect.

B. Tolls and duties were a serious handicap to the development of commerce.
    1. Duties on highways, bridges, and fords were exacted by lords as merchants passed through their dominions. Although the charges were small they caused many delays.
    2. Methods of collection were unfair for monks and lords took the best goods in payment of duties, and what was left was often damaged.

C. There were also dangers in sea travel such as:
    1. Pirates, especially numerous in the North Sea, were often well organized by men of high rank who thought the business no disgrace.
    2. Strand laws stipulated that stranded ships with their cargo became the property of the owner of the coast.
        a. Ships often became stranded.
        b. Lighthouses were few, and dangers of coasts were increased by false signals of wreckers.
    3. The Hanseatic League became famous.
        a. Towns formed unions for mutual defense.
        b. They formed several leagues: the Hanseatic was the best known, and one of the most influential.

D. Means of travel were poor.
    1. Restrictions prevented the full use of the ready-made system of highways, mainly the streams and rivers, and there were few others.
    2. The roads were poor, as the Roman highways were worn out, while most of the others were mere trails, ungraded and unpaved.
    3. Lack of bridges was a serious problem.
        a. Finally, bridges were built as a pious act, usually by monks.
        b. The London Bridge was the most famous of the period. It was begun in 1179 and completed in 1209.

V. One of the most important results of the development of towns and commerce was the rise of the Third Estate.

A. The rise of the Third Estate caused a decline in the importance of the nobles and clergy.
   1. Kings favored the wealthy merchant who aided in the collection of taxes.
   2. Merchants became more independent of church and state.
      a. They lost their dread of the church.
      b. Soon, they began to ridicule the ideals of both clergy and nobles.

B. Another important development grew out of a need for law in the medieval town.
   1. Each town developed courts and its particular customs gradually were codified into laws.
   2. The merchant class also developed a valuable body of trade laws, (the "law merchant") especially in the Italian cities. These form the beginning of much of our present day commercial and maritime law.
   3. Individuality was the outstanding characteristic of the medieval cities.

C. The merchants assumed an elevated position in political and social life.
   1. They became a recognized class.
      a. The literature of the time indicates that they were often educated, and books were written to meet their needs.
      b. They enjoyed the luxuries of the nobles.
   2. The Third Estate supported a strong government, for they demanded security.
      a. Protection of property and communication was essential.
      b. They assisted the state in suppressing lawlessness.
   3. In brief, the rise of the Third Estate was one of the most important changes of the thirteenth century, and its development may be directly traced to success of the cities and towns.

> " 'All these differences in the arrangement and the development of the medieval cities are new proofs of the inexhaustible riches of medieval life, of the infinite variety in the society of that time . . . . The endeavor to find one form for the medieval cities is a mistake against the very nature of the Middle Ages.' " *

* *From* Thorndike, The History of Medieval Europe, p. 371. Copyright 1917. *Used by permission of* Houghton Mifflin Company, *publishers.*

CHAPTER XXVIII

EDUCATION AND THE BEGINNING OF THE UNIVERSITIES

"When a teacher of eminence appeared, such as Abelard or Peter Lombard at Paris, or Irnerius at Bologna, a concourse of admiring students flocked round him; and the members of the studium generale formed themselves, for mutual support, into a corporation, on which the general name of universitas came to be bestowed. In this way, the oldest universities arose spontaneously." *

I. The later middle ages witnessed a period of great educational progress.

A. Learning had been practically lost by the seventh century.

    1. In this century intellectual life in western Europe was at its lowest ebb.

        a. The schools were entirely monastic or episcopal. They trained for the "Holy Orders" entirely.

        b. Humanistic culture survived, however, in the Irish monasteries, from which point it later spread back to the continent.

    2. However, there was a definite intellectual revival of a certain sort in the time of Charlemagne.

        a. Roman and Grecian works were recovered; although they had been forgotten they had not been destroyed.

        b. The Mohammedans aided in bringing much forgotten literature to western Europe.

        c. From this time on, the amount of knowledge constantly increased[1] and the quality of instruction improved.

    3. Comparatively, the amount of learning was very meager.

        a. Education was based primarily on manuals and summaries compiled by the church fathers of earlier centuries.

        b. Good works were few, and teachers were incompetent to use those available.

        c. Grammar, rhetoric, and logic were studied as formal rules and definitions.

---

*From Library of Universal Knowledge (1880), Vol. XIV, p. 619.

[1] This was true except for a brief interval following Charlemagne's death. This break was caused by the inability of others to immediately assume a leadership for which they were not qualified or well prepared.

      d. There was very little study worthy of the name.

    4. Western Europe inherited the Roman system of education through the church and monasticism.

      a. The lower Roman schools taught grammar, reading, arithmetic, and music; the higher, rhetoric, declamation, literature, and some law and philosophy.

      b. Capella first distinguished the seven liberal arts: grammar, rhetoric, logic, arithmetic, geometry, astronomy, and music.

      c. Boethius divided these into the humanistic trivium, grammar, rhetoric, and logic; and the scientific quadrivium, the remaining four.

B. Substantial advances in learning were apparent everywhere by the twelfth century.

    1. The curriculum had been greatly enriched.

      a. Grammar now included a study of larger technical grammars as well as the classics of Roman literature.

      b. Dialectics was the greatest rival study of grammar; it was based on the logic of Aristotle.

      c. Mathematical subjects such as arithmetic, algebra, plane geometry, and astronomy were studied.[1]

      d. Law study including Roman law was entered into by many, especially in France and Italy, with the center of its teaching at Ravenna.

      e. Theology and philosophy were considered the most intellectual and noble of any of the subjects.

    2. As a result of the enriched curriculum the "seven liberal arts" were now considered as higher studies.

      a. This was the case mainly in the larger cities, especially in the Cathedral or bishop's schools.

      b. These were the forerunner of the universities in which appeared the "faculty of arts." Then professional studies such as theology, medicine, and law appeared.

II. In the twelfth and thirteenth centuries the works of Aristotle greatly influenced the study of philosophy and logic.

A. There were several stages in the development of philosophy.

    1. The early period, to about the year 400, incorporated Greek philosophy with the Christian doctrines.

    2. The second period, during the middle ages, indicated that scholars had lost most of the Greek philosophy. Logical

---

[1] Many of the natural sciences were included in the curriculum under the term, "mathematics."

methods were sometimes applied to religious questions, but with inadequate results.

3. The third period, during the later middle ages, indicated that people had regained a knowledge of the works of Aristotle.
   a. Aristotle's system of reasoning made a lasting impression upon the schoolmen.
   b. The system was eventually adopted by theologians, and became the basis of the new systematic church system, Scholasticism.

B. The systematic theology of this period, called the Scholastic Method, or Scholasticism, is a most important phase in the development of education.
   1. Abelard, 1079-1142, became familiar with the logic of Aristotle and did a great deal of original thinking.
      a. He criticized the accepted interpretations of theology, and submitted the doctrines of the church to the test of reason.
      b. His ideas were not accepted by orthodox churchmen, on the ground that they were a serious menace to the faith.
   2. Abelard's "sic et non" was his chief contribution to scholasticism.
      a. This method resembled a modern debate, for on important questions he collected statements pro and con and the conclusion was left for the student to determine.[1]
      b. The following quotation illustrates his method: "The master-key to knowledge is to keep asking questions."
   3. St. Thomas Aquinas, a Dominican friar, 1227-1274, was, perhaps, the greatest mind of medieval philosophy.
      a. His great work, "Summa Theologica," well illustrates the scholastic method.
      b. He takes up each point in church doctrine and examines and proves it[2] to the satisfaction of most of his contemporaries.
   4. The characteristics of the scholastic method are interesting and important.
      a. Complete authority of the church in matters of doctrine was accepted.

---

[1] It was really a collection of conflicting statements of church fathers on identical subjects. It was used effectively to discredit those who tried to convince by quoting authority.
[2] He attempted to produce a system of philosophy which would harmonize with the logic of Aristotle and the revelations which constituted church authority. He is the last of the great "system makers" until Herbert Spencer.

      b. Aristotle was revered as a master of logic and reason.

      c. However, the formal logical method was a very poor means of acquiring new knowledge.

III. The founding of the universities,* beginning in the twelfth century, was of the greatest significance.

A. The first, the University of Paris,[1] had its origin from the formation of a union or guild of teachers who became numerous in Paris.

    1. The guild was called *universitas*, which was the usual name for corporations in the middle ages—thus the name, university.

      a. Both church and state granted many privileges to both teachers and students.

      b. *Studium generale* was the name given to the universities in the middle ages.

    2. There were only four universities in Europe in the twelfth century.

      a. Paris was especially noted for its work in theology.

      b. Oxford was the first of the great English universities, and resembled the university of Paris in many ways, but its development was later than the other three mentioned here.

      c. Bologna[2] was famous as a law school.

      d. Salerno became famous as a school of medicine.

B. The educational movement received great stimulus in the thirteenth and fourteenth centuries.

    1. Many universities were founded on the model of the original four.

      a. Seventeen universities were founded in the thirteenth century, and thirty-five in the fifteenth century.

      b. Standard curricula were early established, and the requirements of masters became uniform.

    2. The academic degree in early medieval times prepared persons for teaching if they desired, but the bachelor's degree itself did not so qualify one. It was in the nature of a certificate indicating the student had finished his apprenticeship and could begin work on his master's degree and, with such, qualify to teach his trade.

---

* For a good brief discussion of the character of the medieval universities, one should consult *The History of Western Civilization* by H. E. Barnes, pages 741-747.

1 The college had its origin as a dormitory. The first was the Sorbonne at Paris in 1257.

2 In Italy the university was a guild of students and not of masters.

   a. However, in the thirteenth century many desired honor-
       able titles of master or doctor, but did not care to be-
       come professors in our sense of the word.
   b. The titles, master, professor, and doctor all meant much
       the same thing in the thirteenth century.
3. Methods of instruction were at first simple.
   a. There were no university buildings, and no laboratories,
       as there were no experiments.
   b. The lecturer explained the text sentence by sentence.
       The students listened and took detailed notes.
4. The study of the classics declined and education became
    sterile, for students confined their studies to required sub-
    jects and neglected others.
   a. Education was planned for fitting men for their life-
       work. Few studied for the joy of knowing.
   b. Toward the end of the middle ages men began to study
       for pleasure, and, in addition, because education in-
       creased one's social standing.

C. The government of a university was in the hands of a double
    organization: the nations and the faculties.
   1. Students from the same country banded together for pro-
       tection and social life. These bands were called "the
       nations." At Paris there were four.
   2. Faculties varied in different universities, but there were
       usually faculties of liberal arts, theology, medicine, and
       law.
   3. A rector was at the head of the university.
      a. In a university of masters he was a master.
      b. In a university of students he was a student.
      c. His term of office was short, but his power was great.

D. Discipline in the universities was generally lax.
   1. The students were often unruly.
      a. They were not required to attend lectures.
      b. Usually they did not take examinations, except to ob-
          tain a license to teach.
      c. Occasionally the students from different nations en-
          gaged in battle.
   2. The students were frequently involved in trouble with the
       citizens of the town.
      a. The citizens tolerated the students, because of the money
          they spent.

b. Students were impatient of authority and took advantage of their privileges.
c. Students were often irreverent, and therefore brought themselves into disrepute.
d. Gregory IX in 1231 published a statute which outlined the privileges of the students and masters.

3. Heresies arose in the universities, for the students frequently discussed heretical propositions, even though certain topics were barred from discussion.

E. Universities aroused great interest throughout Europe, and were founded in large numbers in most countries.

1. The students had a great desire to learn.
2. Oftentimes the students endured hardships and dangers to continue their education.

> "The mediaeval student would know everything about
> his narrow curriculum; the modern . . . . would dis-
> claim all academic responsibility for anything out-
> side his 'course.' . . . . The student of the old order
> had the mill, but not the grain; the modern student
> has inherited a rich harvest of knowledge, but is not
> so well equipped with a mill to grind it fine." *

---

* *From* Shaw, Trends of Civilization and Culture, pp. 243-244. Copyright 1932. *Used by permission of* American Book Company, *publishers.*

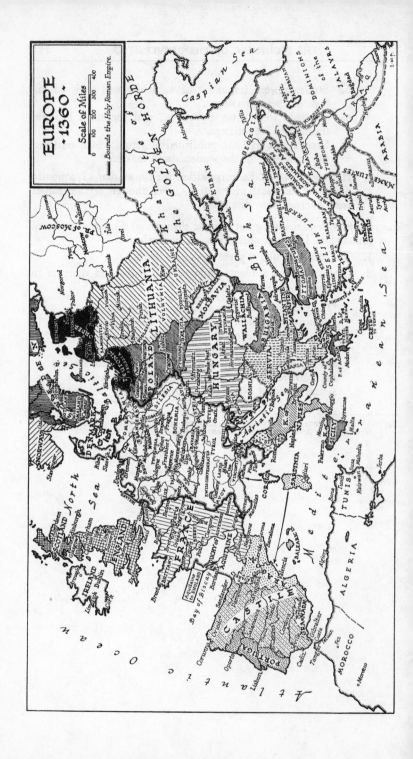

EUROPE
· 1360 ·

Scale of Miles
0   100 200 300 400

───── Bounds the Holy Roman Empire.

CHAPTER XXIX

FRANCE AND ENGLAND DURING THE FOURTEENTH CENTURY

"It is difficult to characterize this long and troubled period without becoming swamped amid a mass of names and details." *

I. Among European nations France and England occupied the most prominent place. Both enjoyed prosperity for a time.

A. England and France gradually transformed themselves into modern national states.

    1. Progress was especially marked in England.

        a. Political feudalism had never gripped England as it had France.

        b. England had evolved a single legal system known as English common law.

        c. Furthermore, the English parliament had often proved itself an ally of the king, and so prevented the establishment of a strong feudal system.

    2. The French king was very strong in parts of France, but in others he was little more than king in name.

        a. The king was absolute in the royal domains which made up about one half the area of modern France.

        b. Outside of the domain lands, the king was weak, and in several provinces there was little real loyalty.

        c. The Estates General held practically no power.

        d. National feeling was not yet marked in France, but was growing. Feudalism was losing ground, and evidences of decay were everywhere.

    3. There were numerous examples of weaknesses both in France and in England.

        a. Unfortunately, both countries were too often governed by weak rulers.

        b. Economic revolution caused by the decay of economic feudalism produced social unrest and bitter class warfare.

---

* *From* Davis, A History of France, p. 82. Copyright 1919. *Used by permission of* Houghton Mifflin Company, *publishers.*

   c. Finally, the Hundred Years' War indicated weakness in
       both countries.

B. England developed rapidly between 1272 and 1377.
    1. The reign of Edward I, 1272-1307, was eventful.
        a. Territory was added.
            (1). Wales was conquered in 1282, and English
                 customs and laws were introduced.
                 (a). Edward presented his son to the Welsh as
                      their prince.
                 (b). Since then the title 'Prince of Wales' has
                      usually been conferred upon the heir to the
                      English throne.
            (2). Scotland proved more difficult to conquer. Edward
                 I left this task to his successors.
        b. The Model Parliament, 1295, is sometimes called the
            first modern parliament.
            (1). Representatives of the people (known as com-
                 mons) met with lords and clergy.
            (2). The innovation was introduced by Simon de
                 Montfort.
            (3). Edward adopted the plan and it became known
                 as Edward's Model Parliament.
    2. Edward II, 1307-1327, had neither capacity nor taste for
        government.
        a. He did not follow up the conquest of Scotland which
            was temporarily lost to the English by the victory of
            Robert Bruce at Bannockburn in 1314.
        b. Disorder spread throughout England until finally
            Edward was deposed by parliamentary action, 1327,
            but this action did not bring good government.
    3. The coronation of Edward III, 1327-1377, gave England
        renewed hope.
        a. He was a minor upon his accession. Power was in the
            hands of his mother, Isabella, and her lover, Mortimer.
        b. In 1330 Edward was of age and obtained power.
        c. He governed England well until the outbreak of war in
            1338.
    4. Economic resources were strengthened everywhere.
        a. Foundations of the English woolen industry were laid.
        b. England entered a period of unparalleled prosperity—
            as expressed by a chronicler, "A new sun seemed to
            have risen."
        c. French prosperity was due to over a century of com-
            parative peace.

        (1). There was an increase in population (20,000,000, four or five times that of England).

        (2). France showed steady growth.

II. However, the Hundred Years' War, 1338-1453, delayed progress and deferred prosperity both in England and France.

A. Territorial holdings of England in France were an important cause for conflict between the two nations.

  1. The old Norman Empire on the continent was a menace to French nationalism.

    a. King John of England had lost Normandy and other lands of the Plantagenet realm on the continent.

    b. England still retained Guienne.

  2. England's possessions in France caused constant friction.

    a. The king of England owed homage to the French king for his continental holdings.

    b. French kings were determined to destroy the power of their vassals and establish national unity.

    c. The English kings still thought they were entitled to certain French territory as a result of their Norman heritage.

B. A second cause of the war was the question of French succession.

  1. The three sons of Philip IV ruled from 1314 to 1328, but left no male heirs; hence the barons of France assembled and gave the crown to Philip of Valois in accord with the alleged Salic law.

    a. Philip V, 1316-1322, and Charles IV, 1322-1328, left only daughters, and French lawyers declared that "custom prohibited the succession of a woman, and, consequently, also of her son, to the throne of France."

    b. When Philip of Valois (VI), nephew of Philip the Fair, ascended the French throne, the Capetian dynasty of French kings came to an end, after presiding for more than three centuries over feudal France.

  2. At first Edward III yielded, but reopened the question later and claimed the French throne as the grandson of Philip the Fair.

C. The Hundred Years' War has been called a social war as well as a civil and foreign war.

  1. French and English sailors were continually raiding each other's commerce, which was a minor but persistent source of trouble.

  2. Crimes were disguised as patriotic endeavors.

D. One of the direct causes of the war was certainly economic.
   1. The Flemish towns wanted independence.
      a. Philip VI aided the Count of Flanders against the towns.
      b. Therefore, the Flemish townsmen were ready to desert Philip and aid Edward III if he would declare himself King of France.
   2. Commercial relations between Flanders and England were important to both parties.
      a. Flanders was the most important commercial and manufacturing country in western Europe.
      b. The prosperity of Flanders depended upon England, where their wool was procured.
         (1). In 1336 all Englishmen in Flanders were imprisoned. This was supposed to have been instigated by Philip.
         (2). The English retaliated by placing an embargo on English wool.
   3. The rupture was complete when Edward III refused to deliver to Philip of Valois, Robert of Artois; and so, sent letters of defiance, dated October 19, 1337.
      a. Edward had foreseen the support of the people of Ghent (Flanders) in demanding an economic alliance with England.
      b. The excuse was political, but Edward had been encouraged by the action of Flanders which was almost entirely economic.

III. Several important battles marked the first period of the war, 1338-1380, which ended favorably for France.

A. Up to 1360 the war was in favor of the English.
   1. England won a naval victory over France at Sluys (Sluis) 1340, in Flanders.
      a. The French fleet met the invading English fleet.
      b. At the crisis a reinforcement of Flemish vessels won the battle for the English.
   2. The Battle of Crécy, 1346, was hard fought.
      a. There had been a period of inactivity after the Battle of Sluys.
      b. In 1346 Edward landed in Normandy, marched almost to Paris, but then retreated northward.
      c. The English met Philip's army at Crécy.
         (1). This battle revealed the strength of the longbow, a new English weapon; English arrows fell "thicker than snow flakes."

(2). The French mounted knights were helpless before English archers.

(3). Later French losses were due largely to their failure to master the use of the longbow. The days of feudal cavalry were over.

3. Calais was captured by the English in August, 1347, which was a matter of great importance for them.

   a. The siege of the city lasted about eleven months, the English entrenching themselves before the city.

   b. Calais remained, until 1558, in English hands, for whom it served as a valuable port of disembarkation.

4. The Battle of Poitiers, 1356, resulted in complete defeat for the French.

   a. John the Good succeeded Philip VI as King of France, 1350.

   b. Edward's son, the Black Prince, who had pillaged throughout France, met the French army, led by King John.

   c. The French were dealt another crushing blow at Poitiers (King John was captured and carried off to England).

   d. As one writer has said: "Crécy was only a defeat; Poitiers was a disaster."

5. The Treaty of Bretigny, 1360, was in a sense only a truce, accompanied by setting the king at liberty upon payment of ransom.

   a. By this treaty Edward surrendered his claim to the French throne and received in return full sovereignty of Calais, Poitou, Guienne, and Gascony. A ransom was also to be paid for John the Good.

   b. The treaty was really a truce necessitated by English and French exhaustion.

   c. Neither France nor England intended to carry out the terms of the treaty.

B. The French met with success during the years 1360-1378, but it did not bring the improvement for which the French people had hoped.

   1. The reign of Charles V, the Wise, was marked by French successes.

      a. The new French king was a poor soldier, but an excellent statesman.

      b. He caused the army to be reorganized.

      c. His diplomacy was of a high order.

   2. Bertrand du Guesclin was the greatest leader of his day.

      a. A capable Breton, he was charged with recruiting a new French army.

      b. He inaugurated new methods of warfare which were successful.

      c. The army became filled with efficient freebooters.

      d. The English renewed the war in 1369, but the French would not meet them in open battle.

   3. By 1375 the English were exhausted, and upon the intervention of Gregory XI, the seventh Avignon Pope, a truce was concluded.

      a. The truce resulted in the recovery of territory by the French.

      b. The celebrated Black Prince, the Prince of Wales, died in 1376.

      c. Edward III, whose strong personality had supported the war, died in 1377.

      d. By 1378 the English had little territory left in France; in fact, they retained only Bayonne, Bordeaux, Brest, Cherbourg, and Calais.

   4. There was little organized fighting from 1380 to 1415, and the war was continued in theory only, except by unorganized bands of pirates and robbers.

IV. The second period, 1380 to 1415, was one of disaster because of internal strife, although the war between the two nations was practically at a standstill.

A. The "Black Death" swept over western Europe, 1348-1349.

   1. It came from Asia, appearing in Europe as early as 1348.

      a. Soon it reached Florence, then France and Germany, then England.

      b. By 1349 it had attacked every part of western Europe, leaving disaster, panic, and grief in its wake.

   2. This dreaded scourge added to the horrors of war, for those stricken usually died.

      a. It took a great toll, although reports vary as to the percentage of the population lost.

      b. Parts of Europe were at a standstill, because of a lack of population.

B. This was a period of political and economic unrest in England.

   1. Results of the war created unrest in England.

      a. Edward III had been somewhat of a failure as a ruler.

      b. Social, political, and economic change was inevitable, but war and the Black Death added to the unrest.

      c. The war was at first popular, but as taxes mounted enthusiasm waned.

      d. Soldiers returning from the battlefield were not able to find their way back into the normal life of the country.

2. Labor was restive.

      a. The decreased population meant a shortage of labor; hence wages were raised and the lot of the peasant was improved.

      b. Statutes of laborers, 1351, was a government effort to force laborers to work at established wages, but the efforts of parliament were unsuccessful.

      c. Medieval manors began to break up, for the serf regarded dues paid to lords unjust. This discontent gradually became general.

3. The peasant revolt of 1381 resulted in the destruction of much property, particularly the registers enumerating dues which were due the lord.

      a. The new poll tax of 1379 caused irritation. This money was used to pay expenses of war.

      b. Revolts began in Kent and Essex. Finally, marchers, led by Wat Tyler, started for London, increasing their numbers as they went.

      c. The gates of London were opened to them, and Richard II promised to abolish serfdom.

4. By 1450 serfdom had practically disappeared from England.

      a. The king did not keep his promise, but serfdom decayed rapidly.

      b. Serfs were paid in money instead of work. Landlords failed to collect full dues, and finally serfs gained their freedom.

5. The period was one of misgovernment.

      a. At first Richard II, 1377-1399, reestablished order and authority, but later became very despotic, and in 1399 was deposed.

      b. The action of parliament was negative.

          (1). It could prevent poor government, but could not bring about good government.

          (2). Most of the gains of parliament came through force.

      c. England did not have a strong monarchy and was not ready for self-government.

C. Prosperity and orderly government had nearly disappeared from France.

1. The Estates General attempted reform.

      a. The French people attributed their early defeats to inefficient leadership.

b. A great list of reforms were drawn up which provided that the body should meet regularly, whether called by the king or not, and also that it should supervise the collection and disbursement of public revenue.

c. The reform movement failed as supporters of the movement degenerated into a mob which brought about a reaction in which 25,000 peasants, suspected of participation in the revolt, were executed.

d. Thus, the growth of popular institutions in France was prevented.

2. Order was temporarily restored by Charles V.

a. He was the successor of John II, 1364, and constantly labored to rebuild his country.

b. Most of France was freed from English rule. There was a period of comparative order and prosperity.

c. Charles VI, 1380-1422, began the establishment of strong government with the help of middle class advisors, but in 1392 he became insane and France relapsed into chaos.

> *"Thus the end of the fourteenth century in England, as everywhere, was marked by the stirrings of a new age. Medieval institutions and conditions were beginning to break down and to give way to newer forms in every field; political, social, religious, and intellectual."* *

---

* *From* Thatcher and McNeal, Europe in the Middle Ages, p. 380. Copyright 1920 *Used by permission of* Charles Scribner's Sons, *publishers.*

CHAPTER XXX

FRANCE AND ENGLAND DURING THE FIFTEENTH CENTURY

"Evidences of a feeling of common nationality among the various peoples of France first appeared in the early decades of the fifteenth century . . . French patriotic sentiment was born of anti-English feeling, just as English patriotic sentiment was originally anti-French." *

I. The third period of the Hundred Years' War, 1415-1453, was renewed by Henry V (1413-1422) of England.

A. The war had been only intermittent during the reigns of Richard II and Henry IV, 1377-1413.

    1. Richard II was controlled by the great noblemen of England.

        a. His reign was a period of misgovernment.

        b. He was deposed in 1399 in favor of Henry IV.

    2. Henry's office was based on parliamentary decree.

        a. As a result, popular government was inaugurated.

            (1). His position depended upon the pleasure of parliament.

            (2). He was guided by the wishes of the people.

        b. Two important principles were adopted in this reign.

            (1). Bills for revenue were to originate henceforth only in the House of Commons.

            (2). Money grants were to be made only after all grievances had been redressed.

B. Henry V, young, intelligent, and ambitious, was responsible for renewing the war, because of his claims to the French throne.

    1. Civil war in France gave Henry V an excellent opportunity.

        a. The question of succession in France was again an issue.

        b. Charles VI became insane, and the right to rule was contested between his uncles and other members of the royal family.

---

* *From* Ault, Europe in the Middle Ages, p. 524. Copyright 1932. *Used by permission of* D. C. Heath and Company, *publishers.*

2. The duke of Orleans was murdered by order of the duke of Burgundy.
   a. They were both contestants for the throne.
   b. This led to civil war in France.
   c. It saved England from attack by the duke of Orleans.
3. Henry V of England had no real basis underlying his claim to the French crown.
   a. Edward III had surrendered his claim. Furthermore, the Lancastrians were not the legal heirs of the Plantagenets.[1]
   b. He wanted to make his house popular by deeds of valor.
      (1). He landed on the outskirts of Harfleur, France, in 1415.
      (2). This is the beginning of the last period of the war, 1415-1453.

C. By the treaty of Troyes, 1420, Henry V of England became king of France.
   1. The battle of Agincourt, 1415, resulted in an overwhelming victory for the English.
      a. It was a repetition of Crécy and Poitiers.
      b. Two years later Henry returned to France and began the conquest of Normandy.
   2. The Treaty of Troyes provided an unhappy chapter in the history of France.
      a. Just when Burgundians and Orleanists were uniting to fight the English, the duke of Burgundy was killed by Orleanists.
         (1). The affair seemed to have been accidental.
         (2). The duke's son swore revenge and succeeded only too well.
      b. The new duke of Burgundy, Philip the Good (who became known as "The Good Duke of the West") then joined the English against the Dauphin (who was to become Charles VII of France) for he believed him to be responsible for his father's murder.
      c. Thus Henry V was enabled to force the French to sign the Treaty of Troyes.
         (1). The treaty provided that Henry V, King of England, was to marry Catherine, the daughter of Charles VI, and would be recognized as heir to the throne of Charles VI, who had long since been mad except at rare intervals.

---

[1] Henry V, as well as Henry IV and Henry VI, were later declared usurpers by parliament.

(2). The treaty further provided that Charles VI would keep the title and revenues of the crown during the remainder of his deadened life, but the English king was to rule.

3. Henry V of England was recognized as king in northern France only.

   a. Henry V of England and Charles VI of France both died in 1422.

   b. Henry VI, only a few months old, succeeded to the thrones of both France and England.

   c. Through the efforts and ability of the duke of Bedford, the English conquered and ruled well all of France north of the Loire.

   d. The south was loyal to the Dauphin (later Charles VII of France.)

4. The Dauphin Charles was weak and indolent and did nothing to prevent the capture of France by the English, but even so, almost half of France was loyal to him.

II. Joan of Arc[1] was destined to arouse the French patriotism and so drive the English from their French possessions.

A. Joan's relief of Orleans led to the complete routing of the English.

   1. Joan, a peasant girl, grieved greatly over the plight of France.

      a. Joan was born about 1410 in Domremy, in northeastern France.

      b. She was led by "voices" to save her country.

      c. Strengthened by faith and divine guidance, she set out to relieve Orleans.

   2. The French, led by this "inspired" girl, were victorious at Orleans, the key to southern France.

      a. At the head of her force, Joan slipped into Orleans, restoring confidence and enthusiasm to the French forces.

      b. By a series of attacks upon the English surrounding the city, Orleans was saved, and Joan had become a national heroine.

B. Joan of Arc triumphed in her mission, but met her death at the hands of the English.

   1. Joan conducted the Dauphin to Reims where he was crowned Charles VII, July 17, 1429.

---

[1] Davis (History of France, p. 95) argues: "It seems wholly unscientific to say Jeanne (or Joan) 'of Arc.' There was no village named 'Arc' near her birthplace, and her people were humble peasants with no claim to the nobleman's 'de.' 'Darc' was simply an ordinary surname." Copyright 1919. *Used by permission of* Houghton Mifflin Company, *publishers.*

        a.   All France became loyal to Charles VII.

        b.   Probably aggressive action by Charles could have ended the war, but instead, the war dragged on until 1453.

   2. Joan was declared a heretic, and was burned at the stake.

        a.   Joan is said to have wished to return home as her mission was fulfilled, but was persuaded to continue to fight for the cause of France.

        b.   In May, 1430, she was sold to the English by a Burgundian leader into whose hands she had fallen.

        c.   Charles could have saved her had he wished, but he made no effort although he probably owed his crown to her.

        d.   On the 29th of May, 1431, declared by churchmen to be a relapsed heretic, she was summarily condemned to be burned at the stake.

        e.   The effects of this incident upon the English are best expressed by the following quotation: "We are lost—we have burned a saint." The prediction was true, for her spirit remained with the French armies.

C. By 1453 only Calais remained of the English possessions in France.

   1. The fortunes of the English rapidly declined.

        a.   Parliament granted money sparingly.

        b.   In 1435 the duke of Burgundy, Philip the Good, deserted the English and joined Charles VII, and the capable English Regent of France, the duke of Bedford, died.

        c.   In 1436 Paris was captured by the French; then town after town was recovered.

   2. Charles VII showed himself an admirable organizer.

        a.   He was supported by wise counsellors.

        b.   During the truce of 1444-1449 the French armies and finances were reformed.

        c.   Duke Philip's (duke of Burgundy) reconciliation with the king of France made England's efforts futile.

   3. The war had run its course by 1453.

        a.   The war was renewed in 1449.

        b.   In 1450 the English were expelled from Normandy; in 1453 they lost Guienne; hence they retained only Calais.

        c.   The great question of 115 years' standing was settled: England was unable to retain her continental possessions.

d.   The date 1453 is generally given as ending the war; but not until Nov. 3, 1492, by the Treaty of Étaples, did it officially end.

III.   Following the Hundred Years' War, England was engaged in a civil war, known as the War of the Roses, 1455-1485.

A.   The rival houses of Lancaster and York[1] struggled for the crown.

1.   Both houses were supported by wealthy nobles.

a.   The duke of York attempted to dethrone Henry VI, of Lancaster.

b.   Many nobles related to the respective houses were drawn into the conflict.

c.   These nobles, through the inheritance of vast estates, had become wealthy and powerful.

2.   The war was fought almost entirely by the great barons who relied largely upon retainers, or hired soldiers.

B.   With the accession of Henry VII, in 1485, the first Tudor king, the war ended.

1.   The War of the Roses was for the most part a series of petty skirmishes and battles, but there were also certain major engagements.[2]

a.   It lasted for thirty years.

b.   For the most part the battles were murders and unimportant skirmishes.

2.   Edward IV, 1461-1483, was the Yorkist leader.

a.   He assumed the crown and was recognized by parliament in 1461.

b.   Edward became a strong monarch, although the earl of Warwick forced him to seek refuge with the duke of Burgundy for a short time.

c.   He died in 1483, leaving Edward V to succeed him, but this youth never reigned.

3.   The reign of Richard III, 1483-1485, was one of turmoil.

a.   Upon the death of Edward IV the government fell into the hands of Richard, duke of Gloucester, who soon seized the crown.

b.   Both of Edward IV's sons were murdered and Richard became very unpopular. (It is certain that Richard had knowledge of these murders.)

---

[1] The badge of the House of Lancaster was a red rose; that of the House of York a white rose. The Tudor monarchs adopted a double rose, red and white, to indicate they had inherited both Yorkist and Lancastrian claims.

[2] Myers states that 100,000 were engaged in the battle of Bosworth Field. He calls this the greatest battle since Hastings.

4. At the battle of Bosworth Field,[1] 1485 the people turned against Richard.

    a. Richard was killed, ending the direct Yorkist line.

    b. Henry Tudor, supported by the Lancastrians, became king as Henry VII, the first of the Tudor line.

5. Tudor despotism broke the power of the great nobles which was by no means a calamity, as the strong central government of the Tudors, despite its excesses, started England on the road to becoming the greatest national state in Europe.

    a. People were tired of disorder and accepted strong government.

    b. Nearly half the nobility of England perished in the war, and the Tudor dynasty was left to govern without an effective check.

    c. The English government was a despotism for more than a century.

IV. Under Louis XI France became a centralized nation-state.

A. Royal authority had declined somewhat during the Hundred Years' War.

    1. In the two centuries preceding the war there had been progress in concentration of power.

        a. Progress, however, had been checked, and retrogression resulted.

        b. During the closing years of the war the army was strengthened.

            (1). The king's power increased.

            (2). At the end of the war the army became a lawless band, a scourge to the country.

        c. When Charles VII attempted to again build up royal authority, he found two chief obstacles.

            (1). The authority of the States-General.

            (2). The power of his vassals, some almost as powerful as the king.

B. However, constitutional limitations upon the power of the king disappeared after the middle of the fifteenth century.

    1. During the Hundred Years' War the States-General had acquired partial control over revenues.

        a. It was first summoned in 1302 by Philip IV to secure money to carry on his quarrel with the pope.

---

[1] See footnote 2 on preceding page.

      b. During the fourteenth and fifteenth centuries the States-General frequently contested royal policy and demanded reforms.

  2. The influence of the States-General declined.

      a. It did not have the background of the English Parliament.

      b. Neither did it have the support of the nation.

      c. When the body was no longer called, little opposition was offered.

      d. The States-General had lost its control over finances, then over legislation; consequently, France became, in principle, an absolute monarchy.

  3. The power of the king depended upon his personal qualities.

      a. An effective centralized administration was yet to be developed.

      b. Charles VII made his influence felt, but was overshadowed by his son, Louis XI.

C. Louis XI, 1461-1483, broke the power of his vassals, making France a well organized state.

  1. The granting of "appanages" had created a new and powerful line of feudal nobles.

      a. The chief of these were the houses of Anjou, Bourbon, Orleans, and Burgundy. The house of Burgundy under Charles the Bold was to create the most trouble for Louis XI.

      b. Older feudal families were shorn of their power in the thirteenth century, but since the time of St. Louis newer houses had been formed by granting whole provinces.

  2. The defeat and death of Charles the Bold greatly strengthened the French monarch.

      a. The League of Public Welfare, a coalition of princes, faced Louis XI.

          (1). This strong coalition forced concessions from Louis.

          (2). Louis XI immediately began his program to break up the League.

      b. Charles the Bold had ambitions of setting up a separate kingdom.

          (1). He held great territory and continually added more.

          (2). Finally he was outmanoeuvered by Louis.

      c. In 1476 Charles was defeated by the Swiss, and the next year died.

          (1). Neither the French king nor the emperor, Frederic III, sympathized with Charles' plans.

(2). The German princes and Swiss confederation became apprehensive of Charles' projects, forming a league of defense against him.

3. The gains for the French were not as extensive as Louis had hoped.

   a. Mary, daughter of Charles the Bold, married Maximilian of Hapsburg, and Louis was forced to yield to the Hapsburgs the Netherlands,[1] Franche-Comte (county of Burgundy), and other territory lying outside of France.

   b. However, Louis added more to the territory of France than a part of Burgundy. He made himself heir to Maine, Anjou, and Provence, which eventually were incorporated as French territory.

4. The work of Louis XI left the French monarchy stronger than ever before, but France was not a well-organized state in the modern sense.

   a. The spirit of the feudal princes was broken.

   b. The king was the undisputed head of the government.

   c. Louis's aims were usually worthy, but his means were not beyond reproach.

V. France and England emerged from the Hundred Years' War with strong national governments.

A. A great amount of territorial confusion was eliminated.

   1. This was really a period of transition from medieval to modern Europe.

   2. The kings of England no longer held territory in France as family possessions, which meant that they ceased to rule a great part of France.

B. England and France became national states.

   1. Feudalism had been destroyed. Royal government was becoming more powerful.

   2. National wealth increased; revenues were plentiful to carry on the work of government.

   3. A strong national feeling was developing.

C. The military pretensions of the knight, the back-bone of the system of chivalry, were demonstrated to be hollow.

   1. The spectacle of the yeoman with his longbow repulsing the knight in mail armor, altered deeply the conceptions of warfare and military organization.

---

[1] The Netherlands finally came into the possession of the emperor, Charles V, making a constant source of conflict between France and the Hapsburgs of Spain and Austria.

2. The kings could not recruit a standing army from among the common people and defy the feudal lords whose power and prestige were derived from their military service to their overlord.

D. In short, the Hundred Years' War and the War of the Roses hastened the transition from decentralized feudal political organization to centralized national government.

> *"'In going my way I found myself in a very desolate and deserted country, because there had been war between the inhabitants of the country for a long time, and they were very poor and few in number; for, I may tell you, it seemed rather a place for wild beasts than a habitation for people'*—JEAN DE BUEIL. *Such was the Hundred Years' War."* *

---

* *From* Funck Brentano, The Middle Ages, p. 438. Copyright 1923. *Used by permission of* G. P. Putnam's Sons, *publishers.*

CHAPTER XXXI

OTHER STATES OF EUROPE IN THE THIRTEENTH AND FOURTEENTH CENTURIES

*"And what was the Germany of the later middle
ages? She was 'an amorphous heterogeneity of
microscopic particles', an 'ensemble of which the
parts did not make a whole."* *

I. Germany underwent several important changes.

A. Germany became decentralized as the Holy Roman Empire disintegrated.

   1. The idea of the universal empire was still an important political fiction.

      a. The period of the "fist law" or the Great Interregnum, 1256-1273, convinced both the Germans and the pope that an emperor was necessary.

      b. Thus, Rudolf of Hapsburg was elected, preserving the bond between Germany and Italy.

   2. Several great houses, or families, gradually became of increasing importance.

      a. Among the greatest of secular princes were:

         (1). Luxemburgs.

         (2). Hapsburgs of Austria.

         (3). Hohenzollerns of Brandenburg.

         (4). Wittelsbachs of Bavaria.

      b. Ecclesiastical princes were also becoming more influential.

         (1). Among the most important were the Archbishops of Mainz, Cologne, and Trier (Treves).

         (2). These three were members of the electoral college, named in the Golden Bull of 1356.

   3. Independent imperial cities were developing, such as Lubeck, Bremen, Rostock, Nurnberg, and Augsburg.

      a. These cities, added to the already too numerous states, divided the country still further.

      b. Great economic and commercial growth took place in these cities.

---

* *From* Ault, Europe in the Middle Ages, p. 547. Copyright 1932. *Used by permission of* D. C. Heath and Company, *publishers.*

4. Switzerland, the first modern democratic state, came into being during this period.
   a. The Swiss Confederation developed from the allied cantons of the western Alps.
   b. The formation of this new country decreased the possessions of the Hapsburgs.

B. The medieval empire was revived to a degree in 1273 with the election of Rudolf of Hapsburg, but succeeding emperors held little real authority.

1. From 1273 until 1519 the emperors were, for the most part, either from the House of Hapsburg or the House of Luxemburg.[1]
   a. During this period the emperors gave up the idea of controlling Italy.
   b. Even in Germany the emperor's power was slight.
      (1). His rule was merely nominal.
      (2). There were many powerful lords; several were rulers in their own right.[2]
   c. Although divided politically, Germany expanded territorially.
   d. In spite of handicaps many German towns reached great prosperity.

2. Political developments indicated further decentralization of government.
   a. The office of emperor was elective.
      (1). The right to elect was held by seven leading lords, three ecclesiastical and four secular princes.
      (2). The power of the electors was confirmed by the Golden Bull of 1356, which fixed the supremacy of the princes.
   b. There were many petty states which were often ruled by nobles claiming to be independent sovereigns.
   c. "The territories of lords and princes resembled a patchquilt, winding in and out, which resulted in overlapping, conflicting jurisdictions, and lawlessness."

3. The Vehmic (Fehmic) courts remedied the chaotic condition by extra-legal means.
   a. This society, originating in Westphalia, supplanted the work of the regular courts.
   b. The meetings were secret for the most part, all members taking oath to serve summons and execute the sentences of the organization.

---

[1] After Frederick III, 1440-1493, all emperors were Hapsburgs.
[2] The emperor retained, however, the powers of "escheat" and "forfeiture" which enabled him to build up his personal possessions.

c. It became very popular.
    (1). It counted as members entire cities, lords, and bishops.
    (2). Even the Emperor, Sigismund, 1410-1438, was a member.

4. During the Great Schism of the church, imperial power was, perhaps, at its lowest ebb.
    a. The Emperor Sigismund was weak.
        (1). He could not maintain order, and was absent from the empire much of his reign.
        (2). He was, however, largely responsible for the Council of Constance, which healed the Great Schism in the papacy.
    b. Private leagues strove to preserve order, as did certain of the lesser nobles.

5. The marriage of Maximilian of Hapsburg with Mary of Burgundy was of the greatest importance during the latter part of the fifteenth century.
    a. Maximilian, son of Frederic III, became emperor in 1493.
    b. His marriage with Mary prevented France from obtaining valuable lands of Charles the Bold, duke of Burgundy.

II. Italy was not yet a nation-state in any way.

A. Italy was merely a "geographical expression" during the fourteenth and fifteenth centuries.

1. Although nominally a part of the empire, emperors were not respected.
    a. Emperors still went to Rome to be crowned, but they did not take part in the government.
    b. The papacy contributed to the weakness of the emperor by insisting upon the elective principle, instead of permitting an hereditary empire to develop.

2. The Italian cities completely dominated Italy.
    a. They often treated the emperor with contempt.
    b. These cities were not working for a strong Italy, but were contending with one another for supremacy as petty city-states.
    c. The most important of the city-states were Florence, Milan, Venice, and Genoa.

3. However, Italy became the center of civilization.
    a. In the twelfth and thirteenth centuries France had been the center.

b. The Italian cities developed a culture comparable to any period before or after. They were leaders in the new Renaissance movement.

c. Gradually Italy became a leader in modern European politics.

B. Instead of a united nation-state, Italy was divided into many petty states.

    1. In the two preceding centuries many republics had come into being, especially in Northern Italy.

        a. They possessed a spirit of liberty, and enjoyed an unusual degree of prosperity.

        b. Eventually, however, they fell into the hands of despots.

        c. By the early part of the fifteenth century only a few towns retained republican governments.

           (1). These were: Florence, Venice, and Genoa.

           (2). The remaining free towns and republics were conquered by Milan, which was dependent upon the German emperor.

    2. In the south were the two kingdoms of Sicily, but power was to pass into other hands.

        a. In the island of Sicily the House of Aragon had established itself.

        b. On the mainland power lay in the hands of the House of Anjou.

    3. In central Italy were the papal states.

        a. The territory was small.

        b. It has been described as an unorganized monarchy under the rule of the pope.

    4. In addition there were several more or less important minor states. One of these, Piedmont, was eventually to bring about the unification of Italy.

III. Spain gradually changed from a feudal into a modern state.

A. Spain, as a united state, did not come into existence until the latter part of the fifteenth century.

    1. There were several reasons for its early lack of unity.

        a. Geographically it was mountainous, and the many rivers set up natural boundaries.

        b. The Moors and Jews were mixed with the native stock, which meant that foreign customs and ideas were adopted, although some became Christians.

        c. The forces of feudalism worked against consolidation.

      d. The church and the king were the only factors working for unity, and for a time the king exerted little influence.

  2. There were four principal kingdoms making up the Spanish peninsula: Portugal, Granada, Aragon, and Castile and Leon, which were united.

      a. Granada was the Moorish kingdom; the other three were Christian.

      b. Frequent dissensions among the Christian states prevented unity of action against the Moors.

      c. The conflict with the Moors had not brought about unity, but it had developed a race of soldiers filled with religious zeal. These characteristics were later to greatly influence Spanish history.

B. The uniting of Castile and Aragon made possible modern Spain.

  1. Ferdinand V ascended the throne of Aragon in 1474. Having previously married Isabella of Castile, the two most powerful Christian states of Spain were united.

      a. The Spanish people had long planned to expel the Moors from Granada in southern Spain.

      b. The war for that purpose began in 1481, and by 1492 the Moorish dominion in Spain was at an end.

      c. By 1512 Ferdinand had invaded and conquered all of Spain, and for the first time Spain was united.

  2. Ferdinand and Isabella laid the foundations for an absolute monarchy in Spain.

      a. Their plan was to some extent copied from that of Louis XI of France.

      b. State police were organized to take place of the former local police.

      c. Many estates of the church and nobles came under royal control.

      d. The royal council of twelve was divided into a council of three: justice, state, and finance.

      e. Royal officials were sent into local communities where they gradually extended royal authority.

  3. The monarchial system, although accomplishing its purpose, proved ruinous to the Spanish nation in the seventeenth century.

      a. Unfortunately, the rulers did not use their new power wisely.

      b. The mercantile system was a poor one resulting in commercial and industrial starvation.

    c. The Moors, constituting the great industrial class, were driven out. Spain came to live upon the precious metals which poured in from the new world.

    d. It must be remembered, however, that she was handicapped by a lack of natural resources.

    e. Her foreign policy was too ambitious for a new nation, and finally, when the royal family became united with the Hapsburgs, they were drawn into wars which spelled their doom.

IV. The Scandinavian countries developed slowly.

A. As late as the ninth century the Scandinavians lived a tribal life.

    1. They belonged to the Indo-European race, spoke a language similar to German, and their customs, institutions, and beliefs resembled those of the Germans.

    2. During the ninth and tenth centuries a process of consolidation took place among these Northmen.

        a. Little tribes were united to form kingdoms.

        b. For about 400 years this process of consolidation took the form of international wars and civil strife.

    3. In 1397 the conflict was brought to an end by the Union of Calmar, which was not completely satisfactory to any of the three countries involved.

        a. Under this agreement the three countries, Norway, Denmark, and Sweden, were brought together under one ruler, Queen Margaret.

        b. Theoretically, the three countries were equal, but Denmark, being the strongest, dominated the other two.

        c. Finally the Swedish resentment to Danish dominion brought their independence in 1523 under the leadership of Gustavus Vasa.

B. The Northmen took to the sea, plundering as they went, but eventually established many colonies. Their value to civilization in this regard has too often been exaggerated.

    1. Many of the tribal chiefs were unwilling to submit to the movement of unification.

        a. They were superior to other northern people only in the arts of war and seamanship.

        b. The rest of Europe became acquainted with the Northmen through their many invasions.

    2. Although at first their invasions were in the nature of plundering expeditions, they later made permanent settlements in many countries, often in those they had previously devastated.

     a. They settled in Scotland, Iceland, Greenland, and even visited the coasts of North America.

     b. Colonization took place in Ireland and Russia, and they explored as far south as Africa.

     c. Their Norman settlement was by far the most important.

        (1). William, Duke of Normandy, who became King of England in 1066, was one of the greatest.

        (2). Later Norman dukes built up strong kingdoms in Southern Europe.

           (a). Sicily was the most important.

           (b). Their power was felt in other places as well.

        (3). Among the leaders of the first crusade were Normans, such as Bohemond and Tancred.

V. Other countries of Europe made many changes during these centuries.

A. Hungary early occupied an important place among the nations.

    1. The history of this kingdom dates back to Stephen I, 997-1038.

     a. Stephen accepted Christianity, developed a centralized government, and added new territory.

        (1). Although his government resembled that of Germany, the customs of the country were somewhat different.

        (2). Stephen acquired Slavonia, Croatia, and Dalmatia; and brought under his submission Roumania, Bosnia, and Servia.

     b. By the thirteenth century the kingdom was well organized, but soon relapsed into barbarianism.

    2. The Hungarians were led back to civilization by Charles I, 1310-1342, and Louis I, 1342-1382, only to again fall into decay a hundred years later.

     a. After the death of Mathias, 1490, the country relapsed into medieval chaos.

     b. Although the revolt of the oppressed peasantry was put down with terrible ferocity, the trouble was far from being ended.

    3. The sudden decline of Hungary was brought about by two forces: the Turks, and the divisions within the kingdom.

     a. In 1526 the Hungarian army was completely annihilated by the Turks in the battle of Mohacs.

     b. Then came the division of Hungarian territory, part going to Austria, part to the Turks, and part remaining as an independent kingdom. This partition of Hungary continued until about the end of the seventeenth century.

B. Slavic countries played a minor but definite part during these centuries.

  1. Bohemia or Czech changed from a semi-independent state to a part of the empire.

      a. German influence was always dominant in this country, although Philip of Swabia granted the title of king to their prince in 1198.

      b. When the Bohemian royal family became extinct there was a long struggle for the territory, which finally went to the Hapsburgs and remained a part of their empire until 1919.

      c. All phases of their life were dominated by the Germans, but their influence was not harmful.

  2. Poland had a short and eventful history as an independent state.

      a. At the close of the middle ages Poland seemed destined to become one of the powerful nations of Europe.

      b. Poland acquired Pomerania and Lithuania, and extended its territory from the Baltic to the Black Sea; but its situation exposed it to attacks from other nations, especially Russia, Prussia, and Austria, which countries brought about its dismemberment in the eighteenth century.

  3. Russia[1] was hardly a part of western Europe during the thirteenth and fourteenth centuries.

      a. Russia owes its first development to Scandinavian peoples and Greeks.
          (1). The Northmen made the principal settlements.
          (2). The Greeks brought them Christianity.

      b. In the thirteenth century Russia came under the rule of the Mongols, and for two hundred years was subject to the great Khan.

      c. In the fifteenth century the prince of Moscow threw off the Mongol yoke. Russia retained her oriental customs until the time of Peter the Great, 1689-1725.

      d. Gradually Russia began to adopt western customs and come into contact with European culture.

---

[1] Russia, however, in the ninth century had a flourishing trade and a well organized political system. It was made up of commercial cities on the principal rivers. These enjoyed self-government. Defense was in the hands of a prince.

C. The Byzantine or Greek Empire greatly influenced the West.
    1. Before the coming of the Ottoman Turks, the Greek Empire
        dominated Eastern Europe.
        a. Commercially it was supreme in the eastern Mediter-
            ranean, although strong competition was given by the
            Italian cities.
        b. Constantinople was the seat of civilization and the
            strongest European city during most of the middle ages.
    2. Eventually the Empire was unable to withstand the attacks
        of the Ottomans.
        a. The Ottoman Turks came from Central Asia about the
            middle of the fourteenth century. Their brilliant con-
            quests made them, first, masters of Western Asia, and
            then of the Greek Empire.
        b. Turkish advances were temporarily checked, but the
            Eastern Empire was virtually at an end.
            (1). In 1354 the Turks captured Gallipoli and by 1399
                  the eastern emperor was forced to pay tribute.
            (2). Constantinople was temporarily saved because
                  Tamerlaine was trying to revive the Mongol
                  Empire. Thus he defeated the Turks.
            (3). However, in 1453 Constantinople was captured,
                  which brought to the attention of all Europe the
                  Turkish peril, and in 1456 combined forces of
                  western Christendom defeated the Turks at Bel-
                  grade.
        c. Finally, however, a Mohammedan state was established
            in Europe. Constantinople was its capital.

            *"Up to the beginning of the fifteenth century Euro-
            pean nations and governments, apart from England,
            can hardly be said to have existed on a large scale."* *

---

* *From* Wilson, Outlines of History, p. 781.

CHAPTER XXXII

THE BEGINNING OF THE RENAISSANCE

*"One cannot say when the Middle Ages gave place
to the Renaissance . . . . There are always many
foreshadowings of any intellectual movement . . . .
Only very gradually did the new dispensation take
form and shape. It was not announced to a startled
world by the blast of a sudden trumpet."* *

I. The twelfth and thirteenth centuries prepared the way for the Renaissance.

A. Knowledge did not disappear during the middle ages, but most of the period is characterized by mental inactivity.

    1. The barbarian invasions halted the work of civilization begun by the Greeks and Romans.

        a. It was a period of fusion of Roman and German peoples, and time elapsed before they could carry on the work of civilization.

        b. During this period people were little concerned with this world, but were preparing for another.

    2. There were several medieval revivals of learning.

        a. The lowest ebb of learning was reached in the sixth and seventh centuries. Charlemagne was the first to bring about a revival of schools.

        b. Then, in the eleventh century western Europe was influenced by Greek culture. This has been called the second revival.

        c. In the twelfth and thirteenth centuries a more important revival occurred, the age of scholasticism.

B. The thirteenth century was a period of great enthusiasm for learning; it was, in a sense, preparatory to the age of the Renaissance.

    1. Many universities were founded.

        a. Students were attracted from all parts of Europe.

        b. Famous thinkers, such as Albertus Magnus, Roger Bacon, and Thomas Aquinas were developed.

---

* *From* Hulme Renaissance and Reformation, p. 3. Copyright 1917. *Used by permission of* D. Appleton-Century Company, *publishers.*

      c. Practically every country of Europe had one, and some countries had many universities.

    2. Great enthusiasm was shown for learning.

      a. Common people delighted in songs and romances in the vernacular.

      b. Great men were writing their famous treatises in which the people became interested.

      c. Architecture and sculpture were in some instances at their height.

    3. The Renaissance, then, did not come as a sudden re-awakening.

      a. It seems strange that there was not a complete revival at this time, but scholasticism was not given to change.

      b. Europe had to wait for development, for a change in thought and taste, and for a literary sense.

      c. This fundamental change came in the fourteenth century and ushered in the period of the Renaissance.

II. The fifteenth century may be regarded as the threshold of modern civilization.

A. The change was not revolutionary, but gradual.

    1. No definite date can be given when the change took place.

      a. Characteristics of the one age are not entirely different from those of the next.

      b. People of the time did not realize the dawning of a new age.

    2. Scholasticism gave way to a spirit of scientific inquiry.

      a. Old ideas were undermined, and new ideas were accepted.

      b. New institutions developed.

      c. Learning was carried out in a broader spirit, unrestricted by the narrow limits previously set up by conventionality and the clergy.

B. This age was characterized by both intellectual and religious movements.

    1. The period may be divided into two rather distinct movements.

      a. The Renaissance, or intellectual movement, reached its height in the fifteenth century.

      b. The Reformation, or religious movement, developed in the sixteenth century.

    2. However, it is probably more nearly correct to say that the Renaissance in northern Europe became the Reformation.

    a. The movement, beginning in Italy, took the form of "art for art's sake," while in northern Europe the development was more natural.[1]

    b. In Germany particularly the Renaissance was a thing of power; it became the religious Reformation.

III. There were many contributing factors which made possible the Renaissance.

A. Political and Religious.

  1. Towns and cities almost completely disappeared from western Europe during the feudal period.

    a. City culture was lost; there had been a return to agriculture.

    b. The nobles, or privileged classes, ruled society, and, for a time, there was no middle class.

    c. This was a period of extreme political decentralization.

  2. With the development of the towns, beginning about the year one thousand, political advances were made.

    a. A middle class sprang up with the development of trade and industry.

    b. The feudal barons did not disappear, but they did lose ground politically and socially.

    c. The new middle class was destined to free Europe from the bondage of feudalism.

  3. The towns fostered self-government, and at the same time helped bring about a spirit of nationalism.

    a. The new towns were forced to fight for their existence, and in so doing developed self-government.

    b. Towns and cities first gained charters, and eventually some of them became independent.

    c. However, they worked for centralized government in harmony with their monarchs, and in mutual contest with the feudal lords.

  4. With the help of the monarchs, the people not only freed themselves from feudalism, but also from the bondage of the church. The Renaissance was now possible.

    a. The church during the middle ages, although in some ways a great civilizing agency, prevented the development of new ideas. It kept people within narrow limits.

    b. With the increasing power of the monarchs and the development of nationalism came a decline in the power and influence of the church.

    c. Thus people were free; they were now able to think along new lines; they were able to test their new ideas.

---

[1] However, it is true that the interest of many in Italy was merely superficial, a form of dilletantism.

B. Social.

    1. During the twelfth and thirteenth centuries productive occupations supplanted the unproductive; people accummulated wealth through their efforts; a middle class developed, based on the possession of wealth, not on the nobility of birth.

    2. This new class meant a new society.

        a. They were influential and strong because of their wealth.

        b. They were filled with a zeal to learn; consequently, they began to explore the unknown.

        c. In many ways they resembled modern society.

    3. This new society was a great factor in the change from medieval to modern times.

C. Economic and Commercial.

    1. With the development of towns came commerce and industry.

        a. During the agricultural period roads and routes of travel fell into decay.

        b. With the revival of towns there was a revival of trade. The greatest commercial centers were the Italian Mediterranean towns.

        c. The development of trade called for manufacturers, which meant the development of an economic system.

    2. The first development was the guild system which was supplanted by the competitive system and capitalism.

        a. The guild system, effective for domestic trade, became ineffective with the expansion of foreign trade.

        b. As foreign trade developed, profits increased, and a class of great capitalists arose.

        c. This in turn called for cooperative activity, or the joint stock company. The next development was the great class of bankers.

        d. The new developments were in line with the spirit of the Renaissance. People made the most of their opportunities.

    3. The concentration of the "money power" in Italy might properly be said to be the seat of the Renaissance in Italy.

        a. In Italy, the bankers controlled the political destiny of many states.

      b. Wealth explains the Renaissance more logically than any other factor. It was more important than freedom of thought or freedom from the papacy.

      c. Money for wealth's sake became the ideal.

D. Education-Humanism.

    1. Humanism[1] was the name given to the new learning.

      a. People freed themselves from medieval education; they began to study Greek and Roman classical literatures.

      b. They not only studied the literature, but they began to imitate its culture.

    2. The old curriculum was largely vocational and practical; the new became cultural.

      a. New studies were introduced, and methods of teaching improved.

      b. The new learning became secular instead of clerical; the church no longer dominated education.

      c. Architecture, sculpture, and painting were important phases of the new culture.

E. Science, Invention, and Discovery.

    1. The middle ages neglected the natural sciences.

      a. Science was limited to astrology and alchemy.

      b. Development came rather late, but once started spread rapidly, especially in the field of medicine.

      c. With the advent of the experimental method great development was assured.

    2. Invention produced a revolution in Europe.

      a. Invention was not entirely lacking during the middle ages, but was handicapped because of the lack of scientific methods.

      b. Every phase of life was affected by the new inventions of the Renaissance period.

      c. Probably the two most important were gunpowder and printing.

         (1). Gunpowder changed methods of warfare, which meant the loss of power of the feudal castle, consequently social and political changes.

         (2). Printing put education within the reach of the masses.

    3. The new voyages of discovery were the direct result of all other advancement.

---

1 Humanism is derived from the latin *Nomo*, and its use by writers in this connection refers to the interest in man and his activities as an individual being. This is in contrast to the scholastics who were interested chiefly in doctrine and theory.

      a. The new commercial movement called for more extensive voyages; consequently, discovery.

      b. They were made possible through the new inventions and learning.

         (1). Inventions produced new ships and instruments of navigation.

         (2). Learning produced geographical knowledge.

      c. Then, too, the new spirit of the people called for adventure.

IV. In the twelfth and thirteenth centuries France had been the intellectual center of Europe, but this supremacy changed to Italy where the Renaissance began.

A. That the Renaissance did not start in France may be blamed to scholasticism.

    1. Apparently, the Renaissance might have begun in France.

      a. France was one of the first countries to free herself from feudalism. Civil liberty had developed in French towns.

      b. She led in education and the university movement. Her language was the language of western Europe.

    2. But scholasticism had too great a hold upon France.

      a. Her scholars were wrapped up in logic; inductive reasoning was the road to all knowledge.

      b. Experimental methods of study were rejected.

    3. France also lost political liberty, so the Renaissance, excluded from France, began in Italy.

B. Necessary conditions for the Renaissance were found in Italy.

    1. Here was to be found freedom of thought.

      a. Scholasticism did not grip Italy.

      b. The scientific method was accepted.

    2. Social conditions favored the Renaissance movement.

      a. Italy had not suffered to such an extent from feudalism.

      b. She was also comparatively free from the Empire and the church.

      c. Here the individual found self-expression.

    3. Roman and Greek traditions were not wholly lost as in France.

      a. Latin civilization was the heritage of the Italian people.

      b. They came into contact with Greek language and customs.

c. They gradually evolved an Italian language capable of expressing the new thought, but still much of the literature of the Renaissance was written in classical Latin. For a time there was a slavish imitation, almost a worship, of the classical Roman form.

*"Italian humanism restored good standards of style in prose and verse, thereby benefiting not classical studies alone, but modern literature as well; . . . . it achieved a result even larger than its work for scholarship, by diffusing a new spirit, the foe of obscurantism, the ally of all forces that make for light, for the advancement of knowledge, and for reasonable freedom." ***

---

* *From* The Cambridge Modern History, Vol. I, p. 568. Copyright 1924. *Used by permission of* The Macmillan Company, *publishers.*

CHAPTER XXXIII

CULTURAL DEVELOPMENTS IN EDUCATION, THOUGHT, AND PHILOSOPHY

"For future generations the important work of the Italian Renaissance lay in classical studies, education, and the formation of a type of cultivation and refinement which was to have great influence in modern times." *

I. The closing period of the middle ages was characterized by scholasticism.

A. Teachings of the church resulted in the neglect of material life.

    1. The only thing of value was the soul.

        a. Accumulation of worldly possessions and the indulgences in worldly activities was discouraged.

        b. People rejected this world for the better world to come.

    2. The philosophy produced by the university attempted to bring Christian doctrines into harmony with Aristotelian reason.

        a. This philosophy we call scholasticism. St. Thomas Aquinas was its champion.

        b. Even the university movement failed to change this attitude to any degree.

        c. The conflict between faith and reason was finally adjusted by Aquinas, so that each held an important place; still the two did not conflict.

    3. After accomplishing its purpose, scholasticism did not die, but lingered on.

        a. This fact delayed the revival of learning.

        b. School subjects and methods were not adopted to the changing life which was a result of the development of cities and towns.

B. Before a change in education could come, the individual had to regain his place of importance in European life.

    1. Neither Greeks nor Romans fully realized the importance of the individual.

---

* *From* Munro, The Middle Ages, p. 507, rev. ed. Copyright 1928. *Used by permission of* D. Appleton-Century Company, *publishers.*

a. The Greeks only partially realized the importance of individuality: Greek art gives one the impression of high development of the individual.

b. But politically the Greek state came first. This fact is shown by Spartan discipline.

c. In Rome the individual became subservient to Roman law.

2. Individuality, at a low ebb in ancient times, almost disappeared in medieval times.

a. Ideals were high, but the life of the people was narrow.

b. The church called individuality, rebellion and sin; conscience was lost; men must not create; they must imitate; man avoided the world, he was entirely shut in.

c. This age of faith destroyed spiritual individuality.

d. Individuality was also lost in other phases of medieval life: political, social, and economic.

3. In another sense, however, the attitude during the middle ages was one of intense individualism.

a. There were those who committed themselves to the life of the monastery, having in mind the selfish object of saving their individual souls.

b. The low ebb of nationalism might also be interpreted as a spirit of individuality.

c. In the usual sense, however, this was a period of lack of individuality.

II. With the development of individualism, scholasticism gave way to humanism.

A. The emancipation of the individual was a gradual process.

1. The revolt was not a university, but a town movement.

a. People were dissatisfied with the character of existing education; scholasticism was not in keeping with the needs and problems of the new urban groups.

b. Education was entirely professional,[1] not intellectual. There was a demand for a new education to conform to the new ways of living.

c. However, the universities were averse to change; in fact, professors worked against the intellectual revival.

2. As early as the thirteenth century St. Francis of Assisi, 1182-1226, proved by example the new feeling.

a. St. Francis was the founder of the Franciscans, one of the orders of begging friars.

b. He was a true and devout Christian, in sympathy with the ascetic concepts of the middle ages. His followers

---

[1] The three recognized professions of the time were: Medicine, law, and theology.

did not shut themselves up in solitude, but went out
into the world to minister to their fellow-men.

    (1). He was not worldly, but rejoiced in the pleasures
and goodness of living.

    (2). He loved animals, birds, all nature, and above
all, mankind.

  c. St. Francis' example reflected the coming change from
the medieval to the modern man.

3. Dante, 1265-1321, was also a major contributor to the new
thought.

  a. He was an orthodox Catholic, believing this life to be
a preparation for everlasting life, but he also believed
in the fullness of life on earth.

    (1). There was, he believed, a happiness natural to
man which led to eternal happiness in the next
world.

    (2). Further, he believed, everything which destroyed
this natural happiness was bad, and everything
which contributed to a high and noble character
was good.

  b. The Divine Comedy, his greatest work, expressed his
interests and ideas.

    (1). By many, it is considered the greatest poem in
Italian literature.

    (2). Dante's greatest purpose was to teach some use-
ful truth.

B. Petrarch, 1304-1374, has been well named "The Father of
Humanism."

1. He was the first scholar to entirely desert medieval learning.

  a. He led Europe back to a full realization of the value
of Greek and Roman literature.

  b. Petrarch made the Latin classics the basis of a liberal
education.

  c. He has been called "the first modern man."

2. Through Petrarch and his predecessors, intellectual life
and a revival of learning took form.

  a. He advocated study of Greek and Roman authors, and
greatly influenced the movement to recover lost and
forgotten works of ancient writers.

  b. There were many obstacles to the study of the classics,
such as:

    (1). The need of converting people to his new ideas.

    (2). Many works had been lost; those preserved were
only badly written copies.

    c. Through Petrarch's enthusiasm, libraries were founded, intellectual ambitions were aroused, and the classics were again given an important place in the education of the time.

III. Humanism, or the new learning, was characterized by an intense admiration and "Imitation of the Ancients."

A. The new scholars became known as the Humanists.

    1. They not only studied Roman and Greek literature, but every phase of ancient life.

        a. The Latin word, *humanitas*, may be interpreted as culture, especially in the sense of literary appreciation.

        b. People interested in culture attempted to acquire it by restoring the Roman language, literature, ideas, and ideals.

        c. Theology became of less importance; new studies, including Latin grammar, literature, poetry, and history were substituted. These new branches were to become known as the humanities.

    2. The study of Greek and Roman literature was necessary because the countries of Europe lacked literature in the vernacular.

        a. The middle ages had produced little literature.

        b. Of necessity people turned to works of antiquity.

    3. The Italian Humanists often showed pagan tendencies.

        a. The teachings of the church were often attacked.

        b. They ridiculed the self-sacrifice of the monk and the medieval views of preparing in this life for the next.

        c. It was a period of reaction to scholasticism.

B. Humanism had an important effect upon educational progress.

    1. The university had lacked efficiency.

        a. Schools had deteriorated; the course of study and methods of teaching had become sterile.

        b. Education was almost entirely vocational; it did not attempt to develop a well-rounded life.

    2. The Humanists sought to change both the methods of teaching and the subject matter.

        a. To them, culture should be the aim of education.

        b. Text-books then in use were replaced by Roman and Grecian masterpieces. Students read the works of great authors with enthusiasm.

        c. However, the new learning tended to be secular, and the Humanists objected to the domination of the church.

3. The first teachers of the new learning in Italy were Greek scholars from Constantinople.
    a. Chrysoloras, a teacher in the employ of the government of Florence, 1397-1400, lectured on Greek literature. He gave western Europe its first Greek grammar.
    b. There was a renewal of interest in Plato's philosophy and its ideal of beauty. This enthusiasm was carried to an extreme in "Neoplatonism."
4. Thus the classics became the basis of a liberal education.

IV.   It was in the field of religion that man was last to free himself from the medieval ideal.

A. Even in Greek and Roman times individual conscience was replaced by implicit religious faith.
    1. Questions of conscience and religion are closely bound together; both are concerned with right and wrong.
    2. With the advent of Christianity man was free to decide between right and wrong.
        a. This became true in both Greek and Roman civilizations.
        b. At first the emphasis was upon conduct, but later the emphasis was on creed.
        c. In time people were not allowed to decide between right and wrong; neither were they allowed to interpret creeds.
        d. The church became necessary for salvation, which was the doctrine of implicit faith.

B. Individualism led to the breakdown of the doctrine of implicit faith.
    1. People of the middle ages were not satisfied with the workings of the church.
        a. There was continuous struggle for reform.
        b. Economic and political activities of the church were condemned.
        c. Nevertheless, it was not until the Renaissance that change was possible.
    2. In the twelfth century opposition took root.
        a. Abelard, 1079-1142, advocated individual conscience.
            (1). He applied reason to religion.
            (2). He was not the first to do so, but he was the one who gave the method life.[1]
        b. Even Bernard of Clairvaux, 1091-1153, Abelard's chief foe, admitted there was some truth in Abelard's method.

---

[1] John Colet carried on the same type of work in England at a later date.

     c. By 1214 much progress was evidenced against implicit faith.

     d. However, there was a loss as well as a gain: the Renaissance was also a return to paganism to some degree.

  3. The thirteenth to the fifteenth century has been called the Age of the Critics.

     a. Open criticism of the church became common.

        (1). This criticism was well founded, prompted by the immorality of the time, the secular activities and the corruption of the church.

        (2). As a consequence, a great reform movement was started. These reforms were carried on by laymen and churchmen alike.

     b. Reform movements failed, at least for the moment, because they were too advanced and too revolutionary.

C. These reform movements were not in vain, for they were the beginnings of a great movement, the Protestant Revolution.

  1. Reform was not possible at the time, but conscience was developing. It was gradually gathering force.

  2. To change religious life men must wait for new generations.

     a. Religion tends to resist change even in a changing age.

     b. Religion and conduct are interwoven with the most sacred and permanent phases of life.

  3. When the Renaissance struck northern Europe it came not as a secular change, but as a religious change, the Protestant Revolution.

> *"While the humanists imitated the writings of classical antiquity, the artists experimented and worked out new methods. The humanists were scholars; the artists were original geniuses."* *

* *From* Thorndike, The History of Medieval Europe, p. 598. Copyright 1917. *Used by permission of* Houghton Mifflin Company, *publishers.*

CHAPTER XXXIV

CULTURAL DEVELOPMENTS IN LITERATURE, ART, AND SCIENCE.

"The age that witnessed the first efforts of the human mind to escape from the thraldom of religious despotism, witnessed also the revival of literature, and many important inventions in modern science." *

I. **Italian literature reached its greatest height under Dante in the fourteenth century.**

A. Italian literature before the fourteenth century consisted largely of unwritten poems.

    1. Little is known of this poetry today, as it was sung and not read; but it is said to have dealt with the everyday life and thought of the people.

    2. The troubadours gave to Italy the first written literature of any consequence.

        a. The songs of the troubadours, first written in the language of the people of Provence, were carried throughout Italy by the singing troubadours.

        b. Other sections took up the movement, either by imitation or in a dialect of their own.

        c. Before long in every section of Italy, verse was being written in the vernacular.

        d. This led to the development of many dialects.

    3. Finally, the Florentine dialect prevailed over others in the formation of the Italian language.

        a. Other sections of Italy were strong competitors of Florence, helping to develop the Italian language.

        b. There were also many individuals working toward this end, of whom St. Francis of Assisi is probably the greatest.

B. With the advent of Dante, 1265-1321, the Italian language was to reach its greatest height.

    1. Dante was the connecting link between the old and the new age.

---

* *From* Wilson, Outlines of History, p. 784.

      a. He expressed with great conviction the ideas of his time.

      b. He wrote in Italian, not only because he was writing for people who could not read Latin, but also because of his love of this new language as a medium of expression.

2. Two of Dante's greatest works were "The New Life" and "The Divine Comedy."

      a. "The New Life," autobiographical, expressing the new idea of an awakening in Europe, is the first great Italian work in prose.

      b. "The Divine Comedy," the greatest epic of Italian literature, is the story of his own soul's pilgrimage, but its characters are so universal as to possess life for all generations to come.[1]

3. The fourteenth century also produced Petrarch, 1304-1374, Boccaccio, 1313-1375, and Chaucer, 1335(?)-1400.

      a. All of these men helped to develop the European vernaculars.

      b. Dante, Petrarch, and Boccaccio were of Florentine descent; Chaucer was English; and Froissart, another important literati, was a contemporary Frenchman.

      c. Unfortunately, perhaps, these men left no successors, consequently the vernacular literature, so important in the fourteenth century, dropped to comparative insignificance in the fifteenth century.

II. Although Petrarch greatly influenced the development of Italian literature, his greatest work was in the revival of Latin and Greek.

A. Latin and Greek had not entirely disappeared from western Europe during the middle ages.

    1. Latin was the language of the church, of the courts, and of the schools.

      a. It was not the language of the common people, but was used by men of culture.

      b. Latin was used by men of position and authority.

         (1). It was the language of commerce.

         (2). Greek was known by a few.

      c. Latin and Greek were known by some throughout the middle ages, but the civilization of western Europe was unaffected by the classics until the time of Petrarch.

---

[1] Dante represented the last voice of Italian patriotism. He decried the decay of the patriotism which characterized the Roman Republic and predicted the decay of Italy nationally.

2. It remained for Petrarch to give understanding to Latin and Greek; to change medieval into modern Europe.
   a. Others had had a modern point of view, but their influence was not felt.
      (1). Petrarch gave his ideas to the world.
      (2). He has been called the founder of the Renaissance.
   b. Through his influence the Renaissance took form: it became a reality.

B. Petrarch's great enthusiasm for writers of antiquity aroused others, and the new spirit spread.

   1. Petrarch, a great revivalist, was filled with the spirit of ancient writers, and never missed an opportunity to recover some ancient manuscript.

   2. Boccaccio and others assisted greatly in this work, and there developed a great body of men, known as the "wandering teachers of Latin," who inspired and communicated their zeal to their students.

   3. There was, of course, opposition to this new movement.
      a. Latin was not only a new language to most of the scholars of Europe, but it expressed new thoughts and new attitudes toward life.
      b. Consequently, many scholars, especially churchmen and schoolmen, were averse to the change.
      c. Petrarch, opposing the old system of Scholasticism, finally succeeded in getting the ideal of Humanism accepted.

   4. The revival of the study of Greek, although it came later, was even more important than the revival of Latin.
      a. Western Europe during the Renaissance obtained both literary style and model from the Greeks.[1]
      b. The study of Greek progressed slowly at first, because of the lack of Greek grammars written in Latin.
         (1). Greek was usually studied through a Greek-speaking instructor.
         (2). Men with knowledge of pure Greek were rare, even in the East.
         (3). Some Greeks came to Italy, however, for a commercial reason.

C. Florence became the center of Humanism, but practically all Italy patronized the new learning.
   1. Economic prosperity created a new leisure class.

---

[1] The Italian writers were primarily stylists. As far as original thought was concerned the writers of the Renaissance were sterile.

      a. With economic independence came luxurious ways of living.

          (1). Money was spent lavishly.

          (2). Religion lost its restraining influence.

      b. The prime motive of Italian Humanism was love of beauty, whether in buildings, homes, art, or literature.

  2. The support of Humanism became almost universal.

      a. The Renaissance affected great numbers, but it did not materially affect the great mass of Italian people, for the life of the laborer and the peasant was very much the same as before.

      b. The best example of the patrons of literature is the great Medici family, of which Lorenzo was the greatest.

      c. In time the church and even the schools supported the new literature, until it greatly affected the popes and the Christian religion.

      d. Scholars ceased to work individually and founded societies.

III. The fine arts gave expression to the new life and new thought even more than did literature.

A. Medieval or Gothic art shows a sharp contrast to Renaissance art.

  1. The fine arts are a means of expressing the life and thought of the people of any age.

      a. Consequently, medieval art was characterized by the Christian spirit.

      b. When the great town movement began in the eleventh century, architecture, sculpture, and painting took their appropriate place. During this period the church controlled practically every phase of life.

  2. Medieval architecture reflected the spirit of the time. It was characterized by massiveness and great height.

      a. It did not express the classical or modern spirit.

          (1). It expressed the emotions of the soul.

          (2). Mere beauty was not the object.

      b. Renaissance architecture expressed the classical ideal, beauty.

          (1). The predominant lines were horizontal instead of vertical.

          (2). The Gothic pillars were replaced by more slender colonades.

          (3). High roofs of the Gothic were replaced by low and broad ceilings,

3. As with literature, Florence led in the development of Renaissance architecture.

    a. Brunelleschi, 1377-1446, was the first exponent of Renaissance architecture.

        (1). His work resembles the Greek, but coming in a different age, it is really unlike that of the ancients.

        (2). His most beautiful work is not that of the great domes, but the more simple ceilings of smaller churches.

    b. The work of Leo Battista, 1404-1472, more nearly resembled the ancient architecture.

    c. Bramante, 1444-1514, was the greatest architect of the period. He began where the others left off.

B. No less marked were the changes in sculpture and painting.

    1. Renaissance sculptors also expressed the new spirit in their work.

        a. Medieval sculpture, the greatest art during medieval times, was not as much a slave to tradition as was architecture.

        b. Important changes took place.

            (1). Beauty became the predominant motive.

            (2). Even the scenes of the church were permeated with grace.

            (3). Renaissance art gradually broke away from the medieval ideal that it must express a moral or be edifying.

        c. Among the pioneers of Italian sculpture the names of John of Pisa, Andrew of Pisa, and Orcanga are outstanding.

        d. Of later sculptors Ghiberti, Jacopo della Quercia, Donatello, Luca della Robbia, and Michelangelo are among the most important.

    2. During the middle ages the primary motive of painting was to help the church in its teaching; now the motive was the expression of life.

        a. Painting did not advance as soon as sculpture, but its final development surpassed it.

        b. The new painting expressed individuality and life.

            (1). Paintings during the Renaissance period seemed lifelike.

            (2). The faces had expression and feeling, and truly resembled people of the times.

    c. Among the important painters were: Giotto, Fra Angelico, Fra Lippo Lippi, Botticelli, Leonardo da Vinci, Raphael, Titian, and Masaccio.

IV. Natural Science was neglected during the middle ages, but with the coming of the Renaissance western Europe began to recover the science of the Greeks.

A. The medieval man was more interested in philosophy than science.

    1. There was no well-ordered system of knowledge.

        a. No systematic study of man's surroundings took place.

        b. Knowledge was not scientific.

            (1). It was not tabulated, but fragmental.

            (2). There was no orderly, observational or experimental method.

    2. Medieval science was largely limited to alchemy and astrology.

        a. Astrology included a study of the heavenly bodies, but the work did not resemble modern astronomy. The chief concern was in the belief that man's destiny was determined by the stars.

        b. Alchemy probably stimulated the laboratory method, but its chief concern was to turn baser metals into gold.

    3. Restored knowledge of Aristotle worked toward a revival in scientific study.

        a. During the middle ages men were imperfectly acquainted with the works of Aristotle; they knew only his logic, and that not clearly.

        b. The influence of the Mohammedans in Spain did much to restore the true Aristotle.

            (1). They were great scientific students, and scholars from western Europe flocked to them.

            (2). It was then, about the middle of the thirteenth century, that the observational method began to develop.

        c. There were many important contributions to science before the scientific method was really developed. The names of Magnus, Bacon, and Lull are outstanding.

B. Advancement was slow in the scientific method.

    1. The subjective attitude gave way to observation.

        a. With the rebirth of classical literature came abundant knowledge of a scientific nature, but progress was slow.

            (1). This is true especially in medicine, mathematics, astronomy, and physics.

    (2). The most remarkable development occurred in the field of medicine.

   b. Dr. Vesalius of Padua greatly influenced the development of the scientific method.

    (1). Studies of anatomy and physiology were put on an experimental basis—dead bodies were dissected.

    (2). Dr. Vesalius, in 1543, published his famous book, "Fabrica Corporis Humani," in which he held that it was necessary to challenge every past authority and be guided only by facts.

 2. Research became all important and permeated most every field of human endeavor.

   a. Geography and astronomy took the lead.

    (1). Advance in geographical knowledge dates back to journeys of merchants and adventurers who were seeking new markets and giving vent to imagination.

    (2). As early as the thirteenth century the Polos had made their remarkable journeys to China. Information was gathered and spread by them and their successors.

   b. Developments in geographical knowledge led to new astronomical knowledge.

    (1). Copernicus led in this work, developing his hypothesis that the earth and other planets revolved around the sun, and that the earth makes one complete revolution on its axis every twenty-four hours.

    (2). This changed the idea that the earth was the center of the universe.

   c. Research began in mathematics.

    (1). Arithmetic became a deductive science; formerly it was used only in affairs of every-day life.

    (2). Practical geometry had been used by architects, but theoretical geometry did not exist. The influence of the Mohammedans stimulated the study of all branches of mathematics, including trigonometry.

   d. Physics, chemistry, and even zoology and biology began to develop.

    (1). Tradition was left behind in these sciences, and experimentation became important.

    (2). Laws of nature began to develop; the elements became of interest to scholars, and plant and animal life were studied with the scientific spirit.

e. Great attention was then paid to navigation and invention, and even history and philosophy took on a scientific aspect.

f. The importance of this phase of the Renaissance lies in the effect increased knowledge had upon social and economic conditions of living; but it is an error to attribute too many intellectual changes to the Renaissance, for many clung to the deductive reasoning until somewhat later.

"So it was that the revival of science revealed the invalidity of the old method of thought and provided one in its place which, though far from being sufficient in itself to give to men knowledge of the truth of things, was yet an incalculable advance upon the one it displaced." *

---

* *From* Hulme, Renaissance and Reformation, revised edition, p. 143. Copyright 1917. *Used by permission of* D. Appleton-Century Company, *publishers.*

CHAPTER XXXV

THE SPREAD OF HUMANISM—THE END OF THE RENAISSANCE

"Not in literature or in art alone, but in every form of intellectual activity, the Renaissance opened a new era for mankind." *

I. Humanism did not take root in northern Europe immediately.

A. Northern Europe was not as ready for the change as Italy.

    1. The great middle class, strong a century before, lost much of its independence to the powerful monarchs.

        a. The scholastic method destroyed freedom of thought.

        b. Logic was given too important a place to allow the development of Humanism.

    2. During the fourteenth and fifteenth centuries northern Europe clung to its old ideas and customs.

        a. Italian travellers in northern Europe were impressed by the lack of culture. Comparatively, northern Europe was almost barbaric.

        b. The old ideas and the old ways were retained; some seemed to have even more vigor as time passed.

        c. Class distinctions were more evident in northern Europe.

            (1). The nobles and the rich lived extravagantly; the poorer classes lived in misery.

            (2). This was a period of social unrest in northern Europe.

B. When Humanism did spread to northern Europe it took different forms.

    1. Humanism crossed the Alps into central and northern Europe nearly a century after it began in Italy.

        a. Conditions were almost immediately changed.

        b. Aversion to Humanism was displaced by enthusiastic intellectual life.

---

* *From* The Cambridge Modern History, Vol. I, The Renaissance, p. 584. Copyright 1924. *Used by permission of* The Macmillan Company, *publishers.*

      c. Theology was displaced by secular studies, but never in the extreme, as in Italy.

  2. In northern Europe the spread of Humanism was more a process of adaption than adoption.

      a. Fundamentally, perhaps, it was the same in all countries, but each country combined its own qualities and characteristics with those of ancient times.

      b. This was truer of England than of any other country, because of her conservative temperament.

  3. The Renaissance produced more lasting results in northern Europe than in Italy.

      a. Developments in Italy seemed more brilliant, but they were also rather superficial.

      b. The people to the north combined the practical with the classical. People were interested not so much in producing art as in spreading learning.

C. In northern Europe the Renaissance often took the form of religious reform.

  1. The countries to the north did not desert religion and revert to paganism as did the Italians.

      a. In Germany men were more earnest than in Italy.

          (1). There was a return to a more primitive Christianity.

          (2). There was a doing away with abuses of the church.

      b. In England people began the study of the New Testament to learn the true character of the original Christianity.

      c. Nearly every country north of the Alps during the Renaissance period developed this spirit.

  2. Consequently, the Reformation began in northern Europe.

      a. Scholars such as Erasmus, Colet, and More used their talents in attacking existing abuses in the church.

      b. The monks and schoolmen, supporters of the old abuses, were openly ridiculed.

          (1). The Scholars and their writings were generally well-received.

          (2). Men began to see the necessity of reform.

      c. There was also great development of mysticism.

          (1). The mystics were a group who believed in personal communion with God.

          (2). They believed that they should not be bound by either the church or the state.

II. The people of northern Europe, being more patient, led in the work of invention.

A. Among the greatest inventions of the period were the introduction of cheap writing material and improvement in printing.

    1. The older method of producing books was slow, costly, and often inaccurate.

        a. Although paper was invented centuries before the Renaissance period, it was not introduced into western Europe until the Mohammedans brought it into Spain.

            (1). During the Renaissance period it generally replaced the costly parchment.

            (2). Books were still produced by copying, a slow and inaccurate process.

        b. The next step was printing by engraved blocks.

    2. Real advancement came in bookmaking with the development of movable type.

        a. This process developed gradually, and was perfected only after long and tedious experiments.

        b. The chief credit in this work is usually given to Johannes Gutenberg of Mainz.

            (1). He was the first European to use the movable type successfully in printing books.

            (2). His first book was a Latin version of the Bible, appearing about 1455.

        c. With the advancement in printing, books became more common.

            (1). Great libraries were developed.

            (2). Two classes of books were in great demand: religious books and the classics.

B. Inventions were introduced into many fields of endeavor.

    1. With the development of navigation, exploration was stimulated, geographical knowledge was increased, and many coast lines were scientifically charted.

        a. The compass was the most important instrument developed in the aid of navigation. Men became able to accurately direct the course of their vessels.

        b. With the invention of the astrolabe, seamen could determine their position. Later developments were the quadrant and sextant.

    2. Invention brought about great changes in warfare, and helped break up feudalism.

        a. Gunpowder was known in the thirteenth century, but it was not until near the end of the fourteenth that guns were commonly used in Europe.

    b.   The chief difficulty in the development of guns was in the ignition of the powder.

        (1). Gradually improvements were made.

        (2). The bow was gradually displaced by the cannon.

    c.   Improvements also came in tactics and strategy; scientific works on war were written and studied.

    d.   These inventions contributed to the downfall of feudal lords, as the castle could not withstand gunfire.

3.   There were many comparatively minor inventions which were to revolutionize everyday life and scientific endeavor.

    a.   The use of artificial glass made mirrors, optical lenses, and telescope lenses quite common.

        (1). Concave and convex lenses greatly increased the use of spectacles, the microscope, and telescope.

        (2). All of these came into practical use by the seventeenth century.

    b.   Great development came in time-pieces. The sundial, the water clock, and the hour glass had been known, but great progress was made with the use of the clock after the discovery of the law of the pendulum by Galileo. This law was applied to clocks about 1650.

III. Northern Europe also led in the work of exploration, discovery, and colonization.

A. Motivation for exploration and discovery came from several sources:

1.   First, there was the natural characteristic of inquisitiveness.

    a.   Europe had learned of the East through returning Crusaders and by contact with Mohammedans in Spain.

    b.   Men became curious to learn more of Oriental civilization and the fabulous riches of the East; they hoped to share in the splendors of the East.

2.   Further, commerce greatly stimulated exploration.

    a.   During the crusades the West learned to use many luxuries of which it had been deprived.

        (1). To satisfy the new tastes and desires of the age a flourishing commerce had sprung up when the commercial center shifted from the Mediterranean to the Atlantic.

        (2). In the fifteenth century, exploration was greatly stimulated.

    b.   As yet, the new luxuries could not be produced in the West; they must come from the East.

3.   Then the religious elements were intent upon spreading Christianity and strengthening the church.

      a. Many who went on the crusades lacked religious zest. Nevertheless, the crusading movement contributed to the spread of geographical information and was a strong motive in discovery.

      b. Many later leaders in exploration, such as Prince Henry of Portugal, adhered to the idea of spreading the Christian faith.

  4. And in addition, imperial policies of European monarchs motivated exploration and discovery.

      a. Monarchs of Spain and Portugal, and later, France and England, dreamed of great overseas empires.

      b. Early discoveries were to serve as the basis for later claims to continents. Monarchs were furthering the work of discovery by outfitting expeditions and granting great rewards for their success.

      c. Spain particularly was temporarily enriched by her success in discovery.

B. Conflicting explanations have been given for the change from land to water routes.

  1. The change is usually explained through the fact that the Turks are supposed to have interfered with the old established land routes.

      a. They are said to have interfered with the overland routes to the East.

      b. As the only new routes were water routes, they became of the first importance.

  2. The development of water routes was greatly stimulated, although recent investigation shows the former theory may be incorrect.

      a. Professor Lybyer says that the Turks did not deliberately obstruct the overland routes; consequently, they did not make new routes necessary.

      b. According to this theory, the change came about because of the superiority of water routes, so it was not the Turk but cheap freight rates that caused the commercial center to shift from the Mediterranean to the Atlantic.

C. Spain and Portugal took the lead in discovery in the fifteenth and sixteenth centuries.

  1. In the first quarter of the fourteenth century Italian cities opened up communication by sea with the Netherland towns.

    a. As early as the close of the thirteenth century, Genoese seamen were making voyages to the Canaries in an effort to find water routes to India.

    b. About fifty years later they discovered the Madeira Islands and part of the Azores group.

    c. By 1445 Cape Verde was discovered, putting an end to the idea that the torrid regions were uninhabitable.

2. The Mediterranean fleets, touching Portuguese ports, aroused the Portuguese to undertake maritime expeditions.

    a. Portugal continued the work of discovery.

      (1). John I, 1385-1433, greatly aided exploration.

      (2). Prince Henry, "The Navigator," probably the greatest leader in exploration, continued the work of his father, John I.

    b. In 1445 the coast of Guinea was reached. Prince Henry died in 1460, but the work was carried on by Alfonso V.

    c. The spice trade was taken away from the Mohammedans after the discoveries of Diaz and da Gama.

      (1). In 1486 Diaz rounded the Cape of Good Hope.

      (2). In 1498 Vasco da Gama reached Calicut, in Hindustan.

    d. By 1515 the commercial center had definitely shifted to the Atlantic, under the leadership of the Portuguese.

3. The idea of reaching the Indies by sailing west was gradually accepted.

    a. The first plan for sailing west was developed by Toscanelli, a Florentine, who greatly influenced Columbus.

    b. Columbus, sailing under the Spanish flag, hoped to reach Japan, but instead landed on the Island of San Salvador.

      (1). Columbus made three further trips to America.

      (2). When he died he believed he had explored the coasts of Asia—not America.

    c. The climax in exploration and discovery came with Magellan's trip around the world, completed in 1522.

4. Both Spain and Portugal built up extensive overseas empires.

    a. The Spanish empire consisted of South America, Central America, and southern North America, while Portuguese influence extended to Brazil and the East.

    b. By the end of the sixteenth century the Spanish began to lose their hold on the Americas, and England and France came to the foreground in discovery and colonization.

5. The age of discovery was important because of the commercial and political results, but no less important were the resulting social and religious changes.

IV. The age of the Renaissance was one of remarkable intellectual progress, but the closing years of the period were in the nature of a transition to the Age of the Reformation.

A. At the close of the fifteenth century, Europe was apparently entering a period of great change.

    1. Humanism had entered every country of western Europe.

        a. Everywhere new ideas and new interests attracted the attention of both scholars and the common man.

        b. Europe had laid the foundations for a remarkable civilization.

            (1). Industry, commerce, and the fine arts gathered great momentum.

            (2). It seemed that Europe was about to enter another Golden Age.

    2. The vision was not only in developing Europe, but other lands as well.

        a. Contact with the Orient had been established.

        b. New continents had been discovered, and already the work of transplanting European civilizations had begun.

        c. Doubt in the minds of men had been dispelled by new theories which told them of the correct place of the earth in the solar system.

B. The Reform Movement resulted in a series of civil, and finally, international wars.

    1. These wars affected almost every country of Europe.

        a. Discovery increased the interests of the nations involved; consequently, Europe was to experience a series of international wars due to conflicting interests.

        b. The religious movements in northern Europe (movements to eradicate abuses from the church) met with bitter resistance.

    2. Thus, the period of the Renaissance gave way to the period of the Reformation.

        a. Men no longer thought of science and knowledge, but of other great changes which seemed inevitable.

        b. The period of the Renaissance came to an end, and further development of civilization was postponed until the seventeenth century.

> *"While the revival of learning . . presents varying aspects in the several countries to which it passed from Italy, the essential gift which it brought was the same for all. That gift was the recovery of an inheritance which men had temporarily lost; one so valuable in itself that human life would be definitely poorer without it, and also fraught with such power to educate and to stimulate, that the permanent loss of it would have been the annulment of an inestimable agency in the development of human faculty."* *

---

* *From* The Cambridge Modern History, Vol. I, The Renaissance, p. 583. Copyright 1924. *Used by permission of* The Macmillan Company, *publishers.*

CHAPTER XXXVI

MARTIN LUTHER AND THE BEGINNING OF THE PROTESTANT REFORMATION.

"The Reformation of the sixteenth century had its birth and growth in a union of spiritual and secular forces such as the world has seldom seen at any other period of its history. On the secular side, the times were full of new movements . . . and spiritual forces aimed at making religion the birthright and possession of the common man." *

I. In the beginning of the sixteenth century the church was still medieval.

A. In other lines of thought the middle ages had come to an end.

    1. The Renaissance had brought great change in European life and thought, but the church was not materially affected.

        a. Politically, Europe was entering the modern age.

        b. Economically and socially, people had raised themselves to a higher plane of living.

        c. Intellectually, there was great advancement.

        d. But the church remained the one great restraining influence.

    2. Medieval popes exercised great power, not only in religious matters, but in secular as well.

        a. The pope put into practice the theory that all power comes from God; and he, being God's earthly vicar, proclaimed that all government, civil and ecclesiastical, was vested in him.

            (1). The pope was not always able to force this position upon rulers.

            (2). His position was usually outside and sometimes above national government.

        b. By the fifteenth century growing national monarchs had weakened papal authority, but had by no means superseded it.

    3. The church was determined to remain medieval, and all efforts to change it had been unsuccessful.

---

* *From* The Cambridge Modern History, Vol. II, The Reformation, p. 104. Copyright 1924. *Used by permission of* The Macmillan Company, *publishers.*

B. There were several unsuccessful attempts to reform the church before the advent of the Reformation.

    1. That there was no change was not because there was no effort in that direction.

        a. The general period of change was bound to come into conflict with the church.

        b. The church was strong.

            (1). It was endowed with position, money, and men of great ability.

            (2). It firmly resolved to resist all change.

    2. The Albigensians made the first great attempt in southern France in the thirteenth century.

        a. This sect was condemned by Catholics and Protestants alike, while the Waldenses conformed to Protestant theological doctrine.

        b. The Albigensians were fearfully punished and were finally exterminated by the Inquisition.

        c. The Waldenses, however, survived persecution, and with the coming of the Reformation joined forces with the Calvinists.

    3. A revolt in England occurred in the latter part of the fourteenth century.

        a. People demanded reform, which resulted in Wat Tyler's insurrection.

        b. This was a period of literary revival, and John Wycliffe used his talents in opposition to the papacy.

            (1). He condemned the papacy itself and many of the teachings of the church.

            (2). Wycliffe's greatest importance is his later influence upon continental Europe.

            (3). In England, when his influence gradually died out, he was deserted by the aristocratic classes.

    4. The next great rebellion against the church occurred in Bohemia under the leadership of John Huss.

        a. Huss followed the ideas of Wycliffe, making an attempt to introduce new customs into the church.

        b. He was finally burned at the stake, but as a political expediency the church conceded some points to his followers.

        c. The revolt was ended by a compromise.

    5. These revolts had little effect upon the organization and practices of the church, but they show the tenor of the times; Europe was thinking of changes in the church as comprehensive as in other institutions.

II. The reformation was inevitable; it was the outcome of intellectual, social, economic, and political, as well as religious development of the fifteenth century.

A. There were many contributing factors which may be termed causes of the Protestant Reformation.

1. The worldliness of the church constituted the greatest cause.

   a. Church taxes were burdensome with the tithes, the dues, and the fees. These were objectionable enough, but the principal source of trouble came from improper use of church money.

   b. Further, some people objected to the absolutism of the papacy and the formalism of church ceremony.

   c. The worldliness and scandalous conduct of church officials were further causes for scorn, for many of the clergy were more interested in comfortable living than in performing Christian services.

   d. However, these conditions alone would not have precipitated the revolt.

2. A second cause was political and economical.

   a. Lay rulers were busily engaged in extending their power and influence.

   b. By 1500 the clergy were almost the only class independent of their influence. By seizing the power and property of the clergy the authority of the rulers would be greatly enhanced.

   c. Emperor Charles V was the one ruler strong enough to stamp out the revolt, but he was prevented from doing so by outside distractions. Consequently, the movement gained such momentum that its extinction became impossible.

   d. Furthermore, so much wealth was flowing to Rome that other countries were impoverished to a greater or lesser degree.

3. A third cause was intellectual development and individualism.

   a. The clergy no longer held a paramount place in education.

      (1). Education was diffused throughout the various countries.

      (2). Knowledge became the heritage of the common man.

   b. The leaders of the time had at hand methods of research, enabling them to carry on investigations that they might discover the truth.

    c. The individual had regained a place of importance; he had come to believe in the scientific method of approach.

    4. Thus, the religious phase of the Reformation was merely an outgrowth of a demand for changes in the church to meet the new political, social, and economic conditions of western Europe.

B. The Protestant Reformation began with Martin Luther, 1483-1546.

    1. Movements were taking form in other countries about the same time as in Germany.

        a. Both Lefèvre d'Étaples in France and Ulrich Zwingli in Switzerland were organizing groups interested in the new doctrines.

        b. Luther was by no means the only leader in reform; but he attracted greater attention, for his plans were better formulated. However, the Reformation properly began with him.

        c. The fact that these movements were developing in different countries at approximately the same time, and all working independently, is indicative of the inevitability of the Reformation.

    2. Luther, a monk, failed to find relief in the monastery; he felt that sin was still upon him.

        a. Luther's father was comfortably fixed as town councillor of Mansfield. He was able and determined to educate young Martin as a lawyer.

            (1). Luther attended the University at Erfurt, where he became greatly interested in logic.

            (2). Instead of entering law school, he entered a monastery in 1505 and became a mendicant friar.

        b. Luther left the world behind him, admitted his sin, and attempted to absolve himself from his guilt. He followed the rules of the monastery, but found that "good works" did not set his soul at peace with God.

    3. Luther's theological beliefs brought about a new idea in Christianity.

        a. He adopted the ideas of St. Paul and St. Augustine, saying that the way to salvation was in trusting in God's goodness and mercy, and not in relying on "good works."

        b. "Justification by faith" became his theological doctrine, through which his soul became comforted.

c. His first work was in the saving of souls and not in destroying the old order; but finally, realizing the abuses of the church, he resolved to reform the whole structure.

III. Luther's attack upon indulgences led to open rebellion.

A. At first Martin Luther had no idea of attacking the church, and did not realize that his ideas ran counter to the Catholic Church.

1. In 1508 he became professor of theology at the University of Wittenberg.
   a. Here he became preacher and lecturer, comforting those who held doubts the same as he.
   b. Here also, he preached his doctrine of justification by faith.

2. In 1511 Luther visited Rome in the interests of the mendicant order.
   a. He was greatly inspired by what he saw, but also greatly shocked at the worldliness of the church.
   b. It seemed to him that everywhere in the church capital there was impiety, extravagance, immorality, and a general laxity of living.
   c. Although he realized the weaknesses of the church he was not yet ready to break with it.

B. Luther, in his earnestness for reform, posted his ninety-five theses on indulgences.

1. The nature of indulgences are important.
   a. The Catholic Church taught that the results of sin were two: guilt and punishment.
      (1). Guilt could be removed by confession.
      (2). Punishment still remained.
      (3). The confession did not free the sinner from the punishment which God or the priest might impose.
      (4). It was taught that the punishment might be undergone by the penitent sinner either on this earth or in purgatory.
      (5). The indulgence, then, was a pardon which removed or reduced the punishment which was expected to be undergone in purgatory.
   b. Indulgences might be granted upon several conditions.
      (1). For prayer, good works, such as pilgrimages, or for money to be used for the church.
      (2). It was the sale of indulgences to which Luther objected so strenuously.

2. The sale of indulgences had become common.
   a. Pope Leo X, wishing to rebuild the Church of St. Peter, relied on the sale of indulgences not only for the living but also for the dead.
   b. People generally did not fully understand the theory of indulgences.
      (1). Luther attempted to clarify the matter by preaching against them.
      (2). Finally, agents selling indulgences became so numerous that Luther resorted to the posting of his famous theses against indulgences.

C. Luther's ninety-five theses, posted October 31, 1517, aroused great popular interest.
   1. With the appearance of Tetzel, the vendor of indulgences, Luther decided to take action.
      a. At this time he did not completely deny the usefulness of indulgences, but attacked only their being used in a secular way.
      b. He wished to have the question openly discussed, so on All Saints' Day, in Wittenberg, he tacked to the door of the church, his theses.
         (1). This was a custom of the time.
         (2). It simply meant a challenge to debate the question.
      c. The theses were quickly translated into German and circulated throughout the country.
      d. Discontent with the church, so long suppressed, was now to be openly shown. The people had found a leader in Martin Luther.
   2. Luther, condemned by Pope Leo X, was summoned to Rome to explain his charges against the church.
      a. The Archbishop of Mainz sent a copy of the theses to the pope. The theses were considered heretical, and Luther was summoned to Rome.
      b. Fortunately for Luther, the powerful elector of Saxony defended him, and it was agreed that the papal authorities of Germany would treat with Luther.

D. Later developments led to open revolt.
   1. In 1519 the great debate between Dr. Eck and Luther took place at Leipsic.
      a. The great question resolved upon the infallibility of the church and considered the powers of the pope.
      b. In the debate Luther attacked established church practices, and went so far as to admit that the great Council of Constance, held in 1414, had condemned Christian teachings.

     c.   Luther had not meant to break with the church, having previously condemned Huss, but now he realized that a break was unavoidable.

  2. Luther soon found he had many supporters.

     a.   Ulrich von Hutten was Luther's chief ally and ably defended the revolt. Luther also enlisted the support of the Humanists who were always ready to attack the old theological beliefs.

     b.   However, Erasmus refused to enter the conflict. He did not believe in revolt, but advocated that time would cure the evils of the church.

     c.   Luther wrote profusely, setting forth his ideas.

        (1). Among the greatest of his writings were the "Address to the Christian Nobility of the German Nation," the "Babylonian Captivity of the Church," and "The Freedom of a Christian Man."

        (2). These and many others were printed and circulated freely throughout Germany and other countries.

IV.   Luther was called before the Diet of Worms in 1521.

A. Luther was excommunicated in 1520.

  1. In the summer of 1520 Pope Leo X issued a bull declaring Luther excommunicated unless he became reconciled to the church by the next winter.

     a.   Luther had been declared a heretic and would have been arrested, but German authorities, instead of carrying out their duties, became offended at the pope's issuing orders to them.

     b.   Luther had many supporters, including the elector of Saxony.

  2. Luther met the challenge of the pope by burning the papal bull; and to give full meaning to his actions, he also burned the books of Canon Law.

     a.   The break with the church was now complete.

     b.   Luther, reckless in action and violent in speech, was ready for what might come.

     c.   No one realized the seriousness of the situation more than the pope.

B. Emperor Charles V summoned Luther before the Diet of Worms, 1521.

  1. Among the most important questions to be considered befor the Diet were:

     a.   The war with France.

     b.   The form of government of the empire.

    c. The succession of the House of Hapsburg in Germany.

    d. The disposal of Luther's case (the most important from the standpoint of this chapter).

2. Charles was an enemy of the German reformers.

    a. He was convinced of Luther's guilt, but dared not take action without giving him a trial, for fear he might arouse a large percent of the German people.

    b. Luther was warned of the danger of appearing before the Diet, but proceeded fearlessly. On his journey to Worms he was met everywhere with approval.

    c. Charles, only twenty-one years of age, was too young to deal effectively with so important a problem.

3. Luther was condemned by the imperial edict of Charles.

    a. Although he admitted the authorship of his books and his attacks upon the church, he refused to recant.

    b. After a day's delay Luther reaffirmed his position by saying, "I must allow my conscience to be controlled by God's word. Recant I cannot and will not, for it is hazardous and dishonorable to act against one's conscience."

    c. The negotiations having failed, Charles issued, on May 26, 1521, the Edict of Worms, which pronounced the ban of the empire against the heretic.

    d. Charles then turned his attentions to the French war.

        (1). He thought, upon leaving Germany, that the religious revolt had been crushed.

        (2). When Charles returned to Germany about nine years later, the revolution had gained such momentum that it was impossible to stamp it out.

4. On his way back to Wittenberg, after the Diet of Worms, Luther was seized by emissaries of the elector of Saxony, and kept in safety until the troubles were over.

    a. He was in friendly hands, and was encouraged to continue his work.

    b. During this period there was, of course, opposition to Luther; but his supporters were as numerous and strong as ever.

    c. The Edict of Worms had not brought the revolution to an end.

5. His disappearance did not mean that he was no longer a leader, but rather "it marks the time when the Luther revolt merges into national opposition to Rome."

"It may be an exaggeration to say, as is sometimes done, that this religious side of the Reformation began in the inward religious growth of a single per-

> sonality—*the river comes from a thousand nameless
> rills and not only from one selected fountain-head;
> yet Luther was so prominent a figure that the im-
> pulses in his religious life may be taken as the type
> of forces which were at work over a wide area, and
> the history of these forces may be fitly described in
> tracing the genesis and growth of his religious
> opinions from his early years to his struggle against
> indulgences."* *

*.*From* The Cambridge Modern History Vol. II, The Reformation, p. 104. Copyright 1924. *Used by permission of* The Macmillan Company, *publishers.*

CHAPTER XXXVII

THE SPREAD OF THE REFORMATION IN GERMANY TO THE PEACE OF AUGSBURG, 1555.

> *"New religions are wont to start in the backwoods. One started in an unimportant province of the great Roman Empire nineteen hundred years ago, and grew in power from its humble beginnings in Nazareth until to-day it nominally embraces the Christian world. So, too, in Saxony, a frontier province of the German Empire, crude and undeveloped, touched but lightly as yet with the transforming humanism of the time, a new religion was born."* *

I. Although Charles V was a great enemy of Protestantism, he was unable to enforce the Edict of Worms because of foreign wars.

A. Charles, a Hapsburg, was not in sympathy with Luther's ideas, and had it not been for his political difficulties would have put an end to Protestantism.

   1. Charles was brought up as a good Catholic.

      a. He had spent his life in Spain and the Netherlands, where he had been taught to support the church.

      b. Even though Charles knew of existing abuses in the church, it would have received his support.

   2. The main principles of Hapsburg policy were:

      a. To maintain the Catholic cause against the Protestants.

      b. To bring the papacy under control and limit the pope's right to interfere with the churches of the Hapsburg domains.

      c. To prevent the expansion of French influence on the continent.

      d. To defend Europe against the invasions of the Turks.

   3. The pope, Hadrian VI, was an advocate of reform, but instead of reforming the church was drawn into Charles' political difficulties.

      a. Hadrian had been the Emperor's tutor.

---

* *From* Hulme, Renaissance and Reformation, p. 240. Copyright 1917. *Used by permission of* D. Appleton-Century Company, *publishers.*

b. He believed that the Reformation was due to Divine judgment, resulting from the wickedness of the time; but he denounced Luther as a foe of Christendom.

c. An understanding developed between Charles and the pope, and the latter cooperated with the emperor in expelling the French from Italy in the wars which followed.

B. The war with France prevented the enforcement of the Edict of Worms.

1. In 1521 when the war began, Charles' single foe was Francis I of France, but soon others were involved.

a. At first the French were driven out of Milan, but later reconquered the lost territory.

b. Apparently the French were in a position to recover Italy, but with the siege of Pavia, Francis was captured and hence was forced to submit to the terms of Charles in the Treaty of Madrid, January, 1526.

c. Then the tables of war turned, and Charles was forced to fight the new pope, Clement VII, the Venetians, and Francis I.

2. Because Charles could not risk civil war in Germany, the Edict of Worms was again suspended.

a. Charles needed the resources of all Germany in fighting the new alliance.

b. It was agreed by the first Diet of Speyer that each state of Germany might decide upon its religious conduct as it "thought it could answer to God and to the emperor."

c. With the support of all Germany the city of Rome was captured and the pope taken prisoner.

d. The war was ended by the Treaty of Cambray, 1529.

(1). When French strength again showed itself the French army was reduced by plague.

(2). The French then withdrew from Italy.

II. With the closing of the French War the time had come for Charles to deal with Protestantism.

A. The second Diet of Speyer was summoned to meet in February of 1529.

1. Peace had been concluded between Charles and the pope, and between Charles and Francis I.

a. The time seemed ripe for settling the religious question in Germany.

b. It seemed nothing was to interfere with Charles' plans on this occasion.

2. The Diet decided upon the enforcement of the Edict of Worms.
   a. It was decided that the decision of the first Diet of Speyer was now invalid; and that instead of each state adopting its own religious policy, the edict would be immediately enforced.
   b. Now a new opposition arose, the supporters of Luther, the Protestants.

B. Many different types of reform measures were being advocated as remedies for the alleged ills of the church.
   1. The German people read with interest the many pamphlets which were being written.
      a. Luther's translation of the Bible stimulated the writing and printing of books and pamphlets.
      b. Questions of the day were discussed by all classes.
         (1). This was the first opportunity of the common people to influence the times through public opinion.
         (2). The commoners made good use of their opportunity.
      c. Many questions of the day were discussed, chief among them was the religious question.
   2. Many men were inclined to advocate radical methods of church reform.
      a. Everyone knew that something should be accomplished, but few had any real plan.
      b. People generally misunderstood Luther, and even he sometimes doubted if his new ideas were justifiable.
      c. The most radical of the plans of reform was the one advocated by Carlstadt.
         (1). It provided for the dissolution of the monasteries.
         (2). This plan had gotten well under way when Luther came out of hiding and began preaching moderation.
   3. Luther advocated peaceful reform.
      a. It was dangerous for Luther to reappear on the scene; nevertheless he returned to Wittenberg in 1522 and began his series of sermons in an attempt to check radicalism.
      b. Luther thought the changes should not be in the nature of a revolution, but that they should come gradually.
      c. Theoretically, Luther's plan seems correct, but it proved to be impracticable. People would not content themselves in revising the old; they wished to destroy and build something new.

4. Disregarding Luther's preaching, his adherents became the leaders in acts of violence, bringing discredit upon the religious movement.
    a. This movement came in the form of an uprising of the Rhenish knights in an effort to overpower the princes.
        (1). It was more of a political and economic outbreak than religious.
        (2). It discredited Luther and the reformers..
        (3). The Rhenish princes, both lay and ecclesiastical, crushed the rising of the knights.
    b. Franz von Sickingen and Ulrich von Hutten became the leaders of the movement, and they, being friends of Luther, caused the reformers to be blamed.

C. The revolt continued to spread, resulting in two distinct parties, the Catholics and Protestants.
    1. The Diet of Nuremberg in 1522 would not allow the enforcement of the Edict of Worms, but little respect was shown for Luther.
        a. The general conviction among Germans that the abuses of the church were real saved Luther from arrest.
        b. However, certain limitations were placed upon Luther.
            (1). His books were not to be published.
            (2). He was ordered to cease open attacks upon the church.

    2. Through the influence of Pope Clement VII there grew up a definite religious division in Germany.
        a. All attempts to bring the country under the control of the pope had failed, so a meeting was held at Regensburg attended by rulers friendly to the pope.
        b. Germany separated into two groups.
            (1). By granting certain concessions, the pope was able to secure the support of the south German rulers.
            (2). Generally speaking, the south became Catholic and the north Protestant.
        c. The concessions gained from the pope by the south German rulers removed many of the old abuses; it was really the beginning of church reform from within.

    3. The term "Protestants" originated from the protest of Luther's followers against the decision of the second Diet of Speyer.
        a. By 1529, and the meeting of the second Diet of Speyer, the Protestants were organized.
        b. This Diet had recommended the enforcement of the Edict of Worms.

(1). Against this action Luther's supporters entered a formal protest.

(2). They declared that duty to God and conscience took precedence over duty to their sovereign.

    c. Thus Charles V faced new opposition in enforcing the Edict of Worms which had remained a "dead letter" since 1521.

III. Luther was again condemned at the Diet of Augsburg in 1530, but the Turkish invasion again prevented religious war.

A. Before the convening of the Diet of Augsburg the Protestants were asked to state their position in writing—the Confession of Augsburg.

    1. Charles V was decided in his course of action, but, as in 1521, allowed the Protestants a hearing.

        a. As Luther was under the ban of the empire, Melanchthon was commissioned to formulate in writing the creed of the Protestants.

        b. In a famous document, the Confession of Augsburg, Melanchthon set forth the beliefs of the Protestants.

        (1). This document was of a conservative nature, making the differences seem as few as possible, and showing that both Catholics and Protestants held the same fundamental ideas of Christianity.

        (2). This document still remains the fundamental creed of the Lutheran church.

    2. After listening to the Protestants' defense of their case, Charles ordered the issuing of a refutation of the Confession.

        a. The Catholics admitted the orthodoxy of some of the Protestant views, but firmly denounced that part of the document dealing with church reform.

        b. Charles then commanded the Protestants to accept the Catholic view, giving them six months to obey the refutation and come back into the Mother Church.

        c. It was plainly understood that if the Protestants did not submit, force would be used.

B. Religious war seemed inevitable, but the Turkish menace postponed the civil struggle.

    1. The Turks were threatening the city of Vienna. If this city were captured all Europe would have been in danger.

    2. Charles again needed the support of all Germany, accordingly the truce of Nuremberg was concluded in 1532. It was

agreed that religious differences would be referred to a General Council of the church.

3. For the next decade Charles was engrossed in political affairs in southern Europe, during which time he dared not interfere with Protestantism.

   a. Because of a Franco-Turkish alliance Charles renewed the war with France.

     (1). Charles had just completed an expedition against the Turks in 1535.

     (2). The war with France broke out the next year.

     (3). After another expedition against the Turks, Charles fought another war with Francis I, 1542-1544.

   b. During this period Protestantism went unchecked in Germany.

IV. Finally, temporary peace was restored in Germany by the famous Peace of Augsburg, 1555.

A. The Protestants refused to attend the Council of Trent, the General Council of the church, which opened in 1545.

1. The pope was opposed to a general council of the church.

   a. These councils generally encroached upon the power of the pope, consequently he tried to prevent their meeting.

   b. The pope looked with satisfaction upon the many difficulties of the emperor, as these troubles limited royal power.

   c. Finally, Charles overcame his obstacles and forced Pope Paul III to summon a council which met in Trent in 1545.

2. It was now too late, however, to conciliate with the Protestants.

   a. They were determined upon their course of action.

   b. They did not wish compromise any longer, but had decided to break with the church.

3. This action by the Protestants was pleasing to Charles, as he was now free to settle the religious differences by force.

   a. The Schmalkaldic War, the first religious war in Germany, broke out in 1546.

   b. This war was of short duration. Seeming at first decisive in favor of Charles, it proved the beginning of his defeat and downfall.

B. Luther's death occurred about the time of the beginning of the Schmalkaldic War.

1. Luther died February 18, 1546. He was buried at Wittenberg, in the church to which he had previously nailed his famous ninety-five theses.

2. It is difficult to formulate a true estimate of Luther's works.

   a. As to Luther's sincerity there is little doubt; that his influence in furthering Protestantism was inestimable cannot be denied; but his doctrine of civil submission is open to criticism.

   b. Luther advocated submission to the civil monarchs rather than to the pope.

      (1). He had deserted the peasants in their revolt.

      (2). He was not a staunch supporter of the Schmalkaldic League.

      (3). He believed that monarchs were God's highest earthly representatives.

   c. Protestants today do not place Luther on as high a plane as would have been the case had he opposed monarchs as well as popes.

   d. However, Luther's one idea, the right of private judgment, greatly overbalances any of his short-comings, both from the standpoint of religious and intellectual development.

C. The emperor was victorious in the Schmalkaldic War, 1546-1547, but by the Peace of Passau he was forced to reestablish Protestantism on the pre-war basis.

   1. The Schmalkaldic War was both political and religious.

      a. Charles claimed the war was to punish political insubordination, while the Protestants claimed their religion brought on the war.

         (1). In truth, the war resulted from the two causes.

         (2). Had the Protestant League seized its opportunity it might have been successful, but the League did not take decisive action.

      b. Maurice of Saxony turned traitor to the Protestant cause, giving military help to Charles. Consequently, Charles closed the struggle with one important victory, the Battle of Muhlberg, April, 1547.

   2. Apparently, Charles was master of the situation, but a general uprising of German princes, both Catholic and Protestant, resulted in his defeat.

      a. Charles found it impossible to carry out his original plans, consequently he adopted a plan of compromise, the Interim.

      b. This document, passed by the Diet, asserted every essential position of the Catholics, but did contain a few minor concessions to the Protestants.

      c. Charles was now becoming very unpopular in Germany, and the intense feeling against him was steadily growing.

          (1). Finally, Maurice of Saxony, who had betrayed the Protestants in 1547, rejoined their cause.

          (2). The Protestants allied themselves with Henry II of France, which alliance forced upon Charles the Peace of Passau in 1552.

D. The result of the Peace of Passau was the religious Peace of Augsburg, 1555.

    1. Charles, broken in spirit, retired from German affairs, turning over the rule of Germany to his younger brother, Ferdinand.

      a. He went first to the Netherlands, later to Spain.

      b. Several years previously, Ferdinand had been chosen by the electors as Charles' successor.

      c. This is the beginning of the Austrian branch of the House of Hapsburg.

      d. Ferdinand now set about preparing for a permanent religious peace. The result was the Peace of Augsburg.

    2. The Peace of Augsburg recognized the principle that religion was a territorial and not a national question.

      a. The Peace permanently established the legal existence of Lutheranism. This meant the abandonment of the unity of the church.

      b. The Catholic church recognized Lutheranism as a heretical departure from Catholicism, but the important point is, Lutheranism was recognized.

          (1). Lutheran princes were granted security by being allowed to choose between the two religions.

          (2). They were empowered to force their choice upon their subjects.

      c. There were two, but only two, legal religions.

    3. There were several weaknesses in the Peace of Augsburg.

      a. Full religious toleration was not granted.

          (1). Only Lutheranism and Catholicism were legalized, and if a subject could not accept either of these religions, he must emigrate.

          (2). If a Catholic Church official abandoned Catholicism his property and title were to be surrendered.

(3). The Lutherans in their negotiations had not considered the followers of Zwingli and Calvin, who
were also Protestants.

b. The Ecclesiastical Reservation and other ambiguities
led to a renewal of the conflict.
   (1). The status of church lords was not definitely determined.
   (2). Bishops were sometimes secular rulers.
      (a). The Lutherans declared they should exercise
          the right of choice of religions the same as
          any other prince.
      (b). Catholics held that the bishop who turned
          Protestant must resign.
      (c). The Catholics won their point and included
          it in the Peace as the Ecclesiastical Reserva-
          tion.
   (3). This Reservation was not always enforced, lead-
   ing, of course, to bitter rivalry between the two
   groups.

c. In reality, then, the Peace of Augsburg was only a
truce, evidenced by the Thirty Years' War, 1618, which
threw western Europe again into chaos.

*"The Reformation began with ideas and ended in
force. In the Germany of the sixteenth, as in that
of the nineteenth century, an era of liberal thought
closed in a fever of war; the persuasions of sweet-
ness and light were drowned by the beat of the drum
and the blare of the trumpet; and methods of blood
and iron supplanted the forces of reason."* *

* *From* The Cambridge Modern History, Vol. II, The Reformation, pp. 278-9. Copyright 1924. *Used by permission of* The Macmillan Company, *publishers.*

CHAPTER XXXVIII

THE SPREAD OF THE REFORMATION TO OTHER COUNTRIES

"Whether a country should remain Catholic or become Protestant would seem to have been determined mainly by political considerations. . . . Before the end of the sixteenth century the permanent lines between Protestant states and Catholic states had been drawn. Since that time no state has transferred its allegiance from the one camp to the other." *

I. Generally, the northern states of Europe gradually turned Protestant, while the southern countries remained Catholic.

A. The Reformation which swept Europe in the sixteenth century was a general, not a local, movement.

　　1. The Reformation had the effect of dividing Europe into two groups of states—Protestant and Roman Catholic. The inevitable consequences of this development were to condition everything that followed.

　　　　a. The Protestant group included England, Scotland, Denmark, Sweden, Norway, Holland, Switzerland, and one-half of Germany.

　　　　b. The Roman Catholic group included Italy, Austria, France, Spain, and Portugal, and part of Germany.

　　　　c. "The defection of so many opulent and powerful kingdoms from the Papal See was a fatal blow to its grandeur and power, as it not only abridged the dominions of the popes in extent — diminished their revenues — and left them fewer rewards to bestow, but it also obliged them to adopt a different system of conduct towards the nations which still continued to recognize their jurisdiction, and to govern them by new maxims, and with a milder spirit."[1]

　　2. The developments of the preceding century were responsible for the movement.

---

*From Hearnshaw, Social and Political Ideas of the Renaissance and Reformation, p. 29. Published by Barnes and Noble, Inc., by arrangement with George C. Harrap & Co., Ltd., London.
[1] From Wilson, Outlines of History, p. 709.

a. The Reformation was not so much a religious manifestation as a politically motivated one; all phases of life were affected: social, political, economic, and intellectual.

b. When Humanism swept northern Europe it had carried with it a desire for religious change or reform.

3. The Protestant Reformation resulted from the demand that the church be adjusted to meet the new conditions.

B. The Reformation spread rapidly; it even gained entrance into the southern countries of Europe.

1. Although the movement was practically universal, it met with stubborn resistance everywhere.

a. In Italy and Spain the resistance was successful.

b. In the Latin country of France, it was largely, though not wholly, successful.

2. In the north of Europe Protestantism became both the religion of the state and the religion of the people.

a. In some countries, such as England and Switzerland, the movement was mainly political.

b. In many cases the religious zeal of the people caused Protestantism to replace Catholicism.

3. There was no definite geographical dividing line between Protestantism and Catholicism.

a. Germany became part Protestant and part Catholic, and remains so even today.

b. For the most part, however, the north of Europe became Protestant and the south remained Catholic.

c. These same conditions exist in present-day Europe.

C. There were several reasons why Protestantism failed in southern Europe.

1. In the first place, the character of the people differed from that of the inhabitants of northern Europe.

a. The Latin people of the south upheld the emotional character of religion rather than the ethical, as in the north.

b. They were temperamental, little concerned with dogma, savoring of paganism, and greatly concerned with ritual and form of worship.

2. Secondly, southern Europeans, particularly Italians, prided themselves on the Papacy.

a. They objected less to taxation on the part of the church, as money poured into Italy, benefiting both the church and the country.

b. Some did object to the exactions of the church, but they did not accept Protestantism.

3. Finally, the Inquisition was devised to stamp out every heresy.

II. The Swiss revolt from Rome was led by Ulrich Zwingli, 1484-1531.

A. By the beginning of the sixteenth century, Switzerland was practically an independent country.

1. During the Middle Ages the territory of the later Swiss Confederation owed allegiance to the House of Hapsburg, being part of the Holy Roman Empire.

    a. In 1291, the three forest cantons of Schwyz, Uri, and Interwalden formed a defensive alliance to fight their enemies, the Hapsburgs.

    b. Gradually, other cantons joined the alliance, until there were thirteen at the time of the Reformation.

2. In 1499 the Count of Hapsburg was forced to sign a treaty, giving the Swiss people practical independence.

    a. The new Swiss Confederation was little more than a loose association for defensive purposes.

       (1). The cantons clung to their individual power.

       (2). The diet of the Confederation was greatly limited in power.

    b. The Confederation gradually conquered other territory, which added to the difficulties of government.

3. Switzerland, a loose confederation composed of German-, Italian-, and French-speaking peoples, was easily thrown into turmoil by the great question of the day.

B. The revolt in Switzerland was contemporary with that in Germany, but of a different character.

1. Ulrich Zwingli, a native Swiss, was the leader of the revolt.

    a. He was born only one year later than Luther, but insisted that he was not influenced by him.

    b. Zwingli came from an influential burgher family, and obtained the best education available.

       (1). He attended the universities of both Vienna and Basel.

       (2). This fact accounts, in part, for the difference in characters of the two great leaders.

    c. Zwingli's discontent came not from spirituality, but through his classical studies; he was a Humanist.

    d. Luther was of a conservative nature, while Zwingli was a radical.

2. Zwingli began his public career as a social and political reformer.

    a. He began by preaching democracy.

      b.   Great objection was raised to the practice of supplying mercenary soldiers for the pope and various European countries.

      c.   He believed that his people should fight for a national cause only.

      d.   At first he did not attack church abuses, as he felt they would correct themselves if given time.

   3.   In 1518 Zwingli was called to Zurich to become a preacher in the Cathedral Church.

      a.   Here he was influential, and soon openly attacked the church.

      b.   The revolt started in the same manner as in Germany, with an attack upon indulgences.

      c.   Finally, he completely denounced the church, and by 1525 succeeded in establishing his Reformed Church.

C. Religious wars, culminating in the Peace of Kappel, 1531, were brought about by the German cantons who were jealous of the rising influence of Zurich, and so supported Catholicism.

   1.   In 1523 Zwingli outlined his beliefs in his sixty-seven theses, but the German forest cantons objected.

      a.   However, the people of Zurich supported their priest in his attacks upon the church.

      b.   The theses were accepted by the townspeople, and Zurich withdrew from the Catholic Church.

      c.   Other towns followed the example set by Zurich, but the forest cantons, fearing the loss of their great influence, opposed the movement.

   2.   Religious war became inevitable, because the forest cantons objected not only to Zwingli's religious teachings but also to his social and political reforms.

      a.   Zwingli and his followers were at first successful, as indicated by his bloodless victory in 1529.

      b.   The trouble arose over religious status in the "common bailiwicks."[1] Each community was allowed to choose its religion, according to the terms of settlement.

   3.   In 1531, the forces of Zwingli were defeated, resulting in the Peace of Kappel.

      a.   Zwingli's death at Kappel was a great, but only a temporary, loss to the cause.

      b.   In the common bailiwicks the settlement favored the Catholics but in the cantons the preferred religion was adopted.

      c.   The Peace of Kappel was very similar to the Peace of

---

1 Conquered territory.

Augsburg, for Switzerland became part Catholic and part Protestant.

4. Zwingli's revolt added a new Protestant party.
   a. Luther and Zwingli had failed to settle their differences at the Marburg Conference.
      (1). Luther could not tolerate Zwingli's rationalism.
      (2). Zwingli would not accept Luther's belief concerning the Lord's Supper.
   b. This new party made a general agreement among the Protestants the more difficult.

III. After the death of Zwingli, Calvin, 1509-1564, became the leader of Protestantism in Switzerland.

A. Political expediency rather than religious belief brought about Geneva's acceptance of Protestantism.

1. In 1504 Geneva began a long war, destined to run twenty years, to gain independence from Savoy.
   a. Freiburg, an ally of Geneva, supported the Catholic Church, while Bern, another ally, and a powerful member of the Swiss Confederation, supported Protestantism.
   b. Geneva was forced to choose between the two parties, and finally decided in favor of Bern. This decision was based mostly on the strength of the two allies; it was more political than religious.

2. The next phase of the struggle for her independence was directed against the prince-bishop.
   a. This resulted in a revolt against the church.
   b. Thus, political independence proved to be the forerunner of religious independence.
   c. In 1535 Geneva ordered the cessation of the mass; this was the official declaration of adoption of Protestantism.

3. Geneva was not a part of Switzerland proper, but the close association of the city with Bern brought it into intimate relations with Switzerland; consequently, the Geneva revolt is usually considered as part of the general Swiss movement.

B. John Calvin, stopping in Geneva on his way to Strassburg in 1536, was induced by Farel—a Zwinglian leader in the city—to stay.

1. Calvin's training was both clerical and legal.
   a. He was of French descent, of lower middle-class parentage, of high intelligence, and well educated.
   b. After studying theology and law he decided to devote his life work to letters.

      c. Calvin's early writings denounced the inefficiency and injustice of the French government, and when persecutions began he was driven into open revolt.

  2. Calvin had turned Protestant in 1533.

      a. In this year he was forced to flee from Paris.

      b. He went to Basel, a city with strong Protestant tendencies, where he published (1536) his famous "Institutes of the Christian Religion," a clear exposition of Protestant doctrine. A few months later he left Basel, intending to go to Strassburg.

      c. As the direct road to Strassburg was barred by war between Charles V and France he went by the southern route which brought him to Geneva. He stayed.

  3. In Geneva, Calvin became the leader of the Protestant movement.

      a. Geneva, after gaining its independence, had set up an oligarchic government. Furthermore, the people had thrown off religious restraint.

      b. The work of Calvin was to reform the government as well as morals.

          (1). He attempted to abolish all pleasure and festivity.

          (2). He became a virtual dictator of the city.

C. Opposition to Calvin's regime resulted in his banishment from the city, but within three years he returned and ruled the city until his death.

  1. In 1538 both Calvin and Farel were banished.

      a. The reforms instituted had been too revolutionary and too sudden in character.

      b. Calvin held an exaggerated idea of sin.

          (1). Rigid regulations were set up.

          (2). Practically every form of amusement was abolished.

      c. His idea was not to induce the people to accept the change, but rather to enforce the restrictions.

  2. Finally, the Calvinist party was victorious in Geneva, and Calvin was recalled in 1541.

      a. Conflicting estimates have been given of the services of Calvin.

          (1). Some give him credit for training the leaders of the coming religious wars.

          (2). Others claim that his policy was entirely in error, and that these men became leaders in spite of Calvin.

          (3). However, the spirit of Calvinism lived and determined, to a great extent, the outcome of the European religious wars.

b.   Calvin developed the natural corollary of Luther's defi-
nition of faith, the theory of "predestination."
c.   He had a clear-cut theory as to the relation of church and
state.
(1). He believed that the church must be autonomous
and must have coercive authority over all its members.
(2). Furthermore, he believed that the power of lay
rulers is ordained by God. The laity should par-
ticipate through elected members in the government of the church.
(3). He founded the Presbyterian system on the ground
that it was present in the primitive Christian
Church.
d.   Calvin's system of lay representation may have established the foundation for popular government. At least
it furnished an organization for popular government.

IV. Germany and Switzerland were important centers in the development of Protestantism, but there were others nearly as significant.

A.   Protestantism in England came as a gradual movement and had
a political motivation from the beginning.
1.   Changes had been taking place in England over a period of
years which made the eventual revolt possible — perhaps
inevitable.
a.   English scholars had questioned certain church doctrines
many years before the revolt in Germany.
(1). Wycliffe, a scholar at Oxford, had begun his de-
nunciation of the papacy as early as the fourteenth
century.
(2). The most famous Englishmen of letters of the first
part of the sixteenth century had been John Colet
and Sir Thomas More.
(3). England was also affected by the writings and
teachings of Erasmus, who had come to England
early in the century.
b.   So, when the revolt came, the people were ready to accept Protestantism. It was not merely to satisfy the whims
of a despotic monarch.
2.   Therefore, the actual break with Rome was not caused by
religious conviction, but rather by political considerations
and Henry VIII's immediate desire to rid himself of his wife,
which was impossible under the Catholic faith without a
special dispensation from the pope.

      a. Henry had married Catherine of Aragon, the aunt of the Emperor Charles V.

      b. Catherine was the widow of Henry's oldest brother, and according to church law could not have become the legal wife of Henry, but the pope had sanctioned the marriage; so, Clement VII could not grant Henry's request for divorce on this ground.

      c. Henry wished a male heir, but the appearance at court of Anne Boleyn,[1] with whom he fell in love, was the immediate cause; yet, it must be emphasized that political considerations were the long-range factors which made revolt possible of practical accomplishment.

  3. Unable to gain concessions from the pope, Henry established himself at the head of the Church of England.

      a. Henry's first act was to force the English clergy to accept him as head of the Church of England.

      b. Parliament then declared Henry's marriage with Catherine illegal and his marriage with Anne Boleyn, whom he had married in the meantime, legal.

      c. With the passing of the Act of Supremacy, the break with the church was completed, 1543.

         (1). This was parliamentary sanction of Henry's headship of the Church of England.

         (2). Henry did not, however, accept Lutheranism or Calvinism.

         (3). He was not a Protestant; in fact, he carried on persecutions, singling out those with Protestant tendencies.

  4. It was not until the accession of Queen Elizabeth, in 1558, that England definitely became Protestant.

      a. Henry's three children — Edward VI, Mary, and Elizabeth — respectively succeeded him to the throne. Two were Protestant and one was Catholic.

      b. During Edward's reign Protestant practices were introduced, but when Mary came to the throne a Catholic reaction set in.

         (1). Edward's reign was marred by destruction and appropriation of church property.

         (2). Mary's reign was marred by the persecution of the Protestants.

      c. In 1558, with the accession of Elizabeth, England definitely became Protestant; but, as in other countries, not without conflict and religious persecution.

---

[1] Who became the mother of Queen Elizabeth, whose reign extended from 1558 to 1603.

B. People in France and Holland were ready to accept the teachings of Luther and Calvin.
  1. Lefèvre d'Etaples had in his writings expressed new ideas in religion before Luther's revolt began.
      a. Lefèvre was a teacher at the University of Paris, and soon had gathered about him a group of scholars who paved the way for teachings of Luther and Calvin.
      b. Luther's influence spread rapidly and greatly increased the strength of the Protestant party in France, called Huguenots.
      c. Calvin's teachings not only brought new converts, but a regular organization and a definite program.
      d. Calvin was one of Lefèvre's pupils.
  2. The Huguenots finally became both a political and a religious party.
      a. Many of the upper classes, including some of the royal family, were Huguenots.
      b. The party occupied an important place in the civil wars following the Reformation.
  3. Protestantism found fertile ground in Holland.
      a. Here the people had developed a degree of self-government and a sense of independence, which they carried into religious questions.
      b. They adhered, for the most part, to the teachings of Luther and Calvin. They were Puritans in belief.
      c. As in France, the greatest importance of the Protestant movement in Holland was the effect upon the religious-civil struggles following the Reformation.
C. Protestantism in the Scandinavian countries was characterized by political revolts of the rulers, rather than by uprisings of the people.
  1. Protestantism in Denmark was contemporary with Lutheranism.
      a. Humanism began to creep into Denmark about 1515, and with Humanism came Lutheranism. The Danish Humanists admired not only Luther but also Erasmus.
      b. During the reign of Frederick I, 1523-1533, Lutheranism made its appearance.
          (1). It was unmolested and made rapid headway.
          (2). Frederick took the fees which had formerly gone to the pope.
      c. In 1536 Christian III summoned a National Assembly which legalized Protestantism of the Lutheran type.
  2. In Norway and Iceland Lutheranism was forced upon the people.
      a. These countries were dependencies of Denmark.

b. There was no popular demand for a change in religion, but Lutheranism became the recognized faith.

3. Lutheranism in Sweden was even more closely associated with politics. It became Protestant in order to regain autonomy from Denmark.

a. Gustavus Vasa was elected King of Sweden in 1523.

b. In 1527 the property of the bishops was largely confiscated, and in 1529 Lutheranism was definitely introduced.

c. The organization of the Lutheran Church in Sweden came during the years 1540-1544. The Confession of Augsburg was accepted as the state religion.

d. Because of the increased power of the monarch, Lutheranism was easily established. There were no wars or persecutions to mar the period of change, as in so many other countries.

e. Finland, dominated by Sweden, was subject to the same religious change, though the change did not come about as peacefully as in Sweden.

"The Reformation produced results of immense importance. By teaching man to think and reason for himself in religious matters, and to acknowledge therein none but a divine authority, it emancipated mind from the thraldom which ages of spiritual despotism had imposed upon it; it extended religion beyond the exclusive domain of the ecclesiastical order, and sent it forth into the wide world of humanity, where, before, it had scarcely been permitted to enter . . . ." *

————————

* *From* Wilson, Outlines of History, p. 800.

CHAPTER XXXIX

THE ROMAN CATHOLIC REFORMATION

"The Catholic Reformation . . . sprang out of the religious soil of the later Middle Ages. St. Catherine, Savonarola, and others had voiced its hopes, and asked, not for change of doctrine, but for renewed religious fervor. The spread of the Protestant movement almost certainly hastened the coming of the Catholic Reformation with its 'exalted devotion,' its 'unquenchable religious hope,' and a 'tenacity which no reversal could wear out.' Its outstanding features were the Society of Jesus and the Council of Trent."

I. **The Roman Catholic Reformation[1] affected every phase of life in the second half of the sixteenth century.**

A. Protestant aggression resulted in "an equally violent outbreak of Catholic zeal." Almost every European country was involved in religious war.

   1. In most cases the wars were civil, but during the later part of the period they often did assume an international character.

   2. France withdrew her interests from Italy and turned to conquests of Germany. There developed great rivalry between France and the Hapsburgs.

   3. Spain engaged in an unsuccessful war to subdue rebellion in the Spanish Netherlands.

      a. This conflict finally resulted in the independence of the Protestant, or northern, provinces of the Netherlands.

      b. Italy, however, came under the power of Spain.

   4. England and Germany were also torn by religious wars.

      a. England emerged as one of the strongest countries of Europe.

      b. In Germany, the Peace of Augsburg was merely a truce; the final conflict was destined to come in the next century with the Thirty Years' War.

---

*From Sellery and Krey, The Founding of Western Civilization, p. 431. Copyright 1929. *Used by permission of* Harper & Brothers, *publishers.*
1 Not infrequently referred to as the "Counter Reformation" but most accurately known as indicated.

B. The Protestant Reformation proved the need for a reform within the Catholic Church. In this movement Spain, under Philip II, assumed leadership.

    1. The Protestants would not have achieved success had there not been a firm conviction that the church was corrupt.

        a. The popes, generally, had not favored reform; it meant the loss of power. However, with the election of Pope Paul IV in 1555 an effort was begun to save the church.

        b. Action of the popes began the Catholic Reformation proper, but the movement had been well under way, especially in Spain, before 1555.

    2. Spain, having carefully laid the groundwork, was in a position to assume leadership.

        a. Spain was not only intolerant, making great use of the Inquisition, but she had a renewed zest for religious life.

        b. She was in readiness to fight the coming battles for restoring the church.

        c. Philip II's reign was characterized by his support and defense of the church.

           (1). Like his father, Charles V, Philip was a staunch Catholic.

           (2). In his mind, the church was more all-important than the state.

C. In addition to the popes and the monarchs supporting the reform movement, the people were ready for reform.

    1. There were many people in Europe working for church reform who did not accept Protestantism.

        a. Many realized existing abuses, but they wished to work from within—not to set up new religions.

        b. Consequently, they did not adhere to the beliefs of Luther, Zwingli, or Calvin.

        c. In fact, this more conservative reform had its embryonic beginning before the Protestant revolt.

    2. The changed religious attitude in northern Europe in the middle of the sixteenth century was due in part to the growing fears of the people. Professor Hulme[1] has indicated that they feared three things most:

        a. *The Turk.* Turkey was a constant source of terror to Europeans. It was thought that the end of the world was near, and that the Turks would ravage western Europe as a punishment for sin and licentiousness.

---

1 "The Turk, The Comet, and The Devil"—The Renaissance and Reformation, by Hulme, Chapter XX.

b. *The Comet.* During this period people believed that signs appearing in the heavens were a warning to mankind. The appearance of comets was thought to signify coming calamity.

c. *The Devil.* The belief in witchcraft was common during medieval times. It was believed that the devil entered the body and that then the individual became an agent of the devil in winning souls. Persecution for witchcraft became common, especially in Germany.

d. This, then, was a period of terror, which was a factor in promoting the cause of the Catholic reaction.

II. The Order of Jesuits, founded by Ignatius Loyola in 1540, played an important part in the Catholic Reformation.

A. The Jesuit order was only one of many similar orders founded during the sixteenth century.

  1. The movement began in Spain and spread rapidly to other Catholic countries.

    a. These orders were associations of men, and even women, devoted to church reform.

    b. Their organization and work show plainly the religious zeal of the people of this period.

  2. Among the earliest of orders were the Theatins and the Capuchins.

    a. The Theatin order was founded in 1524.

      (1). The order was composed of ecclesiastics devoted to the cause of elevating the ideals and practices of the clergy.

      (2). The order was founded in Rome.

    b. The Capuchin order, founded about 1526, was composed of friars who ministered to the people in an attempt to further loyalty to the church.

B. The most important of the societies was the Society of Jesus, sanctioned by Pope Paul III in 1540.

  1. Loyola, the founder, was a well-educated Spanish nobleman.

    a. He was educated at the court of Ferdinand and Isabella and, as was natural, was imbued with the spirit of arms and war.

    b. Loyola was also of a religious nature, and while recuperating from a wound received in battle in 1521 had much time for thought and meditation.

    c. Influenced by religious books which he read he decided to dedicate his life to the service of the church.

      d. His book, "Spiritual Exercises," enabled many to live the true Christian life. The "Exercises" outlined a plan for learning the will of God, and also for carrying out His will.

  2. Loyola soon realized that the new work called for a new education; consequently, he gave up the study of military science and tactics and began the laborious pursuit of Latin, philosophy, and theology.

      a. He studied at Barcelona, Alcalá, and Salamanca, and finally at the University of Paris.

      b. Then Loyola began developing his plans.

         (1). He and his companions planned a trip to the Holy Land with the avowed purpose of converting the "infidel Turks."

         (2). Finally, they made their way to Italy and received papal consent for their journey to the Holy Land.

         (3). In the meantime war had broken out, and their journey was postponed.

  3. Loyola decided to found a permanent organization, the Society of Jesus.

      a. While they were waiting to carry out their plans, Jerusalem and the infidel were forgotten, as there was missionary work to be done at home.

      b. The group had already taken the vows of poverty and chastity, and now took the vow of obedience. So, in 1540, the pope gave sanction to the new order.

      c. The new order was organized along military lines, and was at all times held in readiness to support the church.

C. The work of the Jesuits was varied, and their influence was one of the greatest of contributing factors to the success of the Catholic Reformation.

  1. Loyola, as the leader of the order, carried out his ideas of organization and of service to the church.

      a. The order preferred the active life to the meditation of the monastery.

      b. They carried out the spirit of activity to the letter.

         (1). They converted the heretics in the Catholic countries.

         (2). They won many back to the church in Protestant countries.

  2. The Jesuits engaged in missionary work, preaching, and teaching.

      a. As missionaries they spread their influence over the known world. They were equally successful with heretics, infidels, and Protestants.

      b. They became the most eloquent and devoted of preachers, filled the churches, and were often preferred as confessors.

      c. As teachers they were unsurpassed.

         (1). Under their guidance the most efficient schools of Europe were produced.

         (2). As with all their work, their instruction was free.

  3. In the next century the order was abolished by the pope, but subsequently was restored.

      a. As with all similar orders, there appeared in its ranks unscrupulous and wicked members.

      b. In the eighteenth century not only Protestants but Catholics as well condemned the order, and in 1773 it was abolished. It was, however, restored in 1814.

      c. Even though the order had weaknesses, and has been criticized, it furnished the stamina and guiding principles to Catholic Europe which brought back to the church some of its former religious prestige.

III. The Council of Trent, proposed by Charles V to deal with Protestantism, in its final session, 1562-1563, brought important reforms to the Catholic Church.

A. Charles V had long advocated a general council of the church to deal with religious issues.

  1. During the Protestant Reformation Charles V had been an ardent supporter of Catholicism.

      a. But Protestantism continued to spread.

         (1). It was firmly entrenched in most of the countries of northern Europe.

         (2). Besides, there were heretics in Catholic countries.

      b. The Catholic Church still claimed to be the one and only church, but its resistance had been somewhat passive.

      c. Charles V advocated a general council, but this was distasteful to the popes, lest they lose temporal power.

  2. By 1542 the popes could resist Charles no longer, and Paul III issued the call for the Council of Trent.

      a. Nothing came of the first attempt, the council being adjourned before the first session was held.

      b. From 1542 until 1562 several efforts at reform were made, but the work of the councils during this period was of little consequence.

      c. This failure was partly due to the fear of the popes of the power of the monarchs, and partly to a changed public opinion.

     d. After the Peace of Augsburg in 1555 there was little hope of reconciliation between Protestants and Catholics.

B. The final session of the Council of Trent, 1562-1563, was of great importance.

    1. Pope Pius IV, no longer fearing the council, convened the final session in 1562.

       a. In earlier meetings one of the important problems was that of dealing with Protestantism.

       b. The final session dealt with internal church reform, which it accomplished to a marked degree.

    2. After settling many disputes, mostly political, the pope established himself as head of the council.

       a. Many questions were presented of a purely national character.

       b. The main question, however, was that of establishing supremacy over the council.

          (1). Through the influence of the Jesuits and a few important individuals the supremacy of the pope was established.

          (2). Then the council began its consideration of theological and ecclesiastical questions.

    3. The decisions of the council were set forth in decrees and canons.

       a. The decrees related to discipline. Most of the clerical abuses which had been brought before the council were corrected.

       b. The canons related to church doctrine.

          (1). The dogma of the church was clearly set forth, particularly those points which had come into controversy during the Protestant Reformation.

          (2). Church dogma became more rigid.

    4. The Catholic Church was no longer willing to compromise with the Protestants.

       a. The line between the two religions was definitely set up. Because of the enthusiasm shown in the final session of the council, the church held renewed assurance.

       b. Conciliatory Catholicism had changed to Militant Catholicism.

       c. In the combat which was to come, the Catholics were united, while the Protestants were divided.

IV. Other useful weapons of the church in effecting its Reformation were the Inquisition and the Index.

A. The Inquisition, used in most Catholic countries to suppress heresy, became particularly famous, or infamous, in Spain.

1. The Inquisition had been used in various periods during the Middle Ages.

2. It had been discontinued with the coming of Humanism and the Renaissance.
    a. The period of free thinking had no use for the institution.
    b. But when the Spanish began to consolidate their provinces into one state, the Christians combined against both Moors and Jews. Therefore, the Inquisition was reintroduced into Spain.

3. In 1542 the pope established the Roman Inquisition, which was to operate in all Catholic countries.
    a. The plan called for courts to be set up in the various countries.
    b. However, the work of the Roman Inquisition was confined largely to Italy; the other countries, following the example of Spain, set up their own courts of inquisition.
    c. Other countries did not object to the practice of the Inquisition as much as to this example of increasing papal authority.

4. This was the most infamous method devised for the punishment of heretics.
    a. It was effected with much cruelty and inhumanity, thousands losing their lives through burning and other tortures.[1]
    b. Not only was heresy checked, but much of the gain made by the Renaissance was blotted out.

B. The papal Index was a published list of prohibited books.

1. As early as the middle of the fifteenth century, an attempt had been made to suppress heretical books.
    a. With the invention of printing, books had become common throughout Europe; consequently, ideas considered as heretical by the church were spread rapidly.
    b. The suppression of books was simply an effort of the church to protect its members against unorthodox ideas.
    c. With the closing of the Council of Trent, it was deemed advisable to prepare a new Index, the first having been published in 1559.

2. So, in 1564 a new Index was published.
    a. This work greatly aided the church in dealing with heresy and in furthering the Catholic Reformation.
    b. Although books could be suppressed to a greater or lesser degree, the thought carried in them could not.

---

[1] The punishments meted out, however, were the punishments common to the age. It was an age of brutality.

V. Neither the Protestant nor the Catholic Reformation brought freedom into religion, and it is an error to attribute real tolerance to any religious group in this age.

A. However, it is true that the Protestant Reformation, in certain respects, realized a return to the more simple or primitive Christianity.

    1. This is true in church organization, doctrine, and ceremony.

    2. Many thought, in the time of Luther, that this same result would be effected naturally in the Catholic Church; and, in fact, it was realized to some extent by the Catholic Reformation.

    3. There developed an increased interest in religion.

B. Nevertheless, the Protestant Reformation brought little real tolerance, for such came only with time.

    1. In Protestant countries, state religions took the place of the universal Catholic religion, but persecutions continued unabated.

    2. Intolerance was the order of the day, and conformity an obsession.

    3. The persecution practiced on the nonconformists by the new Protestant sects was almost as depraved as that of the Inquisition.

> *"The Church was reformed and underwent a moral regeneration; but religious and intellectual freedom were left further off than ever. The issues at stake were, however, made clear, and the parties in the great struggle were definitely marked out. A modus vivendi between authority and liberty could not be found. Neither would tolerate the other, and Europe was doomed to be the battlefield of the contending principles. The sword alone could be the arbiter."**

*From the Cambridge Modern History, Vol. II, The Reformation, p. 689. Copyright 1924. *Used by permission of* The Macmillan Co., *publishers.*

SUPPLEMENTARY REFERENCES

Andrae, T. *Mohammed: The Man and His Faith.* rev. ed. New York: Barnes & Noble, Inc., 1956. Highly regarded study of the life of Mohammed by a noted Swedish scholar.

Artz, F. B. *The Mind of the Middle Ages.* New York: Alfred A. Knopf, Inc., 1954. Outstanding account of the intellectual history of the Middle Ages. Valuable bibliography and illustrations.

Baldwin, S. *The Organization of Medieval Christianity.* (Berkshire Studies in European History) New York: Henry Holt & Co., Inc., 1929. Excellent short study of the medieval church.

Barraclough, C. *The Origins of Modern Germany.* Oxford: Blackwell, 1949. Contains best general treatment of Germany in the medieval period in English.

Baynes, N. S. *The Byzantine Empire.* London: Oxford University Press, 1929. Excellent survey of Byzantine history.

Bury, J. B. *The Invasions of Europe by the Barbarians.* London: Macmillan Co., 1928. Best single-volume account of the barbarian invasions, absorbingly written by an outstanding historian.

Cambridge Medieval History. 8 vols. New York: Macmillan Co., 1911-1936. Standard, full-length account of Middle Ages as a whole. At times difficult and detailed, it contains articles on all aspects of the subject by noted specialists. C. W. Previté-Orton has edited condensation of this work, *The Shorter Cambridge Medieval History*, 2 vols. (Cambridge University Press, 1953).

Cambridge Economic History. Vols. I, II. Cambridge: Cambridge University Press, 1952. Contains the most thorough and scholarly treatments of medieval agrarian systems, commerce, and industry.

Coulton, G. G. *Medieval Panorama.* New York: Meridian Books (Noonday Press), 1955. Extensive collection of essays by an eminent medievalist on many aspects of English social scene, 1066-1550.

Farrar, C. P. and Evans, A. P. *Bibliography of English Translations from Medieval Sources.* New York: Columbia University Press, 1946. Invaluable guide for those who wish to read sources in translation.

Haskins, C. H. *The Normans in European History.* Boston: Houghton Mifflin Co., 1915. Brilliant, highly readable account of Norman invasions of western Europe and establishment of Norman Kingdom of Sicily.

——————. *The Rise of Universities.* New York: Peter Smith, 1940. Delightfully written series of essays on development of medieval universities, life of students and rise of professional schools.

Hearnshaw, F. J. C. *Medieval Contributions to Modern Civilization.* New York: Barnes & Noble, Inc., 1949. Lectures at King's College, London University by authorities on medieval religion, philosophy, science, art, English poetry, education, society, economics, politics.

——————. *Social & Political Ideas of Some Great Medieval Thinkers.* New York: Barnes & Noble, Inc., 1950. Essays by noted medievalists on St. Augustine, John of Salisbury, St. Thomas Aquinas, Pierre Du Bois, Marsilio of Padua and John Wycliffe.

Hitti, P. K. *History of the Arabs.* 5th ed. rev. London: St. Martin's Press, 1951. The outstanding work on the history of the Arabs. A shorter treatment has been brought out by the author under the title *The Arabs: A Short History*, rev. ed., Princeton, 1949.
264

Huizinga, J. *The Waning of the Middle Ages.* New York: Anchor Books (Doubleday & Co., Inc.), 1954. Classic interpretation of the decline of the medieval spirit in France and the Netherlands during fourteenth and fifteenth centuries. Remarkable recreation of the intellectual, social and artistic climate of the time.

Lot, F. *End of the Ancient World and Beginnings of the Middle Ages.* New York: Barnes & Noble, Inc., 1954. One of the best volumes on the reasons for the decline and fall of the Roman Empire. Written with great clarity by an eminent French historian.

Luchaire, A. *Social France in the Time of Philip Augustus.* New York: Peter Smith, 1929. An outstanding account of the reign of one of the great kings of France. Highly readable.

Moss, H. S. B. *The Birth of the Middle Ages, 395-814.* Oxford: The Clarendon Press, 1935. Good brief survey of Roman civilization during the last centuries of the empire with an account of the barbarian invasions and establishment of the barbarian kingdoms.

Myers, A. R. *England in the Late Middle Ages.* Harmondsworth: Penguin, 1953. Excellent, readable account of the period 1307-1536 with emphasis on economic and social developments, religious and educational movements and the arts. Maps and useful bibliography.

Newhall, R. A. *The Crusades.* (Berkshire Studies in European History) New York: Henry Holt & Co., Inc., 1927. Excellent, brief treatment of the whole era of the Crusades.

Packard, S. *Europe and the Church under Innocent III.* (Berkshire Studies in European History) New York: Henry Holt & Co., Inc., 1927. Excellent, brief account of a remarkable period in church history.

Paetow, L. J. *Guide to the Study of Medieval History.* rev. ed. New York: Appleton-Century-Crofts, Inc., 1931. The standard, comprehensive bibliography of medieval history. Still useful as a general guide, it is not up-to-date. A revision is in preparation.

Petit-Dutaillis, C. *Feudal Monarchy in France and England from the Tenth to the Thirteenth Century.* New York: Alfred A. Knopf, Inc., 1936. Brilliant discussion of the development of feudal monarchy in France and England.

Pirenne, H. *Economic and Social History of Medieval Europe.* New York: Harvest Books (Harcourt, Brace & Co.), 1956. Highly readable account of the economic life of the Middle Ages by a renowned scholar in the field.

——————. *Medieval Cities.* New York: Anchor Books (Doubleday & Co.) 1956. Short but comprehensive study of the rise of cities during the Middle Ages.

——————. *Mohammed and Charlemagne.* New York: Barnes & Noble, Inc., 1955. Brilliant treatment of early medieval history, emphasizing the interchange of culture between Islam and western Europe.

Poole, A. L. *From Domesday Book to Magna Carta, 1087-1216.* Oxford: Oxford University Press, 1951. Excellent account of the Norman period in English history.

Power, E. *Medieval People.* New York: Barnes & Noble, Inc., 1950. A noted economic historian presents fictionalized biographies of six medieval people, illustrating monasticism, peasant life, travel, trade, women's life. Also published by Anchor Books (Doubleday & Co., Inc.).

Rashdall, H. *The Universities of Europe in the Middle Ages.* rev. ed. 3 vols. Oxford: The Clarendon Press, 1936. The standard account, highly readable, revised by Sir Maurice Powicke and A. B. Emden.

Runciman, S. *History of the Crusades.* 3 vols. Cambridge: Cambridge University Press, 1954. Authoritative and comprehensive history of the crusades by a noted Byzantine scholar.

——————. *Byzantine Civilization.* New York: Meridian Books (Noonday Press), 1956. Compact survey of Byzantine history and civilization.

Shepherd, W. R. *Historical Atlas.* New York: Barnes & Noble, Inc., 1956. The best of the historical atlases, and a valuable companion to the study of medieval history.

Stenton, D. N. *English Society in the Early Middle Ages.* Harmondsworth: Penguin, 1952. Very readable description of English society in the period 1066-1307 with many references to original sources.

Stenton, F. *Anglo-Saxon England.* Oxford: The Clarendon Press, 1950. Excellent study of the Anglo-Saxon period in English history by the outstanding authority in the field.

Stephenson, C. *Medieval Feudalism.* Ithaca: Cornell University Press, 1942. Excellent, brief account of the organization of medieval feudalism. Considered the best treatment of this subject in English.

Taylor, H. O. *The Medieval Mind.* 2 vols. 4th ed. Cambridge: Harvard University Press, 1949. Outstanding study, eloquently written by a noted American medievalist. Devotes a chapter to each of a large number of medieval thinkers, both men and women.

Thorndike, L. *History of Magic and Experimental Science.* 6 vols. New York: Macmillan Co., 1923-41. A monumental work, valuable for reference. See particularly chapter on Albertus Magnus.

Vasiliev, A. A. *History of the Byzantine Empire.* 2 vols. Madison: University of Wisconsin Press, 1928, 1929. Highly regarded as the outstanding work on the history of the Byzantine empire.

Vernadsky, G. *Ancient Russia* (History of Russia, Vol. I) New Haven: Yale University Press, 1944. The most recent, authoritative study of early Russian history, by a noted scholar.

——————. *Kievan Russia* (History of Russia, Vol. II) New Haven: Yale University Press, 1948. Outstanding account of the Russian civilization centering around Kiev between 882-1169 A.D.

INDEX